Thursday, September 1. 1836
Workhouse Diary

C. Barnet — Paid into the hands of Mr. Buckland Treasurer
Sep.r 1.st five Shillings, as p order of the Board

Frank Watkins, returns his thanks to the Board,
and observed it was more than his former
conduct deserved, but he should endeavour
for the future to improve —

Friday — Mr. Dourton & Mr. Thorp, call.d at the Workhouse
C. Barnet — this afternoon, & went over the Premises

Friday — Mary Willey, was discharged from East
East Barnet — Barnet Workhouse, Yesterday, at her own request

Sold Week the Seven in 2 Sep: 1836
11 Bushel Ashes at 2.d Bush.l — ,, 1. 10
paid the Same time

The opening page of Benjamin Woodcock's diary
[HALS: 70876]

Hertfordshire Record Publications, Volume 24

THE DIARY OF BENJAMIN WOODCOCK
MASTER OF THE
BARNET UNION WORKHOUSE
1836–1838

Edited with an Introduction by
Gillian Gear

Hertfordshire Record Society,
volume for the membership year 2008

Hertfordshire Record Society

The publication of this volume has been
assisted by generous grants from:

The Marc Fitch Fund
The Scouloudi Foundation in association with
the Institute of Historical Research

ISBN 978-0-9547561-7-8

Printed and bound in the UK by the MPG Books Group,
Bodmin and King's Lynn

Contents

Illustrations

The opening page of Benjamin Woodcock's diary [HALS: 70876]

Frontispiece

Tables

Acknowledgements

I wish to thank Georgina Oliver for her watercolour paintings used in the design of the cover of this book and to acknowledge the help and advice of Sue Flood, Heather Falvey and Ruth Jeavons with the checking and layout of the text. Hertfordshire Archives and Local Studies, Barnet Local Studies and Archives Centre and Barnet Museum have been of great help, providing access to their collections and giving permission to reproduce many of the illustrations. Volunteers from the Museum, Jane Hartman and Carla Herrmann, kindly assisted with the checking of the Barnet material. The funding provided by the Marc Fitch Fund and the Scouloudi Foundation in association with the Institute of Historical Research is much appreciated.

Abbreviations

HALS	Hertfordshire Archives and Local Studies
BLARS	Bedfordshire and Luton Archives and Records Service
C Barnet	Chipping Barnet
CB	Chipping Barnet
E Barnet	East Barnet
EB	East Barnet
F Barnet	Friern Barnet
FB	Friern Barnet
H H'sted	Hemel Hempstead
S Mims	South Mimms

*An artist's impression of the main entrance of the Barnet Union
Workhouse painted by Georgina Oliver, based on photographic evidence*

Introduction

The New Poor Law, 1834

The early nineteenth century saw an increasing financial burden being imposed on parish rate-payers. The increase was due to the cost of supporting the growing number of poor unemployed people leaving the countryside and trekking to the towns to seek work. This put a disproportionate pressure on the poorer parishes least able to provide the support needed. National government recognised the need for change and intervened in the way that the poor were to be cared for. In 1833 the Poor Law Commission examined the effectiveness of the old system and made recommendations to parliament that resulted in the Poor Law Amendment Act of 1834.

The intention was that the new legislation would provide care, in a fairer and a more economical way for the deserving poor, while providing minimal support to those considered to be undeserving and discouraging abuse of the system. To that end the level of care provided in the newly formed district workhouses was intended to be lower than that which the poorest working man could provide for his family. Economies of scale were to be introduced through the banding together of parishes and the formation of large poor law districts, each with one central district workhouse, under the supervision of Boards of Guardians instead of the small parish-based units that had been administered by the overseers of the poor. The Poor Law Commissioners divided the country into districts, and local Boards of Guardians were appointed to put the new system into effect.

THE DIARY OF BENJAMIN WOODCOCK

The diary

The diary that forms the basis of this book was begun by Benjamin Woodcock on 1 September 1836, two years after the passing of the act and just over a year after Woodcock's appointment by the Barnet Guardians as the master. While the site for the new Barnet workhouse had already been selected, the district's paupers were still being housed in some of the old parish poorhouses.

The diary goes on to cover the period of the building's completion in the late spring of 1837, the transfer of the inmates from the Barnet, Shenley and East Barnet poorhouses to the new building and the establishment of a settled routine for staff, inmates and Guardians. The entry in the diary relating to the transfer from Shenley workhouse is included below. The Chipping Barnet and East Barnet poorhouses appear to have still been used for union paupers but, presumably, they too would have moved in shortly afterwards.

> **Friday 5th May 1837** Removed this Morning, as per orders of the board, the Women & Children together with all the Furniture from Shenley Workhouse, except a 8 day clock & a Night Chair, which Mrs Rogers the Matron says with the approbation of the board, she will pay for at Mr Taplin's[1] Valuation. Got them all safe in Chipping Barnet house to Dinner.

In the diary Woodcock describes his daily routine admitting and caring for the workhouse inmates, his handling of the problems he experienced in creating a smooth-running regime in the new buildings and coping with the demands of the many visitors who took an interest in this newly conceived method of dealing with the poor, amongst whom was the rector of Shenley, Thomas Newcome. On the 23 May 1837 he recorded in his diary viewing Barnet Union Workhouse.[2] On Tuesday 17 May Woodcock wrote 'the Rev Mr Newcome and his two daughters called to view the new house on Tuesday & was much pleased'.

The diary ends on 10 May 1838.

[1] Edward Taplin of High Street, Hadley was an auditor and registrar of marriages, [Pigot's Directory 1839]

[2] Judith Knight and Susan Flood, editors, *Two Nineteenth Century Hertfordshire Diaries*, Volume XVIII, Hertfordshire Record Society (2002) p204

INTRODUCTION

Benjamin Woodcock – the man and his family

Benjamin Woodcock was born in about 1791, possibly in Bengeo, Hertfordshire. There is a record of a Benjamin Woodcock born there on 24 June 1792. Benjamin was appointed master of the Barnet Workhouse in August 1835, aged about 44, and he was probably still in post when he died in 1848, aged 56.

He and his wife lived at Eaton Bray in Bedfordshire prior to their coming to Barnet. Two of their children, Frances and Adolphus, had been born there, in 1823 and 1824 respectively and a search at Bedfordshire and Luton Archives and Records Service showed in the Eaton Bray parish registers the baptisms of Adolphus on 24 September 1824, of Isabella on 11 March 1827 and another daughter, Merinal, on 30 December 1831. In these registers Benjamin was shown firstly as a draper, then as a farmer. He appears to have been reasonably well off. A land tax return of 1831 shows him as occupier of a house and land but also owner of two properties occupied by others. In 1832 he was shown as owner of one house and land as well as owner and occupier of a second house and land. The owner of the property where he lived in 1831 was shown as John Pedley, who owned a vast estate in that parish.[3]

By the time of the 1841 census Benjamin, his wife Elizabeth and three of their children, Frances aged 19, Isabella aged 15 and Merinal aged 11, were all living at the Barnet workhouse.

Although it was usual for the master and matron to be a husband and wife team, it seems Benjamin's wife, Elizabeth, was not actually acting as matron at the time of his appointment. A letter, dated 28 August 1835 and sent to the Poor Law Commissioners by the Board of Guardians, confirmed the appointment of Benjamin Woodcock as the overall master, a Mrs Rogers as matron of Shenley and Mrs Peat as matron of South Mimms workhouses.[4] The latter two places were used to house the women and children, while the men were held at the Barnet workhouse.

---

[3] Eaton Bray register of baptisms, 1823–1831 [BLARS: P63/1/9] and Eaton Bray Land Tax, 1831 and 1832 [BLARS: QDL Eaton Bray]
[4] Guardians Letter Book [HALS: BG/BAR69]

THE DIARY OF BENJAMIN WOODCOCK

In 1836, when Mrs Peat was absent for a few days, Benjamin's daughter acted as the relief matron rather than his wife. Elizabeth was still probably busy with her younger children Isabella and Merinel, who would have been aged nine and five at the time of their father's appointment. However at the time of the 1841 census, when the new central workhouse was operational, Elizabeth had become the matron and their eldest daughter, Frances, was the schoolmistress. Frances was already acting as the schoolmistress in 1839 according to Pigot's Directory and a Thomas Buckle was the schoolmaster.

Following Benjamin's death in 1848 his son Adolphus seems to have taken over as the master; he was described as such in the 1851 census. As a young man Adolphus had been apprenticed as a shoemaker but, after a period as the workhouse master, he became a publican in London and in 1881 was living in Watford and was described as a retired publican.

The Barnet Union is formed

The poor law district selected for the 'Barnet' area ignored the Hertfordshire/Middlesex boundary and linked together a disparate group of ten parishes. It included the whole of the area covered by the manor of Chipping and East Barnet, that is the market town of Chipping Barnet, the old village of East Barnet as well as the rural area between them that underwent development for housing following the opening of the Great Northern Railway in 1850. This latter district had been an undeveloped part of the East Barnet parish and was to become known as New Barnet.

The Barnet poor law district also included the surrounding parishes of Elstree, Ridge, Shenley and Totteridge in Hertfordshire and Finchley [a late joiner], South Mimms, Friern Barnet and Hadley in Middlesex. Many of these areas would have had their own parish poorhouses and the new regime continued to use some of them while organising their replacement with a single large workhouse on one site.

The new district

A section of a map produced in 1852 for the London and Watford Spring Company to show the position of their pipes and the height of various

INTRODUCTION

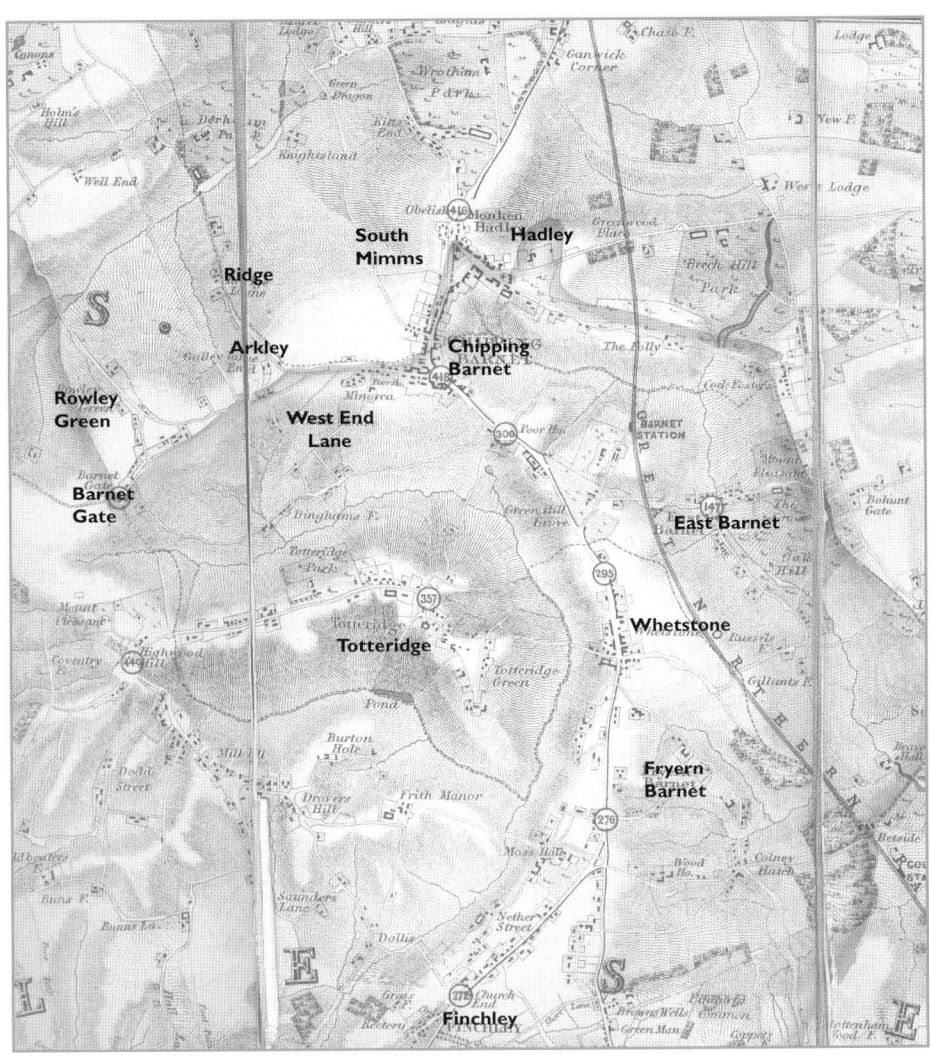

*A section of a map produced in 1852 for the London and
Watford Spring Company [Barnet Museum]*

points above sea level is included on the previous page . It shows just how vast an amount of the district remained undeveloped at this time. Only Chipping Barnet could be described as a town and, even there, the houses were limited to two fairly main roads, Wood Street and the High Street, the upper end of which lay in the parish of South Mimms, Middlesex. The other parishes included in the new district are referred to as villages in their entries in the 1839 Pigot's directories for Middlesex and Hertfordshire. The following extracts provide a little more information.

Chipping Barnet – a town and parish, partly in the hundred of Edmonton, Middlesex, but chiefly in Cashio hundred, and the liberty of St Albans, Hertfordshire, being intersected by the boundary of the two counties; it is 11 miles NW from London, 9 S from Hatfield, and 10 SE from St Albans – seated on a pleasant eminence … .
There are several good inns here, well supported by the number of travellers and coaches passing through; the 'Red Lion' is one of the best, and is the principal posting-house. Much fine hay is produced in this neighbourhood, and sent to the London market.
The church, dedicated to St John the Baptist, stands in the centre of the town: … the living is a perpetual curacy, united to the rectory of East Barnet. A new chapel of ease, having a school and dwellings attached, has recently been erected in part now called West Barnet, (formerly Barnet Common) at an expense of £5,000. A free school was founded here by Queen Elizabeth … . There are twelve alms-houses, in which the inmates are comfortably maintained, and some other contingencies for the indigent . …
Fairs are held here on the 8, 9 and 10 April, for cattle; on the 4, 5 and 6 September, for cattle and pleasure; and an additional fair has lately been established, in November, for the sale of stock and agricultural produce. Pony races are annually held on the last day of the September fair.
East Barnet – a pleasant village and parish in the hundred of Cashio, Herts situate in a valley, ten miles from London, on the right of the north-western road. The country around is fertile, and it is the residence of many respectable families. The church, dedicated to the Virgin Mary, is a small and very ancient structure; the benefice is a rectory, in the patronage of the crown, and incumbency of the Revd Thomas Henry Elwin.

INTRODUCTION

Elstree – a small village and parish in Cashio hundred, 11 miles NW of London, seated upon the confines of the county of Middlesex; a turnpike road, leading to St Albans through Edgware, passing through the village. The village stands on elevated ground, and affords pleasing views – amongst others, that of St Albans abbey church. The church dedicated to St Nicholas, which has been re-edified, has now a neat appearance, but its interior is destitute of any claim to particular description … a reservoir belonging to the Grand Junction Company and rented by the Regent Canal Company to feed their navigation, forms a delightful lake embellishment to the village.

Fryern Barnet – parish and village, situated to the south of East Barnet, in the Finsbury division of the hundred of Ossulton, Middlesex, is of no importance with reference to either business or extent; the village, however, contains some handsome houses, and the environs abound with agreeable scenery. The church, dedicated to Saint James, has been partly rebuilt; the living is a perpetual curacy, in the gift of the dean and chapter of St Paul's London. A national school and alms-houses for twelve aged persons are in the village. In this parish is the hamlet of Colney Hatch, distinguished particularly for the number of respectable and opulent inhabitants, and tasteful residences

Whetstone – a hamlet, partly in the parish of Fryern Barnet, and partly in that of Finchley, distant one mile from the former and two from the latter. A number of coaches proceeding to London, and from the metropolis to the north, pass through this place.

Monken Hadley – The much admired village and parish of Hadley or Monkey Hadley, is in the hundred of Edmonton and county of Middlesex: in the parish, which is adjoining to that of Chipping Barnet, are the mansions of many families of the first respectability. The parish church, dedicated to St Mary is an old structure, chiefly of flint.

Ridge – About one mile from South Mimms, in the hundred of Cashio, lie the village and parish of Ridge, watered by the river Colne. The church is dedicated to Saint Margaret; the benefice, a vicarage, is in the patronage of the Earl of Hardwick.

Shenley – Two miles from London Colney, South Mimms and Ridge, in the hundred of Dacorum, is Shenley village and parish. The church, dedicated to St Botolph, is a neat small edifice of flint and brick, containing some handsome and interesting monuments, and a good organ: the living is a rectory, in the patronage and incumbency of the Revd T Newcome.

South Mimms – a village and parish in the hundred of Edmonton, Middlesex – 14 miles from London, and nearly 4 miles NNW from Chipping Barnet. The village is seated on the main road leading from London to Birmingham, Manchester, Liverpool, etc, and to this situation is to be attributed whatever little business is done in the place; but the majority of the inhabitants derive their support from agricultural employment. The parish church, dedicated to St Giles, is of considerable antiquity; its tower is clothed in ivy, and the interior of the church contains a monument or two of very remote erection. The living is a discharged vicarage, in the patronage of the family of Hammond; the Revd Thomas Price is the present incumbent.

Totteridge – a delightful village and parish in the hundred of Cashio, situated about two miles to the south-west of Chipping Barnet. The church, dedicated to St Andrew, stands near the centre of the village.

Finchley – Finchley village and parish are in the Finsbury division of the hundred of Ossulton, the former being seven miles NNW from London; the parish is nearly eighteen miles in circumference. The great north-western road, through Highgate, passes to the east of the parish church, and is joined by another road from Saint John's Wood, Paddington; several other roads have been formed across Finchley common, which formerly comprised upwards of one thousand acres, now nearly all enclosed. The church, dedicated to St Mary; is a stone edifice, in the later style of English architecture, and contains several ancient monuments; the benefice is a rectory, in the gift of the see of London; the present incumbent is the Revd Ralph Worsley. The other places of worship are a chapel of ease at Whetstone, and others for independents and Wesleyan Methodists. A school, supported by public subscription, and six almshouses, comprise the charities. A market for pigs, held on Monday, was formerly numerously attended; it has long been on the decline – the little business now done is transacted at the 'George' inn.

A table included in *Down and Out in Hertfordshire*[5] showed the number of acres of each parish, its population, the figure at which it was assessed and the level of the poor rate in the years 1832, 1833 and 1834. The table

---

[5] Robert M Gutchen, ed, *Down and Out in Hertfordshire*, Hertfordshire Publications (1984) p12

Parish	Acres	Population	Pop. per acre	Greatest pop.	Assessment £	Ass. Per head £	1832 Poor Rate £	1833 Poor Rate £	1834 Poor Rate £	Average £
Chipping Barnet	1440	2369	1.64	1st	4928	2.08	1075	1031	882	996
East Barnet	1630	547	0.23	9th	3619	6.61	611	666	576	617
Elstree	1370	341	0.25	8th	2891	8.47	323	376	243	314
Ridge	3520	347	0.10	10th	3211	9.25	528	478	482	496
Shenley	4360	1167	0.27	7th	5608	4.80	785	817	818	806
Totteridge	1510	595	0.39	5th	2564	4.30	404	394	326	374
South Mimms	4260	2010	0.47	3rd	12792	6.36	867	926	1072	955
Hadley	2530	979	0.38	6th	3120	3.18	538	476	566	526
Friern Barnet	1330	615	0.46	4th	1836	2.98	347	406	454	402
Finchley	2837	3210	1.13	2nd	13054	4.06	X	X	X	1497

*Table: 1: Population by district showing density and level of poor rate 1832-4
[Robert M Gutchen (ed) 1984]*

on page xv is based on that table with the addition of columns that show
the number of people per acre, the order of the districts in relation to the
density of the population and the assessment for poor rate per head of the
population, together with the average level of poor rate for the years
1832–4.

It can be seen that Chipping Barnet had the highest density of population
per acre, followed by Finchley which had twice the number of acres. Both
Finchley and Barnet had large areas of open common land. Barnet
Common covered the area to the west of the town centre, referred to as
West Barnet, and extended southwards from Wood Street towards Mays
Lane. Chipping Barnet's population was largely concentrated along its
main roads, the High Street and Wood Street. Finchley's population was
more widely spread over several small hamlets. Its common extended
along both sides of the main road to London from just south of
Whetstone.

The least densely populated district was the village of Ridge, followed by
East Barnet, Elstree and Shenley. These areas were very rural but had
some grand houses.

Finchley was the most highly assessed district, followed by South
Mimms. Then came Shenley and Chipping Barnet. Friern Barnet had the
lowest assessment closely followed by Totteridge and then Elstree.
However when the amount of the assessment is calculated as a figure per
head of the population the position changes. Ridge has the highest assessment per head followed by Elstree, then by East Barnet and South
Mimms. Presumably these places had some very rich people and some
much poorer ones.

The Board of Guardians

Each parish elected at least one representative to sit on the Barnet Board
of Guardians with some additional ex-officio guardians. In 1835 the Board
consisted of the following members:

INTRODUCTION

Parishes	Guardians
Chipping Barnet	Charles Bryant, innkeeper John Hopewell, grocer Benjamin Smith, grocer
Shenley	James Ho[a]worth, attorney Benjamin Clayton, Esq, farmer
South Mimms	Samuel Manning, farmer Henry Fox, Esq
Hadley	The Revd John Richard Thackeray James Dickens, Esq
East Barnet	The Revd Thomas Henry Elwin, rector, St Mary the Virgin, East Barnet
Elstree	The Revd William Shove Chalk
Ridge	Frederick Betham, farmer
Totteridge	Samuel Osmond, farmer
Friern Barnet	William Bass, veterinary surgeon
Finchley	(joined later)
ex-officio	George Byng, Esq, MP Alexander [Henry] Dury, Esq, The Revd Abel Lendon, Clerk John Miso, Esq,

Appointments

The first meeting of the Barnet Guardians was held on the 6 July 1835 at the Red Lion Inn which lay on Barnet Hill just south of the church of St John the Baptist. The meeting was held on the orders of the Poor Law Commissioners and in the presence of one of the assistant commissioners, D G Adey. Charles Dickens visited this inn and dined there with his wife at a time when the Barnet workhouse was an innovative project and

Dickens was researching *Oliver Twist*, published in 1838.[6] Dickens demonstrated his knowledge of Barnet when he set the meeting of the Artful Dodger and Oliver nearby.

The Revd Thomas Henry Elwin, rector of St Mary's church, was appointed as the chairman of the board. It was agreed that the first weekly meeting of the Board would be held at the Red Lion Inn, Barnet on Wednesday 15 July at 11 o'clock. Thereafter meetings were to be held on the same day of the week and at the same time, but the venue could be changed. However the Board appears to have continued meeting at the Red Lion until the new workhouse building, with its board room, was completed.

W Norris Franklyn[7] was appointed as clerk to the Board of Guardians at a salary of £60 a year. The Board appointed William Acason[8] as the relieving officer, at a salary of £110. He had to deal with the continuing stream of applications for poor relief, providing outdoor relief as well as residential care in the former poor houses. Acason produced a minute book at the Guardians' regular meetings that gave the names of the applicants, those who were admitted to a poorhouse and when outdoor relief [help without admission] was to be given to paupers. The book was checked by the Guardians and the sum spent debited from the relief charges account.

Responsibility for the financial aspects of the new board fell to James Buckland, a Barnet ironmonger, who was appointed treasurer. The auditor was to be Edward Taplin at a salary of £10 a year who, according to Pigots' directory of 1839, was 'auditor and registrar of marriages' and was listed as residing at High Street, Hadley.

The existing provision

One of the first steps the board took was to set up a committee to assess the existing level of accommodation available in the local parish

---

[6] John Forster, *The Life of Charles Dickens*, Vol 1, 1812–1842, Ch VII p146 (London, Cecil Palmer, 1872–4)

[7] W. Norris Franklyn was an attorney and solicitor in Marylebone [1861 census]

[8] William Acason lived in South Mimms parish on the edge of Barnet Common, and was listed as a registrar of births and deaths [1841 census]

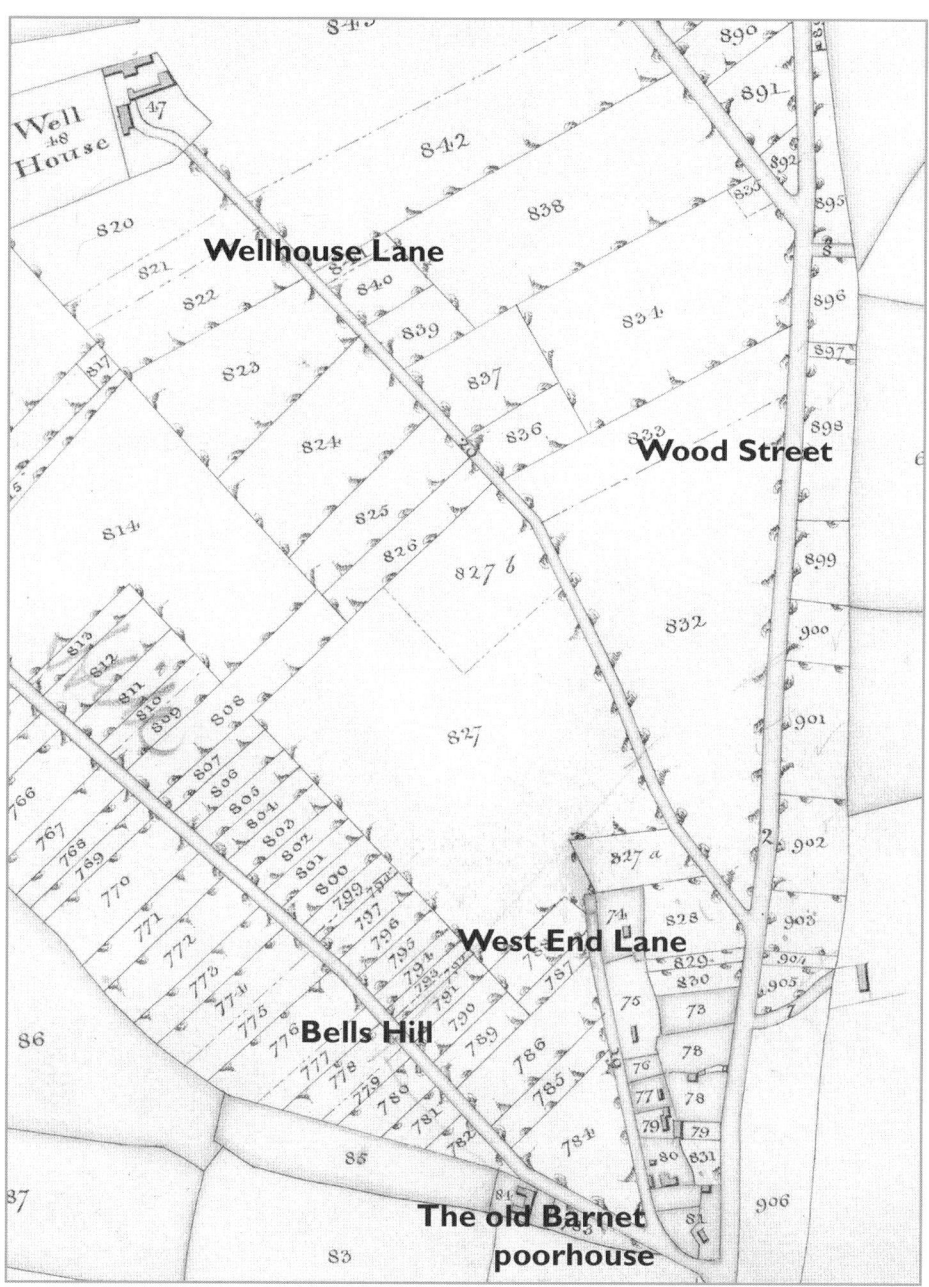

A section of the 1817 enclosure map showing the location of the Barnet poorhouse, plot no 84 [HALS: QS/E13]

poorhouses. They established the following information which has been supplemented with additional detail:

Chipping Barnet – The workhouse had been erected in 1807 and held forty-five people. It had a yard and a garden of two acres. [S H Widdicombe wrote in 1912 that Dr Stewart's house in Wood Street which lay opposite the Ravenscroft almshouses, was once the Barnet parish workhouse.[9] The 1817 enclosure map on page xix shows two cottages on the edge of the common that were used as the poorhouse. They were later used to house orphans of the Crimean war.]

East Barnet – This workhouse belonged to the parish, was mainly built in 1829 and was able to house fifty people. It had a small yard but no garden. [It was formed by two cottages that stood close to the village school directly opposite the end of Capel Road in Church Hill Road.]

Shenley – This building was 'below' the parish, part of it had been erected in 1800. It held about twenty-five people and had a yard and an extensive garden. [On 27 February 1839 Thomas Newcome recorded in his diary the sale of Shenley Workhouse.[10] In 1840 the parish workhouse was bought by the Methodists as a place of worship.]

South Mimms – had a building which was old but in good repair and capable of holding about forty people. It had a yard and small garden.

Elstree Parish – It had been agreed to build a workhouse in 1834 with enough space to house about twenty people with a small yard and a small garden.

Hadley – There was no poor house belonging to the parish. [However there is a reference in 1731 to a cottage near the pound being used as a poorhouse[11] and a survey of 1776 shown on page xxi shows a workhouse near to the area where Hadley Road now joins the Common. It is known that the cottage was used by the Coram Foundling Hospital and as a parish poorhouse.]

Friern Barnet – There was no poor house in Friern Barnet. [However nearby Whetstone put a former poorhouse to good use in 1833 when a new school opened in the building.][12]

---

[9] S H Widdicombe, *Barnet and its History* (1912) p72

[10] Knight and Flood, editors, *Two Nineteenth Century Hertfordshire Diaries*, p505

[11] John Heathfield, 'Some Notes on Hadley Parish Poor House 1768–1835', Barnet & District Local History Society, *Bulletin* no. 35, (1997)

[12] John Heathfield, 'A forgotten Whetstone schoolmaster', Friern Barnet Local History Society *Newsletter* issue no 33 (April 2008) p4

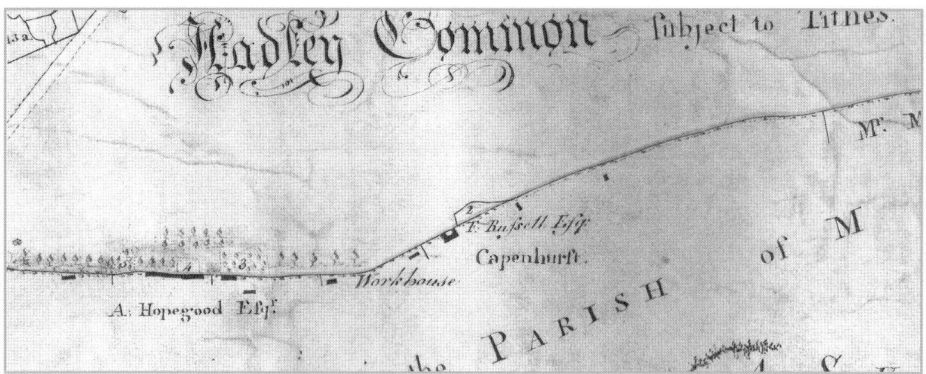

The site of the Hadley poorhouse on a Duchy of Lancaster Survey by Francis Russell 1776 [Duchy of Lancaster]

Totteridge – There was no poor house.

Ridge – was not included in the list [but a note says the poorhouse at Ridge was not to be taken into use by the new union].

The inmates

The new union workhouse was built to house 220 paupers, more than sufficient space for the 194 paupers that were living in the various poorhouses in 1834. They were spread out as follows:

South Mimms had the most paupers at forty-five, while Shenley had thirty-three and Chipping Barnet thirty-one. When the admission

The former Shenley poorhouse, now a Methodist Church

and discharge register began it recorded the circumstances of each person admitted. Fifty-one of the first 250 entries were for paupers who had been admitted before 31 August 1835, and presumably these were those long-term residents, included in the above figures, who stayed on to be housed in the new building.[13]

On 13 June 1835 there were thirteen paupers in the Barnet poorhouse and fifteen men, women and children in receipt of outdoor relief. The former cost 4s a head except for one who cost 10s; the latter were granted sums ranging from 1s 6d to 2s 6d. The last reference in the accounts to inmates and out-pensioners occurred on the 8 August 1835. Presumably by that date all Barnet's paupers were housed in the union workhouse.[14]

Finances

Parishes	No. of paupers	Total cost	Average quarterly cost per head
Chipping Barnet	31	£83.00.00.	£2.12.00.
East Barnet	12	£51.08.04.	£4.07.00.
Elstree	12	£26.03.04.	£2.03.00.
Ridge	21	£41.06.08.	£2.00.00.
Shenley	33	£67.03.04.	£2.00.00.
Totteridge	9	£31.3.004.	£3.08.00.
South Mimms	45	£79.11.08.	£1.15.00.
Hadley	19	£43.16.08.	£2.14.00.
Friern Barnet	12	£33.10.00.	£2.15.00.
Finchley	___	(late joiner, not listed)	—
Total	**194**		

Table 2: The spread and cost of paupers in 1834 and the average quarterly cost under the old poor law system

[13] Barnet Union, Board of Guardians Minutes [HALS: BG/BAR1]
[14] See Appendix II, Workhouse Accounts 25 November 1835 to 4 December 1837

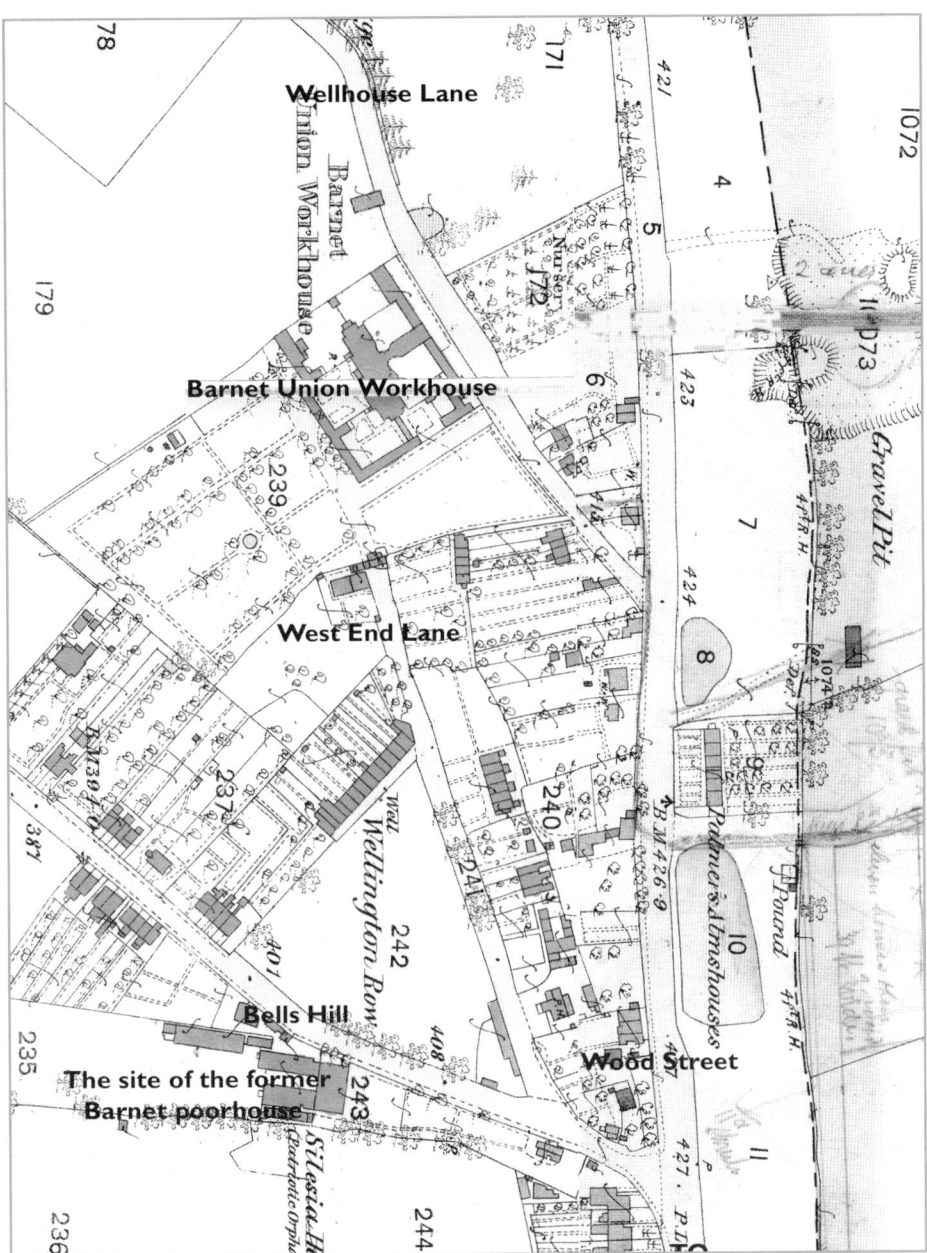

Ordnance Survey map 1881, showing the Barnet Union Workhouse and the site of the former poorhouse which had been superseded by Silesia House, the Patriotic Orphan Asylum [HALS : OS map 1881 sheets XLV3 and XLV7]

In July 1835 the clerk wrote to the overseers of the poor of each parish of the union telling them that an order would be issued on 29 July 1835 by the board, directing the parishes to pay a sum of money equal to one twelfth of their annual average expenditure during the previous three years. [This would have equalled the average cost per quarter for each workhouse and is included in Table 2 and the average cost per head has been calculated and added.[15]

It would seem therefore that Chipping Barnet spent the greatest total amount, closely followed by South Mimms. But the parish that spent the highest amount per pauper was East Barnet at more than four pounds a head. Most of the others spent between two and three pounds a head with Totteridge paying just slightly more.

The accounts held at Barnet Museum for the period from 1835 to 1837 show the names of those paying poor rates and the sums paid out by the Board of Guardians. They also show that the poorhouses continued to be used while the new building was being erected, as did the payment of out-pensioners and the support of named individuals. Woodcock's diary includes entries that demonstrate that the abolition of outdoor relief was not fully appreciated or acted upon. On 5 March, 1837 the Revd Mr Newcome asked Woodcock if the pauper Jiltro, who had been an inmate of the Workhouse for some years, would be allowed out-door relief. Woodcock replied that he was not able to answer the question. He also noted that the pauper Eames, described as 'idiot', who had been admitted to the workhouse but had absconded, had earlier said to him that he did not want to be in the house and would apply for out-relief.

The central workhouse

In 1835 the Board of Guardians agreed that their best course of action was to provide a central workhouse 'to take in classes all of the paupers entitled to relief for this Union'[sic]. Mr Howorth proposed that a central workhouse should be begun and completed with as little delay as possible. It was also agreed that two pieces of land comprising a little over three and a half acres be bought by the Guardians.[16] They were situated

---

[15] Barnet Board of Guardians Letter Book, 1835 [HALS: BG/BAR69]
[16] plot no 827, see map on p. xix

on Barnet Common, near to a track that led to the physic well, later to become known as Wellhouse Lane. The land had earlier been allotted to the poor of the parishes of Chipping and East Barnet under the Barnet Common Enclosure Act, 1815 and was not far from the site of the earlier poorhouse.

As well as providing a site for the new house there was enough land to provide a kitchen garden where those elderly men who were sufficiently able-bodied could work. The clerk was instructed to write to the Exchequer Loan Commissioners asking for a loan of a sum of up to £4,000 to buy the land and build and fit up a central workhouse.

The new building

Despite the Poor Law Commissioners' having submitted drawings of examples of some workhouse plans, the Board agreed to adopt an alternative design by John Griffin, surveyor of Hemel Hempstead, that was similar to that of his own town's house. Griffin had been appointed architect and surveyor in the autumn of 1835. He had designed several workhouses in Hertfordshire, including those at St Albans, Hemel Hempstead and Barnet and had drawn up plans for the enclosure/tithe maps at Berkhamsted and Flamstead.

Griffin wrote to the Board on 25 December 1835 sending plans and specifications of the new workhouse.[17] He asked them to consider when they wanted to have the new building completed and suggested that it would take two months to reach the stage of putting the roof on the main building and a further three months to complete the building. He suggested that work could begin early in February 1836.

The Barnet house differed from the Hemel Hempstead house in just two ways. The first was the projection of a larger section of the front to increase the size of the Board and some other rooms and enlarge the yards. However there was a marked difference in the costs of the Hemel Hempstead and the Barnet houses, despite the similarity of their designs. This was to raise questions from the commissioners. Griffin put the

[17] Barnet Board of Guardians Letter Book, 1835 [HALS: BG/BAR69]

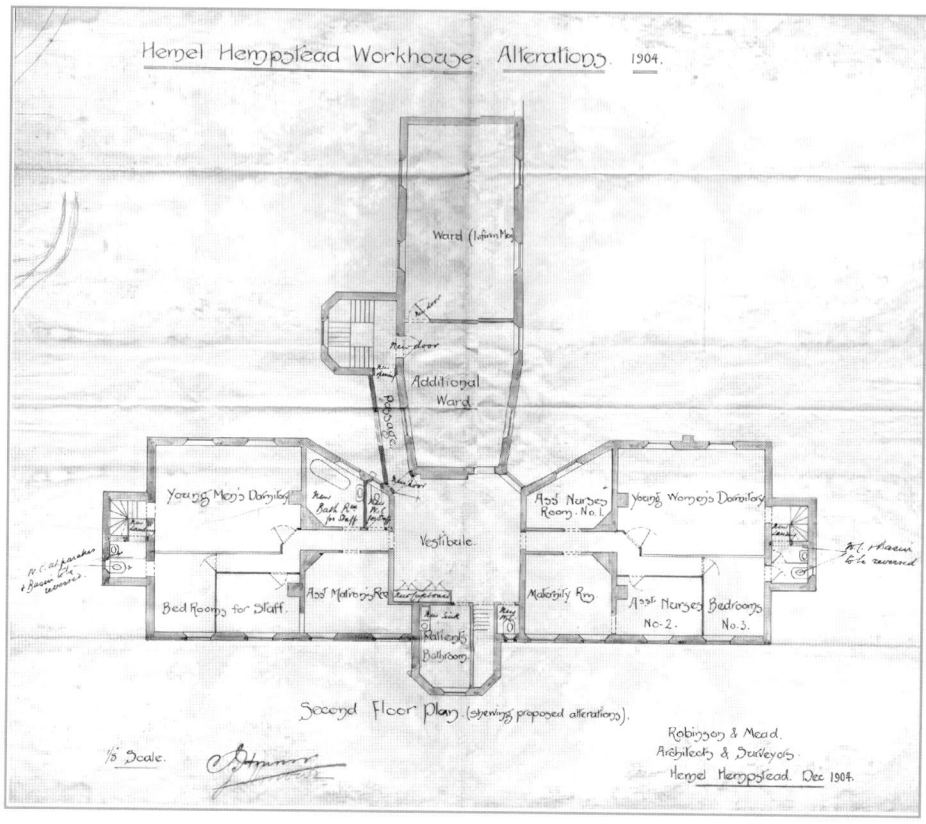

Plan of the Hemel Hempstead workhouse by John Griffin,
dated 1904, when later alterations were planned [HALS: DE/Ma22]

increase down to the accessibility of the Hemel Hempstead site compared
to the Barnet one and the different soil conditions. His explanation to the
Poor Law Commissioners was as follows:

To PLC Adey   9 February 1836

In reply to which I have written them a long explanatory and I think
satisfactory letter, which in substance was this. That in locality and
soil much difference in cost will spend, for instance the price of bricks
delivered at Hempstead by water carriage was 36s per thousand,
while at Barnet they will be by land carriage 44s and the conveyance

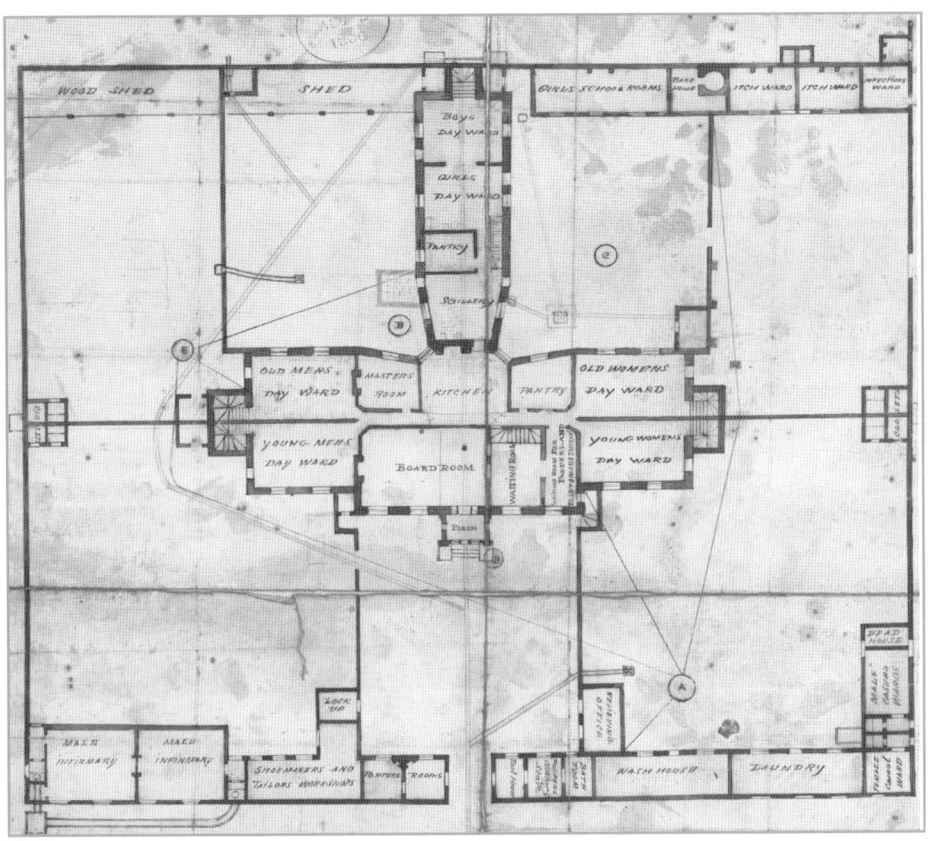

Plan of the Barnet Union Workhouse, August 1856
[Barnet Archives and Local Studies: L7373/1/3]

of Timber, lime lead and other ... materials, will of course bear a proportional difference. At Hempstead the soil is chalk enabling the Builder at two or three feet apart to find a solid foundation, at Barnet it is sand and gravel where a foundation cannot safely be made at less than seven or eight feet, and owing to damp rising for land springs all the ground floors must be raised on brick piers. The drains too are obliged to be carried on a much greater length for in chalk a dumb well is sunk and the drains being conducted into it the contents are so absorbed. I have then added the following statement:

	£	£
Price of Hempstead House		2,900.
Hot water apparatus		
Some extras will be charged for		
Price of Barnet House say	3,200.	
Addition cost of conveyance of bricks		
800,000 at 8s	320.	
Addition cost of cartage of timber etc		
and advance in price of all Building materials	200.	
Additional costs of Foundations and drains	430.	
		4,150.
supposed cost of Hot water apparatus		150.
Surveyors Commission and other incidental		
expenses as Law charges etc		200.
		4,500.[18]

Appointments

The Guardians were anxious to begin building the workhouse without further delay and on 9 May 1836 invited Griffin to meet them to stake out the site of the building. A builder, Mr Bellamy, had already been appointed. Tenders were sought from local tradesmen. Advertisements were submitted to newspapers including *The Times* and *County Herald* inviting tenders for the supply of food, coal, coffins, clothes and candles. The following people were appointed:

Mr Nisbet	butcher of Hadley	meat	Bond £50
Mr John Bangs	South Mimms	coffins	Bond £20
Miss Shuttleworth	Barnet	shoes	Bond £20
Mr Charles Smith	Barnet	clothes	Bond £50
Mr Phillips	Barnet	coals	Bond £40
Mr George Cornwall	nurseryman Barnet	potatoes	Bond £20
Mr Pooley	Hadley	flour, oatmeal and peas	Bond £20
Mr Geo Royer	Hadley	bread	Bond £50
Mr Richard Brodie	cooper of Barnet	pails	—

Positions also needed to be filled to supply religious and medical care.

[18] Barnet Board of Guardians Letter Book [HALS: BG/BAR69]

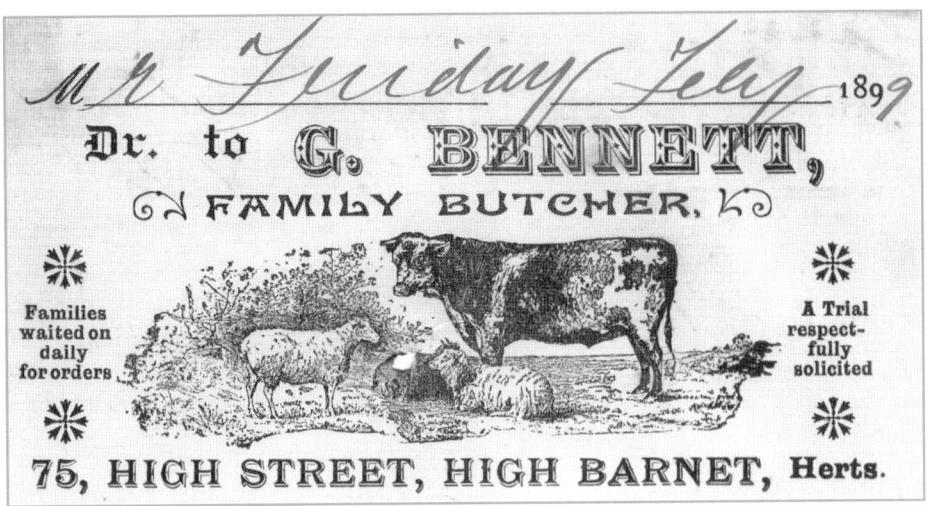

Bennett's butchers, who supplied meat for the workhouse, continued in business in Barnet into the next century [Barnet Museum]

Chaplain

In October 1837 the Revd J A Wood was appointed chaplain at a stipend of £80. His duties included the performance of a complete church service every Sunday morning, to visiting the sick and providing religious instruction to the inmates of the workhouse.

Medical Services

Medical services were needed to ensure the good health of the inmates of the new central workhouse. It was agreed that the Barnet Union would be divided into four medical districts rather than the former parishes. New contracts needed to be entered into with doctors, but not all of those previously employed by the parishes were to be engaged by the Board of Guardians.

An advertisement had been placed in *The Times* newspaper of 19 July 1835 inviting tenders to supply medical services. The medical officers were to be paid £50 per annum plus 10s per case for midwifery. The following doctors applied:

John Humphreys
H B Smith, Shenley, £30 plus 10s 6d midwifery
John Ringrose, Hadley and South Mimms part, £45 plus 10s 6d
midwifery
William Hammond, 4th District Friern Barnet and Totteridge East
Barnet £40

The Board accepted the tenders of William Hammond Esq surgeon, for
Whetstone and that of John Ringrose Esq surgeon, for Potters Bar and H
B Smith, Esq surgeon, for Shenley. The tender of J Humphreys Esq for
Barnet, was turned down. Nearly a year later on 27 May 1836 the Board
wrote to James Carrie Esq surgeon concerning his responsibilities as a
medical officer.

The Board having been informed by an ex-officio Guardian of
Finchley that you now professionally attend the paupers of part of
that parish, I am instructed to apprize you that in its annexation with
this Union on the 16th instant all parochial contracts ceased. This
board however has resolved to ratify your engagement upon the
understanding that it shall terminate on the … Aug next when the
contracts for all the medical officers of the union will expire.

Under the assumption that you do not dissent from the proposition, I
send on the other side some instruction for your guidance in the discharge of your duties as a medical officer.

Instructions

1. To attend no pauper without having received a written order
signed by the Relieving Officer, or a Guardian, or by an overseer
under an order of a Justice of the Peace, Except in cases of sudden, or
urgent necessity, when the authority of a certifiable rate payer of the
parish will be deemed sufficient.
2. To attend Post Mortem examinations of paupers dying in any of
the Workhouses on receipt of an order from the clerk of the Union,
and to attend the Board of Guardians when required.
3. To fill up the accompanying form of Medical return accurately in
all respects, taking especial care to insert at full length the Christian
and Surname of the pauper relieved.

4. To transmit to the Clerk free of charge on Wednesday in every week all the orders for Medical relief with the return made up to Tuesday inclusive. And when any authority has been given by a rate payer or a Justice's order has been issued to write at the foot of the return the name and address of each ratepayer.[19]

Barnet Museum holds a similar set of instructions for the labour master, which are included as Appendix I.

Woodcock's diary includes recommendations from the medical officers that special adjustments be made to the diets of those whom they considered to be in particular need. In February 1837 the medical officer recommended firstly that a woman Burton be given chocolate to drink instead of tea and then that she be given 'a full pint of brandy weekly' as she could not keep anything in her stomach. Another entry on 16 March 1837 shows that the medical officer recommended half a pint of beer should be given each day to the boy Peart, 'who was in a poor way'. A subsequent entry on the 21 March recorded the death of Frances Burton, aged 52, pauper widow of South Mims, following a long illness.

Fitting out the new building

In February 1837 the building was sufficiently complete for Woodcock to record his visit on Saturday the twelfth to ensure that 'the fires were going on right at the New Workhouse'. Presumably this was to help with drying out the building as well as checking that the heating system worked. A week later he had the stoves all taken upstairs and put in their proper rooms as soon as they had come in that morning and fires were lit in them immediately. However the plumbing and heating systems were both not without problems. Woodcock was asking in April 1837 for a tin or wooden spout to be fitted to help in conveying water from the pump to the copper. When Edward Wells aged 50, pauper of Finchley, was admitted on Thursday 25 May 1837 the medical officer was able to recommend the use of the warm bath.

However problems were being experienced with the hot water furnace in the summer of 1837. In January 1838 the Guardians wrote demanding of

[19] Barnet Board of Guardians Letter Book [HALS: BG/BAR69]

Mr Weeks the 'early examination of the Hot Water Apparatus in the Barnet Union Workhouse, which has not acted properly for some time, being out of order'. Woodcock subsequently reported that 'Mr Allen has been at work at the hot water pipes all day but cannot make them to act properly ... we are sadley Pledyd [plagued] with them'. The problems were becoming more acute and the medical officer asked if the chapel could be used as the school until something could be done to sort out the school room. A Mr Nichollas of Barnet, called at the house at Mr Franklyn's request but he said he could not do anything with them without taking them all down. Things went from bad to worse and Woodcock reported in his diary on Sunday 21 January 1838:

> About 12 Oclock on Saturday we was suddenly Alarmd by the Bursting of the Hot Water Pipes. We was obliged to pull the furnice entirely down before they could be repaired fortunately their was no one Burnt. Mr Buckland's Men was at work on the pipes all day on Sunday.

Buckland's men continued to work on the pipes and Woodcock reported on 25 January 1838 'We had the Hot Water Pipes at Work on Saturday, they act better than before'.

Suitable furniture from the existing poorhouses was put to good use in the new building but additional beds and other furniture were needed. The diary records that on 28 April 1837 thirty-six bolsters and thirty beds were bought, that 'goods' from London ordered by Mr Franklyn, arrived on Friday evening and that from Shenley workhouse being sent on the 5 May 1837. The accounts show a sum of £35.11.6d being spent on the furniture for Barnet Union on 5 November 1837.[20]

Visitors to the new workhouse

The building of the Barnet workhouse caused a good deal of interest both from local residents and those interested in establishing similar institutions in their own areas. So many people wanted to visit that Woodcock recorded on Sunday 12 March 1837 that he 'attended at the New Workhouse this afternoon, to admit none without orders from the Guardians to view the New house'. Visitors continued to press to be

[20] See Appendix II

allowed to see the new workhouse. Woodcock recorded that on Saturday 5 April Mr Smith and two gentlemen from another union called to view the workhouse this afternoon and on the Sunday Mr Ray brought two gentlemen who had come 300 miles and was 'much pleased with the Arrangements of the house'. The Revd Mr Wood from Shenley called at the workhouse, just at the inmates dinner hour, on Saturday and expressed himself 'much satisfied with the diet, bedding and healthy appearance of the inmates'. Tellingly he went on to add 'being very different from What was represented to him'. Presumably there had been much talk and some misinformation about this new venture. When Lord Caledon of Tyttenhanger went over the house on the 20 April he expressed himself 'much pleased with the provisions, bedding and general arrangements of the premises'. The stream of visitors continued and a note of annoyance creeps in when visitors expected to be able to attend without first obtaining an order from the Guardians. Woodcock did not allow everyone in. When Lady Hardwick of Tyttenhanger called on the 12 May and wished to go over the house, Woodcock reported that 'not having A Guardians Order We of Course refused'. The use of the word 'we' suggests he felt the need to spread responsibility for this refusal.

Allowing visitors did have some benefits other than approbation. It gained local support and interest and, from time to time, the donation of items for use in the workhouse. When the Revd Mr Thackery, his friends Mr Robarts and his daughters, called to view the house on the 3 June 1837, Miss Robarts asked if there would be any objection if she sent the children some books. Woodcock had written in his diary just the previous day that some children's school books, testaments and prayer books were needed for workhouse use. Perhaps a little prompting had occurred at the visit!

Admission and Discharge Registers

Amongst a number of items received at Barnet Museum following the demolition of the former Barnet Union Workhouse, are two admissions and discharge registers dating from 1836 to December 1839.[21] This is a period that coincides with that of Woodcock's diary.

[21] It is difficult to establish the exact date when the entries were actually written into the book since the early ones appear to cover an existing situation. The handwritten date for the beginning of the book includes no month, merely the year 1836.

THE DIARY OF BENJAMIN WOODCOCK

These first two registers record the reasons for which inmates were taken in together with other details. These include references to the people's state of health, particularly when referring to the elderly, their marital status, their occupation and, for children, whether they were deserted or had lost one or more parents. They also show whether the person was later discharged from the workhouse, the date of discharge and the reason. The date of the admission of the last entry was 23 January 1837.

Volunteers at Barnet Museum have started work putting the information into a searchable database. The first two hundred and fifty entries, covering the period from 1834 to January 1837, have been extracted and examined by the author and an extract of the first four hundred and fifty entries is included in Appendix III.

As has been mentioned the early entries include information from prior to 31 August 1835 and cover references to fifty-one existing inmates, who had been admitted before that date into the existing poorhouses. 140 entries for seventy people who had been admitted twice and thirty-nine for thirteen people who had been admitted on three occasions. The majority of admissions were made on the orders of the Board, forty-three were ordered by the relieving officer and just one admission was by the overseer of the poor.

The reasons for the admissions ranged from ill health, both physical and mental, being aged, out of work or past work, without a home, deserted or having lost father or mother or both. Ninety out of the 250 entries involved some sort of poor physical health, for nine the cause was poor mental health, fifty-seven had either left their employment or lost their job, twenty-five had no home, twenty-two were aged or past work. As far as children were concerned seventeen entries were for children who had been deserted, four had lost one or both parents, one was starving. For a few no information was given.

The ages of those admitted varied from those born in the workhouse and to those aged 91. There were forty-seven entries for children aged 10 and under, forty-three entries for those aged between 11 and 20, eleven entries for those aged between 21 and 30, fifteen aged 31 to 40, fourteen 41 to 50, twenty-nine aged between 51 and 60, thirty-two between 61 and 70, forty-four aged 71 to 80 and ten over 80. There were two entries where no age was given. The religion of all those admitted was entered as 'Church of England'.

Later changes

To deal with changing needs the main workhouse buildings were added to. Additional buildings were put up around the main building including work rooms, laundry buildings, cells for casual paupers and wash-houses. A substantial infirmary was built to the north in 1886 and an equally substantial 'master's and matron's' block was added facing the main entrance to the old workhouse buildings in 1901.

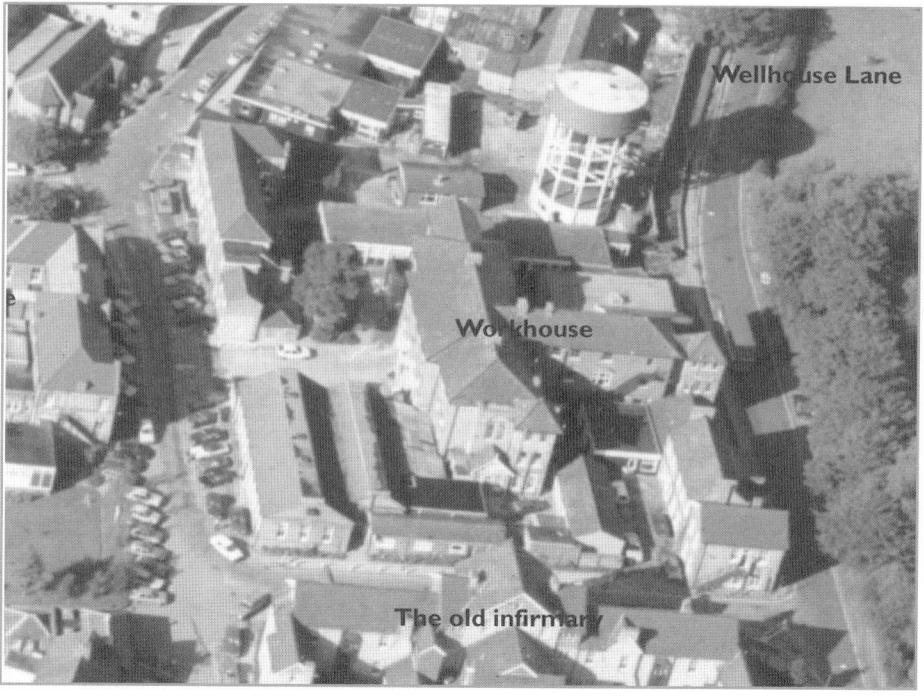

The former workhouse buildings surrounded by later additions in the mid-1950s [Barnet Museum: WE/04]

THE DIARY OF BENJAMIN WOODCOCK

Boys from Queen Elizabeth's Boys' School outside the West End Lane entrance to the union workhouse c1911 [Barnet Museum]

During the First World War new buildings were taken over for the use of injured soldiers. The Wellhouse Hospital was opened by the then former Barnet Board of Guardians as a separately administered unit in November 1920 and a chapel was built nearby. In 1927-8 a one hundred-bed nurses' home was added in the grounds of the hospital. The buildings continued in use as a Poor Law Institution until 1939 and on 5 July 1948 the Wellhouse became a National Health hospital.

However the greatest change of all happened in 2002 when the whole site was almost completely cleared and the workhouse, the former infirmary, the chapel and all the other older buildings were completely demolished. A modern twenty-first-century hospital now serves the local community.

Despite the loss of the workhouse buildings something important does remain in the form of many of its valuable records. These include the diary written by its first master that has been used as the basis of this book. This diary and other records provide a link with the well known story of Dickens' Oliver Twist and the district with a period when the

INTRODUCTION

new Barnet Union workhouse was a visible sign of national changes in the system of the provision of care for the poorest and most vulnerable members of the community.

The main entrance to the former workhouse in 2002

The newly built Barnet hospital buildings in 2002

Editor's conclusion

A close examination of Benjamin Woodcock's diary has led the editor to review many of her preconceived ideas concerning the treatment of the parish poor, at least during the early years of the new union system. While it may still seem one of strict control, when put into the context of the times, there does appear to have been a real attempt to provide a reasonably good system of care. The attitudes to casual paupers and the undeserving poor is less sympathetic but still not unreasonable.

As far as the master is concerned, Woodcock appears to have had no previous experience or training. There is no indication as to why he should have made the career change from a tailor to a workhouse master. He was very much in awe of the Guardians, to whom he appealed for advice and approval on occasions when in doubt as to the action he should take. He and they were not always in agreement but it was the Guardians who had the final say. The medical officers, appointed by the Guardians, were more inclined to express their opinions, frequently asking for special treatment for ill paupers. However they did not always attend as promptly as they might have done and there were occasional delays in treating paupers.

There are times when the loss of the ability to provide outdoor relief is felt by the parish poor and by the officials. There seems to be some reluctance to lose this method of providing support in the pauper's own home from both the paupers and the master.

The location of the new building meant a distancing of its inmates from their former neighbours and families and permission had to be sought for any time absent from the workhouse. The provision of reasonable clothing for the inmates was one in which Woodcock, as a former tailor, seems to have taken a particular interest. He declined to take the inmates to church when he felt they were not sufficiently well dressed and his annoyance is evident when inmates take advantage of the system and leave taking their union clothing with them without permission.

Woodcock does have problems when dealing with particularly difficult inmates. The diet in the workhouse seems to be reasonable and although

INTRODUCTION

the withdrawal of food is used as a form of punishment it does seem to
have been noted and reported to the Guardians when it occurred. Other
punishments were reported in the diary but the advice of the Guardians
seems to have been sought and although the straight coat was used as a
last resort Woodcock was overruled when it came to the use of the cane
with female inmates. Mental health conditions are neither always recognised nor dealt with appropriately.

The editor has come to the conclusion that, at least during the early years
of the Barnet Union Workhouse, that house was not the 'house of horrors'
we are led to believe to be the normal state of union workhouses.

The volume itself

Woodcock's diary is a small, hand-written volume held at Hertfordshire
Archives and Local Studies under reference 70876. Its survival and repro-
duction in full here provide an opportunity for readers to reach a better
understanding of the running of an early workhouse, the views and
actions of the master, the Guardians and the paupers. It should be born in
mind however that the diary was produced to be seen by the Board of
Guardians. Woodcock would therefore want to show his management of
the workhouse in the best possible light. From it the Guardians would
trace their master's progress and in it they could note their agreement
with or disapproval of his actions and intents.

Benjamin Woodcock uses a highly individual style of punctuation
with the regular scattering of hyphens and short wavy lines. They seem
to indicate his pausing for thought or act as a flourish at the end of an
entry. To aid the understanding of the text, the wavy lines and hyphens
have been deleted and replaced with a full stop or comma when appro-
priate. Woodcock almost never uses a full stop and rarely, and not always
appropriately, a comma.

His use of the upper and lower case is equally irregular but the author has
the impression that the use of capitals in unexpected places appears to
indicate his desire to emphasise a word or phrase and these have been
retained.

He abbreviates frequently used place names and officers' titles; for example he uses CB for Chipping Barnet and RO for relieving officer. The editor has extended in full the place names but has tried to retain his idiosyncratic style while completing incomplete words within square brackets where it is felt beneficial to the reader. She has generally left the text unchanged unless there is a need for clarification, but has modernised the punctuation in parts for the same reason. She has also 'tidied up' the headings, dates and comments column to provide overall conformity.

Comments, usually by the Guardians, were generally included in the column set to the left-hand side of the page alongside the paragraph to which they related and where the place, days of the week, dates and item numbers were also located. As the diary progresses this practice becomes more erratic. These details begin to appear within the main entry and the use of the day and the date is replaced by a number relating to the order of the entry. Once the new workhouse is fully operational there ceases to be a need to add a parish location. In order for the reader to be able to identify entries and to provide conformity, the editor has moved this information to the left hand column.

Extracts from the diary were included in an earlier volume produced by Hertfordshire Publications, *Down and Out in Hertfordshire*, in 1984. They were introduced and edited by Robert M Gutchen. The book included two other chapters on associated topics: 'The Operation of the Old Poor Law in the Parish of St Michael's, St Albans 1721–1834' by Eleanor Truwert and 'The Old and the New Poor Law in Hitchin', by Grace Peters.

George Orwell's book, *Down and Out in Paris and London*, described his experiences staying in a range of 'spikes'[22]. Orwell wrote 'There are regular beaten tracks where the spikes are within a day's march of one another. I was told that the Barnet–St Albans route is the best'[23]. The title of the later Hertfordshire book is obviously a reference to Orwell's earlier volume.

[22] workhouses
[23] George Orwell, *Down and Out in Paris and London*, Ch 26, (Victor Gollance, 1933) p143

INTRODUCTION

This book

The opportunity has now been taken by the Hertfordshire Record Society to reproduce Woodcock's diary in full and to include additional information of the same period held at Barnet Museum and at HALS, to help provide a broader understanding of the diary's setting. This material is provided mainly as appendices, and comprises extracts from the early admission and discharge register, a set of early accounts and the undated rules for the labour master. A copy of the rules for the medical officer that are held with the correspondence of the Board of Guardians at Hertfordshire Archives and Local Studies is included in this introduction as well as other extracts and additional information from these sources. Included as Appendix V is an extract covering the period from 1834 to 1838 of a document held at HALS that provides details of paupers who were found work by the Guardians.

A bibliography of both published works relevant to the subject and original sources can be found at the end of this book.

Illustrations include copies of plans of the original architect's design for the workhouse, maps showing the location of the former poorhouses and of the new district workhouse, together with a selection of photographs. Georgina Oliver has kindly produced an artist's impression of the central portion of the workhouse building, based on photographs taken at the time of its demolition, and images based on the cover of the Admission and Discharge Register and plans held at the Barnet Archives and Local Study Centre.

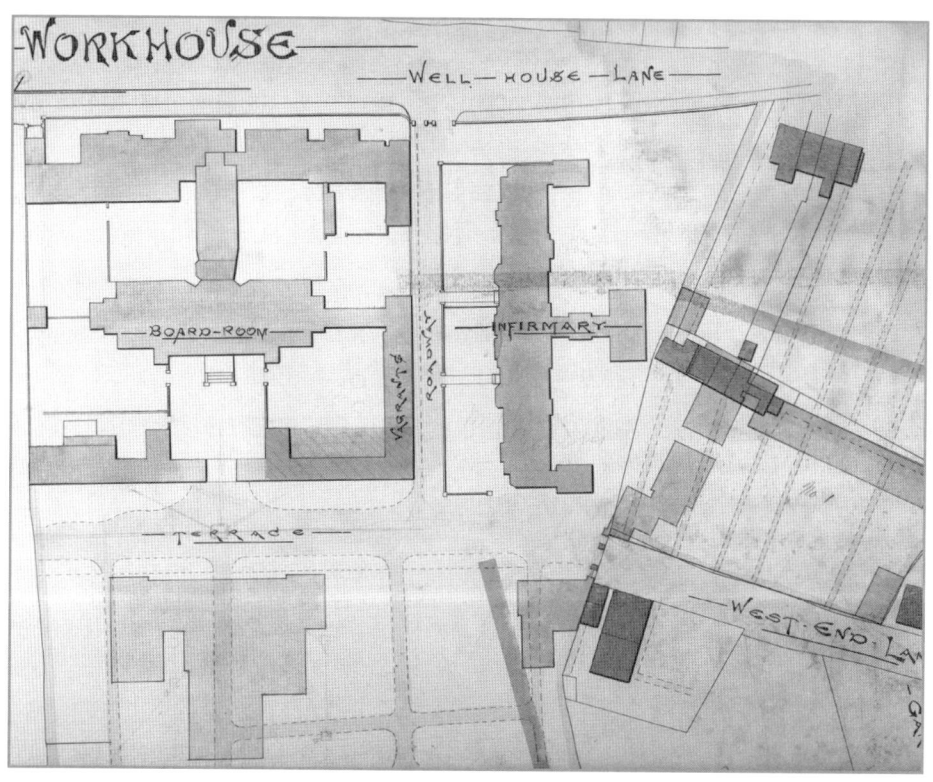

General plan of the workhouse buildings,W H Mausbridge, 1891
[Barnet Local Studies and Archives Centre: L7373/58]

The diary of Benjamin Woodcock
master of the Barnet union workhouse

Thursday, 1 September, 1836

Chipping Barnet — Paid into the hands of Mr Buckland Treasurer Sep[tembe]r 1st five Shillings, as p[er] order of the Board

Frank Watkins, returns his thanks to the Board and observed it was more than his former Conduct deserved, but he should endeavour for the future to improve

Friday
Chipping Barnet — Mr Dowton & Mr Sharp, calld at the workhouse this afternoon, & went over the premises

Friday
East Barnet — Mary Willey was discharged from East Barnet Workhouse yesterday, at her own request

Sold Cheek the Sweep 2 Sep[tember] 1836 11 Bushell Ashes at 2d a Bush[el]l ... 1s 10d paid the same time

Widow Cox, of South Mimms, was requested by the Members of her Late Husband's Club,[1] on the Last Meeting, to attend at the Woolpack Barnet at the quarterly Meeting held in Sept[embe]r, which is Wednesday the 14th. May she have permission to go?

on reasoning with Laura Cooper for her mis conduct this Afternoon towards the Matron, she went off in a fit, without an explanation

[1] Clubs were working-class insurance organisations which, for very small weekly contributions, paid death or sickness benefits. Widow Cox is probably Ann Cox, widow of South Mimms, described as an infirm, aged, poulterer in the admission and discharge register.

THE DIARY OF BENJAMIN WOODCOCK

Saturday
Shenley

the Women & Children, all orderly peaceable & in good health, having plenty of Medicine in the house, in case of immediate Necessity

Sunday
Chipping Barnet

William Head, the youth who was admitted about two months back with broken thigh, was able to walk to Church this afternoon with the assistance of his Crutches, without the least inconvenience

Monday
Chipping Barnet

This was his own Statement

Francis Long of Ridge was discharged this Morning at his own request. His health & strength being so much improved since he has been in the Workhouse that he is again able for Work. During the time he was at home, attended by Mr Smith the Medical Officer, he was daily getting worse.

Monday
East Barnet

The Girl Cooper more orderly. The other inmates all peaceable & going on Comfortable

Monday
Chipping Barnet

Admitted by order of the R[elieving] Officer A casualty named Edward Rockery aged 60 belonging to Scotland, who had met with an accident. As soon as we got him to bed, I sent the usual Notice to the Medical Officer to attend him. The Answer was, Mr. Morrison was from home, & they sent the order back by the bearer. The poor man lay in much pain with his Ancle till 2 Oclock the following day When Mr M[orrison] calld

Tuesday
Shenley

The Coals ordered of Mr Phillips, to be delivered at Shenley Workhouse, on the 1st Sep[tembe]r, was not sent on Wednesday the 7th when I was there

Early this Morning Charles Woodhouse, John Bone & Jos[ep]h Collins got out of the window & left the Workhouse leaving their Union Jackets & Caps behind. I cannot learn from what Cause

**Tuesday
Chipping Barnet**

Mr Clayton the Butcher, having Sent A lean Stickin[2] of Beef this Morning, Contrary to the Contract, the Matron sent it back. The Meat of Late, [h]as been very lean Altogether.

**Wednesday
E Barnet**

Laura Coopers, Refractory Conduct, disturbd the whole house Again this Morning.

all the other inmates orderly, but say the general behaviour of Laura, is most shameful

**Wednesday
Chipping Barnet**

The poor man Warren gets gradually Weaker, the woman Crew Appears much the same but the Shillington Youth has laid up his Crutches being able to walk with two Sticks. All the other inmates in good health except the Scotch Casualty whose Leg Seems much inflamd

Thursday, 8 September, 1836

Shenley

This evening the two runaway boys Woodhouse & Collins returned to the Workhouse after three days Absence. I am waiting for orders from the Board how they should be punished

**Friday
East Barnet**

Admitted, by order of the R[elieving] Officer, to East Barnet Workhouse, Ruth Shepherd aged 28 belonging to Finchley. She has but one hand

Chipping Barnet

Admitted this Evening by order R[elieving] Officer, Ann Gray, till a conve[ni]ent opportunity of having her examined before A Magistrate, for Selling her Union Clothing.

**Saturday
Shenley**

Mr Phillips, having not Sent the Coals to Shenley, According to order, on my return home, I sent another order to Mr Pruden, which was instantly attended to

[2] Stickings are coarse and mutilated pieces of meat.

THE DIARY OF BENJAMIN WOODCOCK

Chipping Barnet   Mr Morrison, the Medical Officer has ordered two Glasses of Wine to be given daily to the Man Warren, instead of one, he being in A very low weak state

Monday **East Barnet**   The Matron, being required to attend the Magistrates' Meeting this Morning, to give evidence in the Case of Ann Gray and it being necessary for some one to Superintend during her absence, I remained in the house, till her return. All orderly

Charles Lambert, returned to the Workhouse this Afternoon, after an Absence of Upwards of A Week, Without leave. I think it may do him good, to bring him before the board, that he may hear his punishment

Tuesday   The Woman Jiltro much better. All the Other inmates doing well, & quite orderly

Wednesday **Chipping Barnet**   Admitted this afternoon, by order R[elieving] Officer An Irish Casualty Woman [Dunn] in the family way. Mr Morrison being not well, Mr Humphreys promptly attended, & shortly deliverd her of A female infant. Both of which are doing well. She fell ill in Hadley

The youth from Shillington [William Head] [who] broke his thigh, is able to be removed to his parish, at the pleasure of the Board[3]

Wednesday **East Barnet**   the woman Burton rather worse, but all the Other inmates better, & quite orderly without Ann Gray

Chipping Barnet   Joseph Warren & Elizabeth Crew, gradually Sinking. The Scotch Casualty better. All the other inmates going on Comfortable

Please to Confirm the enclosed Order

---

[3] Because each parish was responsible for the expenses of its own poor, the costs incurred by the Barnet Guardians for supporting William Head in the Chipping Barnet Workhouse and that of sending him back to his own parish, would be reimbursed by the parish of Shillington, Bedfordshire.

East Barnet   Ester Segrave, [Esther Sygrave] who was pronounced to be in the family way in last week's Medical Report, appears upon A Subsequent examination, not to be Correct

Thursday, 15 September, 1836

Chipping Barnet   Edward Hull, the Younger, pauper of Hadley, Admitted this day by order of Board. Had him strip'd & washed Immediately, & gave him Clean Union clothing, & burnt his old rags, being altogether in a most filthy state

Chipping Barnet
Friday   Thomas Cheadle, who for Several days has Suffered from A relaxation of the bowels was taken worse about two Oclock this Morning. Mr Morrison being unwell I sent for Mr Humphreys, who Attended Immediately & Stopd with him nearly an hour but had very little hopes of his recovery

Mr Sears, & Mr Franklin, calld at the Workhouse this afternoon, & wished to look over the premises.

Friday
East Barnet   Widow Cox States that oweing to some arrangement, by her Late Husband, previous to his Death, she is not likely to receive the twenty pounds from the Club as was expected

Widow Burton's in a very poor way. All the other inmates doing well & quite orderly

Saturday
Shenley   Betsy Williams, Admitted into Shenley Workhouse on thursday, by order of R[elieving] Officer, this Girl who enterd the Service of Mrs Beetham a short time back, was discharged in Consequence of not being Strong enough to do the work

Punished the two runaway Boys, Collins & Master Woodhouse as per orders of the board. All quite Comfortable.

THE DIARY OF BENJAMIN WOODCOCK

Saturday
Chipping Barnet

Thomas Cheadle Aged 76, East Barnet pauper, Died this Morning between 2 & 3 Oclock because of the Bowel Complaint

Sent directions, to the Medical Officer, undertaker & Sexton who promptly attended

Monday
East Barnet

the Meat sent this Morning, from Mr Claytons was in 5 pieces, which must waste in Cooking

Monday
Chipping Barnet

Admitted by Order of R[elieving] O[fficer], John Williams & his wife Eliz[abe]th paupers of Elstree, both of which was in a State of intoxication. The Woman who was certainly the worst of the two, was very pert

Monday
Chipping Barnet

About 6 Oclock this evening, we Buried Thomas Cheadle. Some of the inmates & three of his Relations followed. One of which, his Sister in Law, being desirous to know what money he left, States that About three Months back she gave him two Sovereigns, but I found but 5s in his box the following Morning. Old Tuckfield was very attentive at his Bedside from the time he was taken, till he died but he dennys knowing anything about the money

Tuesday
Chipping Barnet

About 7 Oclock this Morning I started with William Head to Shillington about 6 miles the other Side Hitchin & deliv[ere]d him Safe into the Care of Mr Wilson the Overseer as p[e]r order of Magistrates. They promise to forward the expenses in a few day[s].

Wednesday
Shenley

To have one month's warning

Mrs Ward of Green Street, with the approbation of the Board, is willing to take the Girl Williams into her Service for 12 months at Michaelmas next. She will want A pair Shoes before She goes. To have her Board Lodging & Clothing. All orderly.

Wednesday
Chipping Barnet

To have 2s 6d

the Man Rockery the Scotch Casualty thinks he will be able to go out in A few days & begs the board will be pleased to advance him A few shillings having upwards of 2 hundred Miles to go home

The Casualty, who was confined last week, her infant are both doing well & will soon be able to go out

the Man Warren & the woman Crew are on the decline but all the other inmates much the same as Last report

the 14lb Beef, sent this Moment was in Six pieces, though I have told Messrs Sears & Clayton repeatedly of the same

allowed

Mr Dowton wishes to Know if their will be any objection to his Sending any one to look over the premises

To enquire if any will like.

James Fennell, the Master Sweep at Hadley wants An Apprentice & wishes to Know, if the Guardians will have any Objection to his having one out of the Workhouse

Thursday, 22 September, 1836

Chipping Barnet
Thursday

Francis Long, pauper of Ridge, who was discharged at his own request, only 16 days back, was readmitted by order of the board this afternoon, examind same day by the Medical Officer, whoes of Opinion, he is Consumptive

Friday Shenley

refused to go

Betty Parkes to whom the Board gave leave of absence for a day a little time ago Wants me to Ask if she may go to London for a few days, but I told her, the application would be useless

THE DIARY OF BENJAMIN WOODCOCK

Friday
Chipping Barnet

Deliverd Yesterday Evening by order of Mr Bass, 40 Bushel Sand, at 8d p[e]r bushel, £1 6s 8d paid Same time

Saturday
East Barnet

It being Necessary, that the Woman Burton, should have constant Attendence & the Matron observing she had some difficulty in getting any one to wait on her, I sent on the following Morning Betty Williams, as the most proper person to look after her. Her husband John Williams, would be found very useful to go on errands but I would not send him, without orders.

granted

the meat sent this Morning, being in 5 pieces the Matron observed to the man, She Should not in future take it in. In Answer to which, he said his Master cannot send it otherwise

Sunday
Chipping Barnet

two Gentlemen from London calld this Afternoon to look over the premises

Monday
Chipping Barnet

the Scotch Casualty Drover, being able to walk, was discharged this Morning at his own request having, with tears in his eyes, expressd his Sincere thanks for the great benefit he had received. I gave him the 2s 6d by Orders of the board, together with 10s 6d from the Revd Mr Wimbolt for whom he said by the blessing of God he should ever offer up his humble prayers.

approved

Having received a Letter from Finchley, signd by Mr Jacques & Mr Osman, two parishioners, to certify that Richard Smith, brother to one of the paupers, was dangerously ill, I gave Thomas Smith, one of the inmates permission to go over this Morning And sent A boy to guide him, he being entirely Blind

The Irish Casualty Woman [Dunn], who was safely deliverd in the Workhouse of a female infant on the 14 instant, having talkd of going out of the house this

week I requested she should take her infant to Church
have her Babtized before they where discharged,
which was done Yesterday Sunday According

Monday
Chipping Barnet

Miss Goodwin, Barnet Common, applyd at Chipping
Barnet Workhouse this Morning for A Steady Honest
Middle Aged Woman, to attend upon her Father who
is Confined to his Bed and Widow Gillman at East
Barnet house, being the most likely woman to suit, I

approved

sent her the following Morning as she was wanted
Immediately

Monday
East Barnet

Widow Cox, wishes to meet the Members of her late
Husband's Club, to be held at the Woolpack Barnet
on Wednesday the 5 Oct[obe]r about the burial

refused

Money. Is she to have permission?

Tuesday
Chipping Barnet

Thomas Smith, & the boy, having returned from
Finchley, yesterday Evening, as Steady[4] as they went
out, in the Morning and, having brought me one of
the enclosed notes signd by the Churchwardens and

approved

Overseers, I permitted him to go out the following
Morning. Which I hope will be approved

Tuesday
Shenley
allowed

Mrs Ward of Green Street is perfectly willing to take
the Girl Betsy Williams from old Michaelmas Day,
upon the Conditions proposed by the Guardians

requested

Charles Gwillim, Aged 10, belonging to Finchley,
being quite agreeable on Saturday I askd him the
same question on the following tuesday, wheather he
would like to be apprentice to a Sweep. His answer
each time was yes. Consequently I requested Mr James
Fennell to call at the Workhouse and see the boy &
then wait upon the Board

The woman Jiltro, on the improvement, the other
inmates & Children all in good health & quite orderly

[4] sober

THE DIARY OF BENJAMIN WOODCOCK

Wednesday
Chipping Barnet

The Irish Casualty woman Dunn, & her female infant, Eliz[ab e]th, both being in good health, was discharged from the workhouse this day quite Satisfied

East Barnet

allowed

The woman Burton sinking fast. The Medical Officer, [h]as orderd her Brandy & Water. All the other inmates much the same as last report

Chipping Barnet

Warren Pearce & the Woman Crew much the same. All the other inmates doing well

Thursday, 29 September, 1836

Chipping Barnet

Died this Afternoon between 3 & 4 Oclock Elizabeth Crew Aged 75. Gave the usual instructions to the Medical Officer, Undertaker, & Sexton

Friday
Chipping Barnet

To attend with the
boy on Thursday next

James Fennell, the Sweep, calld at the Workhouse this Morning to say he had seen the boy Gwillim & that he was just the right size but I told him the Guardians had an objection to his being A Sweep. He said he knew Mr Hopewell & would speak to him about it

Friday
East Barnet

Widow Gillman, whom I sent to Mrs Goodwin, would not suit. Consequently she returned. The Woman Burton rather better. The other inmates all Comfortable

Saturday
Shenley

the Revd Mr Newcome calld at the workhouse & told some of the boys they had better be A Drummer or go for A Sailor than be confind there

Saturday
Chipping Barnet

William Pearce pauper of South Mims, aged 76, Died About three Oclock this Morning. Gave proper directions to the Medical Officer, Undertaker & Sexton

Sunday
Chipping Barnet

Eliz[abe]th Crew Buried this Afternoon about 4 Oclock, followed by some of her own Children &

some of the inmates. Having received A note from Mr Benj[amin] Smith, I gave permission for Henry Crew to be out till 7 Oclock at which time he came home

Monday Chipping Barnet

It Appears by the statement of Mrs Wells of Hadley that the Girl, Mary Cooper, being so Idle she could not Keep her but that Mrs Cornwall at the Nursery had agreed to try her

1 of the Sacks of Coals, sent in from Mr Phillips, on Saturday evening, was 7 lbs short weight

Buried this afternoon, about 4 oclock, William Pearce, pauper of South Mims. Thomas & Sarah Balls, his Son & Daughter, with Several of the inmates, followed him to the Grave after which his Daughter Sarah Balls begd I would ask the Board, If she might be allowed to have A Small family trunk, belonging to her Late Father

Wednesday Shenley

the woman Jiltro better, the other inmates all in good health and quite Orderly

Wednesday East Barnet

Ruth Shepherd, one of the Finchley paupers wants to go to Holloway at the request of Mr Lewis, & begs for leave of Absence for 2 or 3 days.

Mr Whaley at the Cross Keys South Mims, wants a Servant. Had I better send Esther Sygrave from East Barnet Workhouse after the place?

the poor Woman Burton, Sinking every day. The other inmates all going on well

Chipping Barnet

the Woman Crew left A Red Cloak, which she begd previous to her death, might be given to her Daughter

Jos[ep]h Warren still sinking all the other inmates doing well

Thursday, 6 October, 1836

Friday
Chipping Barnet

I permitted Henry Crew, one of the inmates, to go out for about 1 hour, this morning to see his Son, whoes Confined to his Bed, dangerously ill

Friday
Chipping Barnet

Died of A Consumption About 8 Oclock this Evening, Joseph Warren Aged 41 of South Mims inmate. The following Morning gave Notice to Mr Hudson, Medical Officer, & the Undertaker & sent a boy to Mr Vincents Lodge at Mims Wash to inform his Father

East Barnet
Friday

Esther Sygrave went this Morning by order of the board, to Mrs Whaley, South Mims, after A Situation but she was too late. It was 6 Oclock before she returnd owing to the rain

Friday

Mrs Peat the Matron, who had been to Barnet, this Morning, on business, returnd to the house about 6 Oclock

Having stated to Ruth Shepherd, that her application for 3 or 4 days Holyday, was refused by the Board, she made some very unbecoming remarks and observed she should give Notice to be discharged on Monday but it appears she left the same evening saying she should return on thursday

Saturday
Chipping Barnet

On enquiry, I le[a]rnt from one of the inmates this Morning that 2 or 3 of the Men, whose regular allowance of Bread, being more than they can Eat themselves, they give it to one of the Women, which I suspect takes it out of the house when she goes to Church on Sundays. How shall I act?

Joseph Warren aged 41 Buried this Afternoon About five Oclock followed by his Father Mother & Neice & Several of the inmates

Shenley
Tuesday

The girl Wllliams goes to Mrs Ward Situation this Evening as p[e]r Orders of the board

I brought the boy Gwillim with me to Barnet this Aftern[oo]n that he may Attend on thursday as p[er] orders of the board.   All the other inmates healthy & orderly

East Barnet
Wednesday

Mrs Peat the Matron left the Workhouse this afternoon for 2 or 3 weeks. My Daughter will Superintend during her Absence, as p[er] order

the woman Burton Still sinking. The other inmates all in tolerable health & quite orderly

Chipping Barnet
Wednesday
medical officer to report [?]

William Green pauper of Hadley, being very much afflicted with the rheumatism, begs he may be allowd A Flannel Shirt & p[ai]r Drawers

Permission given

Thomas Smith the Blind man, begs he may be permitted to attend the funeral of his Brother Richard who now lies Dead at Finchley

the whole of the inmates in Barnet house are in good health & quite orderly

Thursday, 13 October, 1836

Thursday
Chipping Barnet

James Fennell the Sweep calld at Workhouse this Evening to Know the arrangement of the Board with respect to Charles Gwillim. I told him I was directed by the Guardians to Keep him as usual till further orders

Saturday
East Barnet

the Relieving Officer, this morning having informd Ann Gillman of A Situation, She gave up her Union Clothing in the Afternoon, & was Discharged According. Its at Mr Debenham the Well house Barnet Common

THE DIARY OF BENJAMIN WOODCOCK

Saturday
Shenley

Took the Boy Gwillim, with me to Shenley this Morning As p[e]r Orders. All in good health

James Earle whom we have Lodged in the Workhouse for several nights, & [a] pauper of Friern Barnet was leaving the house about the usual hour this Morning, rather in haste. I calld him back, searchd him & found his Coat pockets filld with Potatoes, which he Acknowledged having taken out of the Barn where he Sleptd. He hoped I would forgive him, as he was going to work the following day. He had nearly a whole quartern Loaf of his own, in a bag at the Same time

Monday
Chipping Barnet

Having Askd the Medical Officer, Mr Morrison if it was Necessary that William Green should wear flannel Next his Skin he examined him, & Said by all means. He also said it was Necessary that Abel Marshall should wear flannel Next him

Chipping Barnet

William Peel, Aged 13, having felt poorly on Sunday, we Sent this Morning for the Medical Officer, who pronounced him, to be Sickend for the Measles. We sent him to bed Immediately

Monday
East Barnet

the Old Woman Tuckfield askd me to give her permission, some fine day, to come to Barnet to see her husband. I told her I must first obtain the Sanction of the Guardians

Monday
Chipping Barnet

Esther Sygrave being very desirous to obtain a Situation, and Mrs Wells of Hadley being in want of A Servant, I gave her leave to go After the place on Tuesday but not to be absent more than 3 hours

Having no orders to the Contrary, I lent, at the request of Mr Humphreys the acting Medical Officer the New Surgical machine sent for the use of the Workhouse

THE DIARY OF BENJAMIN WOODCOCK

Mrs Cornwall, with whom the Girl Cooper went to live only A fortnight back, informd me she would not Keep her Another Night in her house. Consequently I thought it better to Admit her in the Workhouse, where she would be safe, till further orders. It appears she has been pilfering, but Mrs Cornwall said she would call at the board and explain the matter to the Guardians. Will it be Needful to bring the Girl up on Thursday?

Mr Bennett   17 Oct[ober]: not paid

2½ Bus[he]l Bones Chipping Barnet 10 bus[he]l

		2s 1d
½ Bus[he]l	ditto East Barnet	5
		2s 6d

Wednesday Shenley

the woman Jiltro, much better. All the other inmates doing well, and quite orderly

Chipping Barnet

The old man Edward Hull, wants permission to go up to London on tuesday Next, to have advice respecting his eyes

The Woman Hedge, also wished me to ask Permission from the Board, to go out for one week to see some of her Children in London

E Barnet
1 pair Shoes
1 pair Stockings
1 Shift;
2 Petticoats
2 Caps
2 Aprons
1 Hand[kerchie]f

Mrs Wells of Hadley has engaged to take the Girl Sygrave upon trial on Saturday next. The Girl begs she may be allowd to take her Union Clothing with her, except the Gown[?d] having none of her own

E Barnet Wednesday

Widow Goadale, 87 of Finchley wishes to go to London to take 10s Bounty money. She tells me Mrs Ray has got the papers

No cane to be used in the case of females

Laura Cooper was Again very refractory this Morning I was about to use the Cane, but she promised to be A good Girl in future

15

THE DIARY OF BENJAMIN WOODCOCK

No improvement in the health of the woman Burton all the other inmates much as usual

William Peel & John Meecham going on Well, with the Measles. All the other inmates in tolerable good health at present, except the rheumatism pains

Mr Morrison the Medical Officer has orderd Francis Long & the blind Man, Tea instead of Gruel

Thursday, 20 October, 1836

Thursday	Took Laura Cooper & her Sister Mary to East Barnet Workhouse this Evening As p[e]r orders of board
Friday	Bought 100 & half fagots ½ of which was sent to Chipping Barnet & half to East Barnet Workhouses
Saturday	Mary Tuckfield was removed from St Pancrass Workhouse this Morning Ill, and readmitted to East Barnet house by the Order of the Revd. Mr Elwin
Saturday	Esther Sygrave was discharged from East Barnet house, this day, As p[e]r orders And gone into the Service of Mrs Welles of Hadley
Saturday	the Old Woman Priscilla Tuckfield Came to Chipping Barnet house this Morning to see her husband by permission of the board & returnd to East Barnet house About four Oclock
Sunday	Thomas Smith the blind man, who had permission to go to the funeral, askd to Stop till the following day as his brother would not be Buried till late in the Afternoon
Monday	the woman Hedge went out of the house early this Morning without leave saying to some of the inmates she would go to see her Children. She has some of the Union Clothing

THE DIARY OF BENJAMIN WOODCOCK

Monday
Thomas Smith, the blind man, on his return this Afternoon said the Resurrection Men[5] had Attempted the previous night to Steal his dead brother and askd me to let him go out the following day as he wished to watch the Churchyard all Night but I of Course refused

Monday
Laura Cooper has again been shewing her Violent temper to some of the other old women by using the most infamous Language and attempting to do her Sister some bodily harm, without the least Cause In the event of any further Complaint of this sort, from the inmates please to say how I am to punish her

Monday
the two boys, William Peel and John Meecham has nearly recoverd from the Measles but Paul Peart fell with the same Complaint this Afternoon. He's doing Well

Tuesday
The man from South Mims parish whom the Guardians directed me, to set to work has not applyd for any employment this week

Tuesday
I promised the men, If they workd well while they where taking up the potatoes, they Should have 2 half pints of Beer a day. Hope I did right. Its hard work

Wednesday
The Women & Children at Shenley, are all in good health, & tolerable orderly

East Barnet Wednesday
the whole of the inmates, in tolerable good health, except the woman Burton, who appears to be Sinking. She tells me, she wants for Nothing. All orderly this Afternoon

---

[5] Resurrection men were people who stole and sold dead bodies for anatomical dissection.

Wednesday Evening	the Barnet inmates all orderly And in excellent health except Paul Peart who is in Bed with the Measles
Chipping Barnet Wednesday	Mr Hunt of Hadley applyd at the Workhouse for a Girl about 15 years but we have none quite Strong enough.

Thursday, 27 October, 1836

Thursday 27	William Smith, Aged 32, Casual pauper,[6] Admitted in Chipping Barnet house this day by order of Board. Examined the Same Evening by Mr Morrison Medical Officer
Thursday 27	Amelia Laura Cooper, Accompanied by the Constable of East Barnet, made her appearance at Chipping Barnet Workhouse About 10 Oclock this Evening, with an order of Admission from the R[elieving] Officer. I placed her in the Strong room all Night, much Against her will where she remained the whole of the following day upon Bread & Water
Friday 28	the inmates of East Barnet house, who appeard all very Comfortable & quite orderly this Afternoon, begd that Laura Cooper might not be sent back to them any more, as she was the whole Cause of their daily disturbance
~~Saturday~~ [crossed through in original]	Mr Humphreys the Medical Officer, has returnd ~~the Machine~~ which he borrowed from Chipping Barnet Workhouse[7] ~~and said~~ he was sorry to say, it did not Answer his expectations

[6] The term 'casual pauper' is, generally, a pauper requesting relief without a right of settle-ment, the parish is not his place of residence or is a destitute wayfarer or wanderer. It does it show whether the casual pauper is an habitually unemployed vagrant with no known parish of settlement, a person travelling in search of work or some other reason. See P F Aschrott, *The English Poor Law System Past and Present* (London, 1888), p. 247 ff. Woodcock sometimes also used the term 'casualty pauper' for the same class of person.

[7] Could this be the 'surgical machine' referred to earlier on page 14 and/or the fracture box Humphreys was authorised to procure by the Guardians on 30 June 1836? [HALS:BG/BAR1]

THE DIARY OF BENJAMIN WOODCOCK

Saturday

The Girl Cooper, whom we have Kept Confind by herself since thursday Night, Appeard very thankful at being liberated this Afternoon and subsequently acknowledged it was more punishment to her than being sent to St Albans [gaol].

East Barnet
Monday
Afternoon

all Peaceable and no Complaints

Monday

May the Sick Woman Burton, who is unable to walk down Stairs, be allowed a Fire in the Matrons room, during the Cold Weather their being no other fire place up Stairs

Tuesday 8

The Women & Children at Shenley all in good health, & doing well. No Complaints from the Matron

Order given

In the event of an order for admission being given to the woman Hedge and the Board think Proper to send her to East Barnet Workhouse, it will be as great a punishment to her, as any thing

Wednesday

the Girl Cooper, whom we have Kept Constantly employd at washing and Scouring, Conducts herself with the greatest propriety at present

Wednesday
East Barnet

the inmates all orderly and in tolerable good health, except the Woman Burton, in whose health their is no improvement, the Medical Officer states, she may continue in this State for 2 or 3 years

Paul Peart, and the other Boys inmates recoverd from the Measles & in good health & quite orderly.

We have clampd nearly 200 bus[he]l Potatoes all we have up

Thursday, 3 November, 1836

Chipping Barnet Thomas Lord, pauper of Shenley aged 57, admitted by
Thursday order of Board, examined the following Morning by
Medical Officer, healthy but Lousy

Chipping Barnet Alfred Meacham, the boy whom I had orders to set to
Friday work on the Common, left it in two hours leaving his
Barrow & Spade under the Hedge I have not herd
any thing of him since

East Barnet Mrs Peat the Matron returnd to East Barnet
Friday Workhouse about 12 Oclock, today

East Barnet Sarah Hedge by order of the Board Admitted to East
Thursday Barnet Workhouse about five Oclock this afternoon.
She observed to some of the inmates she hoped she
should not live a month

Thomas Bennet

7 Oct A/c	del[i]v[ere]d for Bone	2s 6d
3 Nov East Barnet, Bones & Ashes		1s 9d
		4s 3d

½ Bush[e]l Bones, East Barnet	5s.0d
Nov 10 4½ Chat Potatoes	3s 0d
1¼ Bones, Chipping Barnet	1½d
	8s 8½d

Friday Mr Gregory the Contractor for Bread askd me if he
might deliver it at Shenley Workhouse, twice a week
instead of three times as heretofore but I told him, I
must have the sanction of the Board. He wants
Accommodation himself, but is not willing to
Accommodate. For instance, I askd him to send 3lb
Loaves instead of 4lb to East Barnet & Chipping
Barnet there being less waste in Cutting up, but he

said he Could Not. We have had 3lb Loaves before, from the other Contractors. If the Bread is to be deliverd only twice a week, instead of three times, it will lose Considerable in weight at each house before used

Monday East Barnet inmates all orderly and in good general health except the woman Burton.

Chipping Barmet One of the Neighbours calld this Morning and wished me to send them A strong man to turn A mangle for 2 or 3 hours. I said it was not allowd

Tuesday On going to Shenley this morning I met Collins & Woodhouse two of the boys from the Workouse returning from Barnet with Bread for Breakfast, None having been deliv[ere]d on Monday according to order

Shenley Charles Godfrey, one of the boys, having been he[a]rd to say he should like to be apprenticed to A Sweep, I askd him the question but could get no direct answer. All doing well.

Chipping Barnet inmates all doing well & quite orderly & all employd who are able

Thursday, 10 November, 1836

Thursday On my return this Afternoon I deliverd the orders of the board to William Smith the South Mims Casualty, who observd that his leg was going on well and he hopd, in a few days more, to be able to walk to Enfield, without further expence

Thursday Eliz[abe]th Bell aged 72, pauper of Totteridge, admitted to East Barnet Workhouse, by Order of the Board

THE DIARY OF BENJAMIN WOODCOCK

Friday

Frederick Woodhouse, Aged 14½ pauper of Hadley, admitted to Chipping Barnet workhouse, by Orders of the Board. Examined by the Medical Officer the same Evening

Friday

the East Barnet inmates all going on as usual, & quite orderly, this afternoon, paid the Union Monthly A/c

Saturday

Joseph Collins, orphan aged 14, pauper of Shenley, discharged from the Workhouse this Morning by the orders of Board.

The Children all healthy and orderly. Paid the Union Monthly A/C

Sunday

Notice

The old man Tuckfield, while in Conversation with his Son Charles this Evening, was observed by one of the inmates, to give him a Sovereign in Secret to take Care of for him. Previous to the death of Thomas Cheadle we knew he was without money

Monday

should not a reward be offerrd

either Saturday Night or Sunday, some person found their way to the potatoe Clamp in The Workhouse Garden & after Moving the Mound A foot & half thick, stole some of the Potatoes, but we think not many. They Certainly will not be safe to remain their during the winter

Monday

Mary Ann Hale, Widow aged 71, admitted to East Barnet house by Order of the Board, pauper of Shenley

Monday

William Smith the South Mims Casualty, belonging to Enfield, was discharged from the Chipping Barnet Workhouse this Afternoon at his own request, Much improved

the East Barnet inmates all going on Comfortable & quite orderly Monday afternoon

22

THE DIARY OF BENJAMIN WOODCOCK

Chipping Barnet Tuesday

William Spencer pauper of Shenley, Applyd to Chipping Barnet Workhouse for Admission on tuesday the 15 Nov[embe]r , but I did not think it proper to admitt him, his order being dated the 27 October

Wednesday

Mr Dowton wishes me, when the potatoes are all up, to set 2 or 3 of the Men to Ridge the Ground up[8] for the Winter, for which he will give them a little Beer. He hoped the Board would have no objection

Wednesday

the Shenley inmates, all going on well, quite healthy and orderly. No Complaints

East Barnet Wednesday afternoon

the Medical Officer, has not been to examine the state of health, of Eliz[abe]th Bell, & Mary Ann Hale, 2 paupers, admitted by an Order Last Board Day. The two Women Burton & Randall in A very Weak State. The other inmates all going on well & quite orderly

Chipping Barnet

the Man Long, appears likely to follow Joseph Warren, who died sometime ago in a consumption. The others all in excellent health and quite orderly

Thursday, 17 November, 1836

Thursday

William Spencer, aged 71, pauper of Shenley, admitted in Chipping Barnet house this day, by order of the Board. Examined by Medical Officer the following Morning, In a low weak state, for want of food

Friday

A Young Man of the name of Barr, belong[in]g to Elstree, applyd to me this morning, about 8 Oclock for employment, by order R[elieving] Officer. I told him what he was to do, that he was to keep his time, and to do a fare days work otherwise I should report him. He said he would keep away another week & went off

[8] to build up a ridge of earth to cover the crop

THE DIARY OF BENJAMIN WOODCOCK

Ann Buck Aged 70, pauper of Ridge, Admitted to East Barnet Workhouse Yesterday, Thursday, 17th by Order of Board. Examined the following day by two Medical Officers as to her health.

The Woman Randall, Much worse, Burton much the same. The others much as usual Friday Evening. All orderly

Saturday

The Women & Children at Shenley , all Appeard. Healthy & orderly Saturday

Some person paid us another visit on Sunday Night, and stole Just one dozen, of the best Savoy Cabbage, we had in the Garden Chipping Barnet

Ordered

Mr Morrison the Medical Officer, thinks it Necessary, that Jacob Robinson, Thomas Smith, & Robert Briers, should wear flannel next their skin, being all subject to the rheumatism.

Tuesday

the Revd. Mr Wimbolt, being of opinion the Board would have no objection, wished me to let Joseph Hill and Benj[amin] Skipsey, two of the inmates, meet him about 4 Oclock on Wednesday Afternoon, to take the Sacrament with a Sick person of the Name of South in the Neighbourhood. To which i attended

Having received information, from one of the Guardians, on Monday, that the boy Jos[eph] Collins had run away from his employment in London and returnd to Shenley Workhouse on Saturday Night, under Pretence of Illness, the following morning I obtain the opinion of the Medical Officer who proved him to be in good health. Consequently we removed him to Barnet waiting further orders

Having received notice from Mr Benj[ami]n Smith, on Tuesday Evening, that he had made arrangements for Paul Peart the Cripple, to be admitted in the

National School[9] We accordingly sent him, the following morning about 9 Oclock as p[e]r orders of Board.

Notice

Mr Bellamy the Contractor for the New Workhouse[10], calld on Wednesday to say he wished me to go over the New Building and say where the Locks where necessary to be put.
I have not been.

Tuesday Shenley

Sarah Waterton & John Hains are on the Doctor's List. The others are all going on well.

Wednesday East Barnet

the Medical Officer has orderd strong Mutton Broth to be given to the Woman Randall & Tuckfield. The Woman Burton much the same. The rest as usual

Notice

Esther Haynes to Notice

Notice

Eliz[abe]th Bartlett to Notice

Should we take any steps, to secure Ann Gray's immediate return to the Workhouse, on the Day of her being Discharged from St Albans Gaol?

Francis Long has taken to his Bed all the rest healthy & orderly

Thursday, 24 November, 1836

Thomas Bourne 53 pauper of Hadly Admitted in Chipping Barnet this day by order of the Board. We was obliged to Burn the whole of this man's old Cloths, being entirely coverd with Lice

John Brill 30, pauper of Shenley Admitted in Chipping Barnet this day by order of Board, ragged but clean

[9] The Chipping Barnet National School (Elizabeth Allen) was built in 1824 in Wood Street, Barnet and had endowments for teaching forty boys
[10] Probably John Bellamy carpenter of 55 High Street, Hemel Hempstead

THE DIARY OF BENJAMIN WOODCOCK

Friday   Isaac Crane Aged 70 pauper of Chipping Barnet
                  admitted this day by Order of Board, ragged and
                  hungry

Friday   Thomas Deller Applyd at the Workhouse this morn-
                  ing for Work. I lent him some tools & sent him on
                  the New Workhouse Ground with one of the Boys

Friday   Mr Morrison, the Medical Officer, after his examina-
                  tion of the inmates this day, said it was necessary
                  that Francis Long should be allowd 1 pint of Beer
                  Daily.

                  No Alteration in the health of the inmates at East
                  Barnet. All orderly since Last report

                  According to my instructions, after Breakfast on
                  Sunday morning I sent Abraham Knight one of the
Observe   inmates, to London with the boy Joseph Collins, who
upon   delivered him safe to the care of Mr Hicks. The man
                  returnd home to the Workhouse, about 5 Oclock the
                  same afternoon perfectly steady. I gave him 4 pence
                  to get 2 pints of Beer on the Road, and another pint
                  on his return home

East Barnet   the two Sick Women Burton & Randall Much the
Monday   Same. The other inmates all Comfortable and quite
                  orderly

Tuesday   Mrs Ellman from the Black Horse, Wood Street,
                  made application at Chipping Barnet Workhouse this
                  Morning for A Strong Servant Girl about 19 or 20. Is
                  it the pleasure of the Board that I should send Mary
                  Cooper?

                  the extreme high winds, on Tuesday forenoon, blew
                  off A number of Tiles and broke two Squares of
                  Glass. Chipping Barnet house

Wednesday
Shenley

the Woman Waterton & the boy Hains much better and the whole in good health & orderly

Wednesday
East Barnet

no Alteration in the health of Burton & Randall. All the rest in tolerable good health & orderly.

Wednesday
Chipping Barnet

The man Long appears to be sinking, but all the other inmates in excellent health & quite orderly

Mr Bennet

3 Nov	Bones & Ashes		4s 3d
30 Nov	4 ½ Bus[hel]l Flug [?] Potatoes	9d	3s 4½
1 ½	Bus[hel]l Bones –	10d.	1s 3d
			8s 10½d

Thursday, 1 December 1836

About 7 Oclock this Evening I received the enclosed from Mr Humphreys the Medical Officer, stating that Mr Richard, the Landlord of the Wellington, was deranged and very violent and begd I would let him have the use of the Strait Waistcoat belonging to the Workhouse. I hope we did right to send it

East Barnet
Thursday

Jane Carpenter Widow pauper of Hadley, admitted by order of Board in A low Weak State of health

Friday

Randall & Burton much the Same the rest. All going on comfortable

Mary Tuckfield, who has A good p[ai]r of shoes of her own, wants me to send her, A New p[air] of Union shoes

Shenley
Saturday

the women & Children all orderly, but was a little Alarmd, during the high Winds, by the bricks falling down the Chimney

THE DIARY OF BENJAMIN WOODCOCK

Saturday

The Medical Officer, Mr Morrison, finding the man Long gradually sinking, has orderd him two pints of new milk daily, instead of Beer.

John Williams one of the East Barnet inmates, came over soon After Breakfast on Sunday morning to give me Notice of the death on Susan Randall, pauper of Friern Barnet which took Place about half past six Oclock the previous Night. I gave Immediate directions to Markwell the undertaker who said he would attend forthwith

Chipping Barnet Monday

having received directions from the Building Committee I sent four of the inmates this morning to level the new Workhouse Garden Ground.

Chipping Barnet Monday

having received proper instructions, I took John Coleman attended by his Daughter from East Barnet to London on Tuesday morning & reached the London Hospital[11] 10 Minutes before 11, where we remained till near 1 before the Arrival of Mr Scott, who observed this was an Accident, & had he being bro[ugh]t immediately After, he must have been admitted, without An Order. I took him to the Sick Ward, where I left him to the care of the Nurse & the Surgeons

Mr Bryant sent A man with A Cart to fetch the Weighing Machine & weighs [weights?] the Second time, with a written order. Consequently we could not weigh the Bread which came in on Wednesday

Wednesday

Thomas Smith the blind Man had some Blood took from him this Evening, to prevent An inflammation on the brain

[11] The London Hospital was founded in 1740 in Whitechapel and provided services for a wide range of people.

East Barnet

the Woman Randall Buried this Afternoon followed by 8 of the inmates. Burton much the same. The rest all Comfortable

the Shenley inmates all going on right

the Medical Officer says its Necessary the Man Long should have some wine & water, being in a very weak state. All the other inmates healthy & quite orderly.

Thursday, 8 December, 1836

Being of opinion, that Coke would be much Cheaper & answer the purpose as well as coal, to be used in the furnace at the New Workhouse. We sent for one sack upon trial but find it will not Answer to be used without Coal

Saturday Chipping Barnet

Eliz[abe]th Bartlett, Pauper of Totteridge Admitted by Order of Board. This Woman being in hopes of having A Situation before long, we have not sent Fanny Stacking to East Barnet house as was proposed on Board day

About 1 Oclock on Sunday, Ann Gray, made Application for Admission in Chipp[in]g Barnet Workhouse, but had no order having, as she said, come direct from St Albans Gaol from which she had been discharged a few hours before. The following morning we sent for the Medical Officer, as usual, who Certifys that she[']s in a very bad State and for Want of proper convenience in Workhouse, a fit object for the Lock Hospital.[12]

Monday Morning

Paul Peart was unable to attend Prayers this morning oweing to severe Cold. We gave him some Medcine & on Tuesday was better but not able to go to School

---

[12] Lock Hospitals were institutions for the treatment of venereal diseases.

Chipping Barnet Tuesday

About 12 Oclock A Man of the Name of George Jones, with the enclosed note from Mr Tattam of Finchley, was brought to the workhouse for Admission. We received him into the house but was of opinion the order sent was not altogether official. He has lost the use of the right arm. We sent for the Medical Officer, Immediately who calls it the evil

the third day after Ann Gray came into the house I was obliged to put her by herself for two hours for quarrelling with, and striking Fanny Starkins, Another inmate. Her behaviour has been proper since

Wednesday Shenley

the woman Jiltro much better but I continue to send her a little Mutton Weekly. The other women & all the Children in excellent health & quite Orderly. They want Shirts & Shifts but we have no Materials

Wednesday East Barnet

the Woman Burton Much the same. Mary Tuckfield on the Sick list. The other inmates all tolerable healthy & orderly

Chipping Barnet Wednesday

no improvement in the health of Long. The Blind Man much better. All the rest going on well & quite orderly. It appears Ann Gray wishes to be sent to East Barnet house but don't like Attending the Board. I will bring her with me

Thursday, 15 December, 1836

Thursday

John Weedon aged 18, Pauper of South Mims, whom we had lodged in the workhouse for several nights previous As A Casualty By order R[elieving] Officer, was admitted An inmate this Evening by order of Board. We was obliged to clothe him entirely, being in a most filthy dirty Condition. I will send him up on board day for examination

THE DIARY OF BENJAMIN WOODCOCK

Thursday

Ann Gray, pauper of Ridge, was removed from Chipping Barnet to East Barnet Workhouse this Evening, by order of Board.

Friday

East Barnet inmates all tolerable healthy & orderly, except the women Burton Tuckfield & Ann Gray. All of which are on the Surgeons List

Saturday

the Shenley inmates all in excellent health & Spirits, but the Matron having a Cold, has been unable to attend her Domestic duties for several days

Monday

Ann Gregory, widow aged 90, pauper of Ridge, removed from Watford to Chipping Barnet workhouse this Morning and admitted, having a removal Order. Gave notice to the Medical Officer to attend her examination.

Tuesday

Mr Hampton Baker of Shenley, having Complaind to me this Morning that the Boys in the Workhouse had entirely Destroyd his Garden hedge, I talkd to them and promised If I herd any further Complaints they should be all severely punished

Tuesday

I directed the Trades people of Shenley to send into the Workhouse the Roast Beef & the Necessaries for the Plumb Pudding as per Orders

Mr & Miss Nicholls calld at the Chipping Barnet Workhouse to enquire the Character & Speak to the Woman Bartlett, relative to A Situation

The Matron having Complaind, that the Woman Goodale's head was lousy from the quantity of hair & her own Idleness, I told her that unless she Consented to have her hair cut Close off, I should be obliged to report her according

Wednesday   requested the Trades people of East Barnet to send into the Workhouse, Some Roast Beef & the Necessaries to make the Plumb Pudding[13] As per orders. The woman Burton much the same. The other inmates all as usual.

the Bread sent into the different houses this week, has been very indifferent. I told Mr Gregory of it.

Mrs Nicholls calld at the Workhouse on Wednesday afternoon, & wishes the Matron to let the Woman Bartlett to go to her house on Saturday for engagement

the Woman Bartlett wished me to ask If the Board would be pleased to advance her about 25s to get some of her Clothes out of pawn, in the event of her going to Mrs Nicholls situation, & she will pay it as heretofore.

Chipping Barnet   the Man Long going fast. Thomas Smith poorly the other inmates all in excellent health & quite orderly

Thursday, 22 December, 1836

Friday   the Woman Bartlett having waited upon Mrs Nicholls according to appointment this morning. Mrs N[icholls] gave her several Articles of Wearing Apparel, 2s 6d in money, & said she would call at the Workhouse in about a week & give her directions where she was to go up to her Daughter

Saturday   Having herd that Mrs Rogers' Daughter had ill used one of the infant Children at Shenley, I made enquiry of the Matron if such was the case, but she strongly denys it.

---

[13] The inmates of the Barnet Union workhouses were to have a special dinner of roast beef and plum pudding for Christmas.

THE DIARY OF BENJAMIN WOODCOCK

Sunday The whole of the inmates at Chipping Barnet perfectly comfortable & quite orderly on Christmas day

Sunday John Vials Aged 29, casual pauper, was removed from the Rising Sun, Barnet to the Workhouse on Sunday & Admitted, having received Notice from the R[elieving] Officer the day before

Monday Died about ½ Past seven Oclock this Morning at Chipping Barnet Workhouse, Francis Long Aged 50, pauper of Ridge

Mrs Tatham of Finchley sent me A man of the name of Thompson on Monday Evening for Ad[mission] but I of Course refused till I Applyd to the R[eliev-ing] Officer who sent me an order to Lodge him the night

Priscilla Tuckfield Aged 78 Pauper of East Barnet, Died early on Monday Morning, after A few days ill-ness

Chipping Barnet the Man Vials, who was removed from the Rising
Wednesday Sun on Sunday, Died about 10 Oclock on Tuesday Night

the Children & Women at Shenley all healthy happy & orderly

the inmates at East Barnet all Comfortable & tolera-ble healthy except the Woman Burton, in whom their is no improvement

the inmates at Chipping Barnet all quite orderly & much the same as our last report

Is allowed to remain until his wife is buried William Tuckfield, one of the inmates askd permis-sion on Tuesday morning to go to East Barnet to see his Deceased Wife. He had not returned on Thursday, this morning.

Allowed until Monday [crossed through and Sunday substituted]

Markwell the undertaker calld at the Workhouse this Morning by order of the relatives of the Deceased Man Vials, to say it was the intention of his relations to bear the expence of his funeral themselves & wished to know If I would Keep him in the house till Tuesday Next. I said I could not answer this question Immediately

Thursday, 29 December, 1836

Markwell the Undertaker calld at the Workhouse with three Men on Thursday Evening, about eight Oclock & took away the Man Vials. I had previously seen the Undertaker & stated to him the time the Corpse was to remain in the house as p[er] orders of the Board

Friday

Frances Long Aged 50, who Died on Monday Morning, was buried at 12 Oclock this forenoon, followed by several inmates but none of his own family

William Tuckfield returnd to the Workhouse about 4 Oclock this Afternoon, after attending the funeral of his Wife & being absent 4 days

Saturday Shenley

the Matron informs me that every Bedroom in the Workhouse, More or less, has been exposed to the Snow & Wet, during the frost. The Women & Children all doing well & orderly

Monday East Barnet

Paid the Several Monthly Union A/c. The inmates all Comfortable

Elizabeth Bartlett, having seen Mrs Nicholls at Church on Sunday afternoon & received Proper orders to go by Flitt the Carrier at 8 Oclock on Tuesday morning to London, We discharged her from the Workhouse according & sent one of the men in the house to carry her Boxes to the Cart. She left the house quite Comfortable

To be ordered

the Chipping Barnet inmates all except Geo[rge] Smith the blind Man, whoes been indisposed for Several days with a pain in his head, are in excellent health. The Medical Officer has orderd 2 or 3 of the Old Men flannel Next their Skin but we have none in the Store room

Thursday, 5 January, 1837

Thursday

Some thin Calico wanted for mending the old shirts & shifts also some flannel wanted to make three waistcoats, see Medical Report

**Friday 6
East Barnet**

Medical Officer has orderd Ann Gray to Apply Mustard & flour to her Legs & Knees.[14] The woman Burton not so well. The other inmates much as usual.

Saturday 7

The Matron of Shenley, having stated that she had not received her allowance of Bread by 40lb on the last Week of Mr Gregory Contract, He for sometime, insisted it was correct but ultimately acknowledged it was his own mistake and made up the deficiency the same afternoon

Sunday 8

Fanny Starkins, in company with the other inmates, left Chipping Barnet Workhouse this morning for Church at the usual hour, whom I saw seated in her proper place five Minutes before 11, & having missed her on my return home, I le[a]rnt from the other women that she went out of the Church during prayers under pretence of having the belly ach, and has not returnd. The officers from St Albans brought her home the last time she was absent with 12s expenses.

**East Barnet
Monday 9**

Mr Elwin gave directions this afternoon for the Woman Carpenter to be removed on Wednesday morning to Chipping Barnet house, in Consequence of Fanny Starkins being absent without leave. The woman Burton much the same.

[14] A possible remedy for arthritis

Tuesday 10

*To admit her &
bring her up to the
next board*

in the event of the woman Starkins be sent home, or applying to the Workhouse for readmission, please give me instructions as to her treatment till board day

**Wednesday
Chipping
Barnet**

at ¼ Before 11 Oclock this morning, we was obliged to send to the Butchers for the Legs & Shins of Beef for the Soup, which should have been in the Copper by ½ past 9 (this frequently happens)

Wednesday

Admitted this Afternoon, by order from R[elieving] Officer , Henry Brand, Pauper from Finchley, 62. Sent Notice of the Same to the Medical Officer, Rheumatic Complaint

Wednesday

Admitted by order of R[elieving] Officer 11th Jan[uar]y William Barnes Aged 22 Pauper of South Mims. Unable to work from An Accident

Wednesday

William Richards Aged 28, Chipping Barnet Casual Pauper, bel[ongin]g to St Johns Margate, admitted by order R[elieving] Officer on Wednesday, being unable to proceed on his Journey to Northampton. This Man, who can speak the French & Latin Languages, was examined by the Revd Mr Venters at the Workhouse the Same day and proved to be the same, whom he had relieved under Similar Circumstances at Whetstone some months back. He complains of his head but the Medical Officer has not yet been, 10 Oclock Thursday Mor[nin]g

Thursday, 12 January, 1837

Thursday

Thomas Stubbington Aged 45 Admitted in Chipping Barnet house this day by Order of Board Pauper of East Barnet

THE DIARY OF BENJAMIN WOODCOCK

Thursday
Thomas Burton Aged 35 Pauper of Finchley, Admitted in Chipping Barnet Workhouse this day by Order of Board

Friday
[crossed through]
Nathaniel Poulton Aged 45 Pauper of Chipping Barnet, Admitted this day by Order of Board R[elieving] Officer

Friday
Thomas Weatherley Aged 58 Pauper of Hadley Admitted in Chipping Barnet house, this day by Order of Board

Saturday
Sarah Godfrey Aged 14 who was in Shenley Workhouse A time back but now in the Service of Mrs Tibbott, has got bad eyes. The Medical Officer think[s] her a fit object for the Hospital

Sunday
William Richards the Casual Pauper, who was Admitted by Order R[elieving] Officer to Chipping Barnet house on Wednesday last, in Consequence of hunger & Illness, being quite restored to health on Sunday, was discharged according. He was not very Willing to go as he said his parish Workhouse, Margate, was very different

Sunday
Thomas Bourne Pauper of Hadley did not return from Church this Afternoon till 7 Oclock. He certainly had had a little beer but being his first offence since his admission, & having Acknowledged his Transgression, went quiet & orderly to Bed. Consequently I did not punish him

Monday
A Stranger calld at the Workhouse this afternoon & wished to see Nathaniel Poulton, one of the inmates. It appears that while Poulton was in the Service of Mr Hillman at the Black Horse sometime ago he placed some earthenware under his care which he afterwards sold and made use of the Money

Monday	Mariah Morris Admitted as Casual Pauper in East Barnet Workhouse on Friday, by order R[elieving] O[fficer]
Tuesday	Mary Tuckfield one of the inmates of East Barnet Workhouse, died this Morning About 6 Oclock
Wednesday	The Clamp of Potatoes[15] & the Savoy Cabbages in the Workhouse Garden was again Visited on Tuesday night or Wednesday morning & a quantity of each taken away. This is the second time
	John Stops Aged 60, Finchley pauper, admitted this day by order R[elieving] Officer, bad Leg
Shenley	All in tolerable good health
Thursday *allowed*	William Tuckfield, wishes to attend his daughters funeral at East Barnet tomorrow. Is he to have permission?

3 Gowns
2 Petticoats
2 Aprons
4 Handkerchiefs
6 Caps, 1 Bonnet
1 Pair Boots
this question to stand over.

A woman of the name of Bumby, Sister to the Deceased Mary Tuckfield has made application to the Matron of East Barnet house to have her Sisters Clothes. Value about 10s or 12s

Thursday, 19 January, 1837

Friday	Pye the [Police] Officer came with a horse & Cart to the Workhouse this morning & took Fanny Starkins to St Albans Gaol, as per order of Magistrate
Friday	Ann Cox, widow, Pauper of South Mims, died at East Barnet Workhouse, about 12 Oclock Yesterday Thursday
Friday	Mary Tuckfield Pauper of East Barnet, Buried this afternoon

[15] A mound of earth and straw in which potatoes are stored to preserve them over winter

THE DIARY OF BENJAMIN WOODCOCK

Friday   John Dickins South Mims Pauper, admitted in Chipping Barnet house this day by order of R[elieving] O[fficer]

George Fanning South Mims Pauper Admitted by Order of Board Thursday 19 Jan[uary]

Alfred Muchum, Chipping Barnet Pauper, Admitted this day by order R[elieving] O[fficer]

Friday   Christopher Lenman Aged 16 Admitted this day by order of Board

Saturday   the Women & Children at Shenley all tolerable healthy this Morn[ing] but the Matron still unwell

Sunday   Hugh Hawkes Aged 60 East Barnet Pauper, Admitted in Chipping Barnet Workhouse, this Afternoon by Order R[elieving] O[fficer]

Monday   Helen Newby Aged 17 Pauper of South Mims, Admitted in Shenley house on Saturday 21 Inst[ant] the inmates all tolerable healthy

Tuesday   Sarah Goodman Henry George & David Harris, her 3 sons, Admitted East Barnet on Monday, Shenley Paupers

Wednesday   the Officer from South Mims calld at the Workhouse this Aft[ernoon] said he had A Charge Against William Barnes one of the Inmates for Stealing some harness & must take him for examination to Morrow, Thursday

the inmates all Orderly

THE DIARY OF BENJAMIN WOODCOCK

Thursday, 26 January, 1837

Thursday

William Barnes, South Mims Pauper, discharged from the Workhouse this day. Same day Committed for Trial by Mr Dewey, the White Hart, Mims

Thursday

the following are a list of the Wearing Apparel, left by the deceased Ann Cox, who died in East Barnet house, on thursday the 19 Jan[uar]y 1837

> 1 Black Stuff Gown
> 1 Crimson Cloak
> 1 Black Silk bonnet
> 3 Caps
> 2 Worsted Shawls
> 2 Aprons
> 2 Hand[kerchie]fs

Friday

John Dickins South Mims Pauper discharged from Chipping Barnet house this Morning, by Order of Board. He had P[ai]r Shoes New Shirt & Shilling

Friday

Removed the 2 Children belonging to the Woman Goodman from East Barnet to Chipping Barnet workhouse this afternoon, by order of Board

Saturday

Sarah Goodman Pauper of Shenley & her 3 Children, Was discharged from East Barnet & Chipping Barnet houses on Saturday afternoon at her own request

Sunday

Nothing Material at Chipping Barnet

Monday

the inmates at East Barnet all somewhat better & orderly.

Tuesday
No, Medical report

Shenley the Women and Children have been most of them poorly, but are all on the Mend today, except A Poor little Cripple female orphan About 10 years of age, belong[ing] to South Mims, who is in a very weak low state, having no Appetite

Wednesday
In Sorting the Potatoes, which we was obliged to put in the Barn, we have been obliged to throw away upwards of 30 bushel, in Consequence of the wet & frost

Wednesday
None of the inmates in Chipping Barnet house, have been laid up in Consequence of the Late General Complaint

Wednesday
complaint against Butcher
10 Minutes to 11 Oclock before the Butcher Sent the Legs & Shins for the Soup Shuld have been in the Copper 1 hour before

Wednesday
East Barnet Medical Officer has taken off the wine & ordered Beer to be given to some of the Sick.

Edward Hull the Younger, this Evening asked permission to go out for 1 hour to see his Mother who lies dangerously Ill at Hadley

The Whole of the inmates, Orderly, & the Sick all on the Mend

Thursday, 2 February, 1837

Thursday
George Salt Aged 60, Pauper of Finchley, Admitted in Chipping Barnet Workhouse this day by order of the Board

Thursday
Edward Shepherd Aged 12 & his Sister Emma Aged 11, belon[g]ing to the parish of Bayford, Admitted in Shenley Workhouse, this day by Order of the Board. They where both in a very filthy state

Friday
East Barnet inmates all improving in health, quite orderly, no Complaint

THE DIARY OF BENJAMIN WOODCOCK

Saturday
Shenley

The Medical Officer has ordered the Matron to let the Child Selisia Holloway have as much Mutton as she can eat. All the other inmates in good general health. The girl Newby is as much trouble to Keep Clean as an infant, all orderly.

Sunday
Chipping Barnet

Nothing Material

Monday

the health of the East Barnet inmates all on the improvement and tolerable orderly

Tuesday

the Women & Children at Shenley much as usual except two, a boy & a Girl, who are not very well, all tolerable orderly

Wednesday

With the Consent of the Revd Mr Elwin, Widow Taylor, Pauper of Shenley, was admitted in East Barnet Workhouse, yesterday without the usual provisional order of Admission

Wednesday

petition allowed

Since the death of Widow Cox one of her daughters has made several applications to the Matron of East Barnet House for a Shawl belong[ing] to the old woman, which of course could not be given to her without orders from the Board. She scarcely even sent to make enquiry after her health during her lifetime.

Wednesday
Chipping Barnet

Paul Peart the Cripple had some blood taken from him yesterday. He is a little better today.
All the other inmates doing well, & quite orderly

Thursday, 9 February, 1837

Thursday

Widow Taylor Aged 65, Pauper of Shenley, admitted in East Barnet this day by order of Board

Thursday

Thomas Cooper Aged 53, Pauper of Hadley, Admitted to Chipping Barnet house this day by order of Board. The Medical Officer examined him the same day, in a filthy state

Thursday

Thomas Camfield aged 76, belong[ing] to Ridge, admitted to Chipping Barnet this day by Order Board. Examined same day by Medical Officer

Friday

After Breakfast this morning Joseph Mitchell and Will[ia]m Green went to East Barnet house as per orders

Friday
East Barnet

Medical Officer recommends Chocolate instead of Tea, to be given to the Woman Burton

Chipping Barnet

Medical Officer recommends Milk instead of Tea to be given to Thomas Stubbington

Friday

In consequence of Rich[ar]d Schofield's filthy habits for several nights I was obliged this morning to make use of the Birch Rod

Saturday
Chipping Barnet

About 12 Oclock this forenoon, I went out to see if the fires where going on right at the New Workhouse. On my return in about ½ an hour I lernt that Laura Cooper & Mary Pedley, two of the inmates, had been quarrelling about a ball of Cotton. After striking each other the Matron separated them, when Laura run out of the house without bonnet or shawl. About 4 Oclock Pye the Police man with some difficulty brought her back to the Workhouse. I lockd her in one of the Casualty rooms, the windows of which she threatened to brake. The fear of the strait waistcoat, I believe was the thing which prevented her doing Mischief.

We find it Necessary to use the strictest Regulations with these two paupers to prevent frequent disturbances from their Passionate tempers

Sunday
Chipping Barnet

Nothing Material

Monday	the Woman Burton whose [who is] Sinking very fast, begs the Board will be pleased to let her have a full pint of Brandy Weekly as [re]commended by the Medical Officer, it being the only thing she can keep in her stomach. It appears the quantity sent from Mrs Bowers [h]as been little more than ½ a pint a week, for which she charges 3s
Tuesday **Shenley**	the Child Holloway is getting better. All the other Children and inmates, doing well, but want Clothing.
Wednesday	In the event of the Man Cooper getting better of his filthy Complaint he will want entirely clothing before we can let him out of the room. He talks of going out. The Medical Officer says he can do Nothing more for him.
Chipping Barnet **Wednesday**	Thomas Camfield & Paul Peart better. The Other inmates all going on well & orderly

Thursday, 16 February, 1837

Thursday	John Rippon Aged 55 Pauper of Hadley, Admited in Chipping Barnet house this day by Order of Board in A dirty Condition. [different hand] Is he in the House now?
Friday *Notice*	Sarah Waterton Pauper of Chipping Barnet having herd that Mrs Acason was in want of a Steady Servant Girl, was desirous to go upon trial. She gave the Matron the usual Notice & was discharged from Shenley Workhouse on friday. She begs she may be allowd to have her 2 Union shifts & 2 Aprons
Saturday *Notice*	Mrs Tibbot gave me notice this morning that she should have no further accation for the Girl Godfrey After Saturday Next, her Eyes being so weak, she was unable to do her work. She went the beginning of Aug[us]t last. Their seems but little improvement

Saturday	in her appearance since she left the Workhouse. Will it be Necessary to have an order for her Admission?
Sunday	Thomas Cooper having been Cured of his filthy Complaint, we gave him some Clothing left by some of the deseased Paupers, & burnt all his old rags.
Chipping Barnet Monday	Nothing Material at Chipping Barnet Workhouse on Sunday
Monday	About 9 Oclock this Morning, Thomas Camfield Aged 76 Pauper of Ridge Died. Sent Immediate Notice of the Same to the Medical Officer also to the Sexton & Undertaker, who Promptly attended
Monday	the East Barnet inmates all Orderly & going on well, except the Woman Burton, who gets Weaker Daily
Tuesday *notice*	Thomas Cooper being in a fit State talks of going out of the house on Thursday next. We have Clothed him from head to toe. He wishes to return the board thanks Chipping Barnet
Tuesday *notice*	We want a few Yards, of Corse house flannel, to Clean the New House
Wednesday Shenley	the Man Newby Calld to see his Daughter Helen Newby. The Children all going on Well
Wednesday East Barnet	Medical Officer recommends A little Gin to be given daily to the Nurse who attends on the woman Burton
Wednesday	The Matron Complains of the Wet Comeing through the Roof into one of the Bed Rooms. The Inmates all going on well but Burton
Chipping Barnet Wednesday	George Salt Pauper of Finchley, having recover[d] wishes to go out to Morrow

Chipping Barnet   Thomas Burton Pauper of Finchley who Came into the house Ill, being now able to work, gave me Notice to be discharged today. I think he will apply to the board for a little assistance
all healthy & orderly

Thursday, 23 February, 1837

Thursday   Thomas Camfield was buried about 4 Oclock yesterday afternoon. His wife Son & Daughter attended & followed him to the Grave

Friday   Had the Stoves all taken up Stairs & Placed in their Proper rooms as soon as they came in this Morning and Fires in each as soon as they where Fixd, as per orders,

Friday
East Barnet   Mary Cooper, a Giddy Girl about 20, having neither home or Situation to go to, talks of going out of the Workhouse. Wats to be done?

Saturday
Shenley   I calld on Mrs Tibbot this morning about the Girl Godfrey, whom I expected was to be discharged according to Mrs Tibbot's own arrangement, but it appears the Girl has gone on much better this last week and her Mistress wishes to Keep her till we remove the Shenley Paupers to the New house

Sunday
Chipping Barnet   Jane Carpenter one of the inmates askd permission to go to Whetstone to see her Daughter, who was ill, this afternoon. She was back in 3 hours

Monday   Thomas Weatherby Pauper of Hadley is Confind to his Bed with the Dropsy. The Medical Officer recommends gin & water by all means. Should he have it?

Monday
Chipping Barnet   The Boy Lenman who was admitted in Chipping Barnet house in consequence of Lameness being

recovered, Mr Claytons Gravel Diggers calld this Evening to say they would give him employment at 4s p[er] week out of which the boy says he will have 1s a week to pay for his Lodging & begs for A little assistance for that Purpose, as he is not safe to be at home with his Father & Mother

Monday
East Barnet

Esther Haynes one of the inmates met with an Accident & Broke her thigh. The Medical Officer was sent for Immediately

Tuesday
Shenley

the boy Gwillim & the Girl Holloway much the same. The other inmates all healthy & orderly

Wednesday
East Barnet

East Barnet Inmates all orderly but several of them, on Sick List,

Wednesday
Chipping Barnet

Inmates all quite orderly. No alteration in the Number since our last report

Thursday, 2 March, 1837

Shenley
Friday

the 3 Boys, Woodhouse, Brand & Peel left the Workhouse about 6 Oclock this morning, but for what Cause unknown. This is the 3rd time

Saturday
East Barnet

the Sick inmates all going on right. The Others all orderly & much as usual

Sunday

Chipping Barnet inmates nothing material

Shenley
Monday

the Revd. Mr Newcome was at the Workhouse this Morning & wished to Know If the Woman Jiltro, who as been an inmate of the Workhouse some years would be allowd out door relief. I said I was not able to Answer the question. The 3 boys had not returned. All the rest as usual

Monday
East Barnet

the Sick inmates much the same. The rest all Peaceable

THE DIARY OF BENJAMIN WOODCOCK

Monday
Chipping Barnet

Old Ned Hull, with whom I have had more trouble to Maintain Proper discipline than any other Man in the house, having Struck Another inmate this afternoon, Contrary to the Rules & orders, I was telling him the impropriety of such Conduct and that I should report him to the board when he made use of the Most Horrid & Abusive Language & said he cared for None of them. For which I pulld his nose, sent him to bed & Kept him the following day without his Dinner. He Smelt very strong of Tobacco having been down the Garden Smoking unknown to me. I hope the Board will be Pleased to award him some little punishment for such conduct, example being the only means to obtain Proper Order with such refractory paupers

Tuesday
Chipping Barnet

About 12 Oclock this forenoon Mr Frost Constable of Finchley brought back 2 of the runaway boys, Woodhouse & Brand. The boy Peel having gone to London. They went away on friday & was brought home on Tuesday with 8s expenses. I have them Lockd up, but have not Punished them in Any Other Way till further orders. The boy Brand, by means of A brick, has erased the B.U. on the buttons of his Union Clothing

Wednesday

Thomas Cooper Pauper of Hadley being Able to Work, will be discharged from the Workhouse to Morrow At his own request. We was obliged to Burn all his old Clothes

Wednesday
Shenley

the 2 Sick Children & Women going on as usual

Wednesday
East Barnet

Mariah Morris the Casual Pauper, was removed to her Legal Settlement Yesterday. The inmates all orderly

Chipping Barnet

We are much in want of A Ladder About 20 rounds. Mr Markwell the Carpenter says he will make A

	good one that Size at 9d a round. We also want 2 or 3 Potatoe Dibbers[16]
Wednesday	The Man Weatherley much better the Other inmates much the same as last report

Thursday, 9 March 1837

Thursday **Chipping Barnet**	Edw[ar]d Hull the Elder after being Dismissd from the Board on Thursday, was about the town for some time and was seen to come out of A Beer Shop instead of going direct back to the Workhouse
Friday	the Sick inmates much the same. The others all peaceable
Saturday **Shenley** *Notice*	Mrs Ward of Green Street, with whom the Girl Williams went to live, about 6 months back, calld on the Matron a few days ago to say she would have no further occasion for her Service, after 25 March
Sunday **Chipping Barnet**	Attended at the New Workhouse this afternoon, to admit none without orders from the Guardians to view the New house.
Chipping Barnet *Notice*	between Saturday Night & Sunday Morning, some person broke through the Clamp & stole A quantity of potatoes in the Garden. They seem extremely fond of the Sort. This being the third time they have been visited
Monday **East Barnet**	the Woman Burton sinking fast. Esther Haynes much the same. All the other inmates orderly except Mary Cooper; who was a little disorderly on Saturday Night
Tuesday **Chipping Barnet**	Nothing Material

16 Tools with which to make holes in which to plant potatoes

Shenley
Wednesday

the Child Hollaway going on right. The boy Gwillim much better. The Children & Women all healthy & orderley

Wednesday

the Man Weatherley still confined to his bed. Paul Peart in a very poor way & the boy Woodhouse laid up with his old Complaint a bad leg. The Man Hull & all the other inmates very orderly this week

Thursday, 16 March, 1837

Thursday

James Fearman aged 37 & Harriet Fearman his wife, Aged 35, paupers of South Mims. Admitted in Chipping Barnet house, this 16 day March by Order of Board. Examined the following Morning by the Medical Officer, the man ruptured

Friday

The Woman Fearman, who was admitted in the Workhouse yesterday by order of the board ask[ed] permission to go back to London to make some arrangement & that she would return the following day & attend to her sick husband but such has not been the case

Friday

The Medical Officer recommends ½ a pint of Beer to be given daily to the boy Peart whoes in a poor way

Friday
Shenley

Inmates all going on as usual. No Complaints from the Matron

Friday
East Barnet

Sick inmates much the same. The Others behave tolerable orderly. This being pudding day, the Matron was obliged to send one of the Men to Barnet for the Suet though the Contractor has had the order in the house a week. The dinner was 2 hours behind time

Saturday

Chipping Barnet Inmates Nothing Material their behaviour being quite proper

Sunday
Chipping Barnet
I attended at the new house this afternoon, to Prevent the Admission of improper Persons

Monday
Shenley
Edward & Emma Shepherd, the two Chipping Barnet Casualty Children belonging to Bayford, was removed to their proper Settlement this morning by order of Board

Tuesday
East Barnet
Frances Burton, widow South Mims Pauper, aged 52 Died this Morning, After A long Illness

Tuesday
Chipping Barnet
the Medical Officer recommends 1 Pint of Beer to be given daily to Tho[mas] Smith the blind man, the same to Paul Peart.

Tuesday
East Barnet
Mary Cooper. aged 21 Pauper of Hadley, was discharged from East Barnet house this day at her own request. Gone to Service at Finchley, had flannel Petticoat & two Caps belonging to the Union with her

Wednesday
Chipping Barnet
Inmates all Orderly. Nothing Material Since our Last report. The Woman Feaman has not yet returnd to her husband

Thursday, 23 March 1837

[No entries were made in the original for the above week]

THE DIARY OF BENJAMIN WOODCOCK

Thursday, 30 March, 1837

Friday

John Stops, Aged 61 Pauper of Finchley, was Discharged from Chipping Barnet house 31 March at his own request. He has a bad leg & wished to try the benefit of the Hospital

Friday Shenley

Eliz[abe]th Williams aged 14, Pauper of South Mims, was admitted in Shenley Workhouse on Friday 31 March, having received 1 Month Notice from Mrs Ward of Green Street with whom she went to live

**Friday
East Barnet**

Joseph Mitchell, William Layton, William Green & Neben Enever, 4 Inmates, was removed to Chipping Barnet house this day, As p[e]r orders of the board

Saturday

Paid the Trades Peoples Union a/c at Shenley & East Barnet, on Saturday, As p[e]r Orders

**Sunday
Chipping Barnet**

between Saturday Night & Sunday Morning some Persons opend the Potatoe Clamp in the old Workhouse Garden again, & took Away 4 or 5 bushels. This is the fifth time

I did not send the inmates to Church on Sunday in Consequence of their Clothing being so very insufficient, being advised to do so

Monday

The Matron of East Barnet sent word this morning that the Girl Ann Gray was going to the Hospital the following day & wished me to send her A new p[ai]r Black Stockings, which was sent Accordingly.

Tuesday

Jane Smith Aged 17, Birmingham Pauper, was admitted in Chipping Barnet Workhouse this Afternoon, Order R[elieving] O[fficer], in Consequence of her Illness. The Medical officer Promptly Attended & took some Blood from her. After which she appeard better

Tuesday
Chipping Barnet
The Chipping Barnet inmates all orderly & in good health, except A little Itching.

Tuesday
James Hall, the Casualty who was admitted with his wife by order R[elieving] O[fficer], is still very ill & unable to be removed

Jacob Robinson much better

Wednesday
Chipping Barnet
Sarah Sharp, Pauper of South Mims Lodged at the Workhouse last night by Order R[elieving] O[fficer], having business with the board

Thursday, 5 April, 1837

Chipping Barnet
Nothing Material

Friday
Chipping Barnet
Mr Smith & two Gentlemen from Another Union, calld to View the Workhouse this Afternoon

Friday
Mr Ray brought two Gentlemen who had come 300 hundred Miles & was much pleased with the Arrangement of the house

Saturday
Chipping Barnet
the Revd. Mr Wood from Shenley calld at the Workhouse Just at the inmates Dinner hour on Saturday & expressed himself much Satisfied with the Diet, Bedding & healthy Appearance of the inmates, being very different from What was represented to him

Sunday
Chipping Barnet
Nothing Material

Chipping Barnet
Isaac Crane, pauper of Chipping Barnet was discharged at his own request this morning having got work, Brick Making, at Finchley. He begd he might have his Union Stocking, an old Shirt and Round frock, having neither of his own

Monday   Mr Morrison, the Medical Officer, recommends one Pint of Beer to be given daily to the Casualty Man Hall also the same allowance of Wine to be given to Jacob Robinson for A few days longer, when he will be in a fit state to remove. 2 Eggs p[e]r day to be given to Paul Peart

Monday   Received of Mr Pitkin the Plasterer, whoes at work on the Premises, 2s for two days Labour for one of the inmates. To whom shall I pay it?

Tuesday   The Man Weatherley was tapd this Morning by the Medical Officer & upwards of four Gallons of Water taken from him

Mrs Cooper of Barnet wishes me to send her a Girl out of the house for 3 weeks or a Month only. Is it the order of the board I should do so?

Wednesday   Sarah Godfrey left her Service on Wednesday & was admitted in Shenley Workhouse the same day

Chipping Barnet   Mary Davison aged 33, Mary Eliz[abe]th Davison aged 9 & Rob[er]t Davison aged 2, paupers of Hadley, was admitted this day by order R[elieving] O[fficer]

Thursday, 13 April, 1837

Thursday   William Peel, the runaway boy, returnd to the Workhouse this morning much distressed

Thursday   George Salt Pauper of Finchley, who was discharged at his own request on the 23 Feb[ruar]y, was readmitted in Chipping Barnet house this day as p[e]r orders of the board, weak for the want of food

Thursday   Christ[opher] Lenman was discharged this day at his own request, having got employ at Brick Making.

THE DIARY OF BENJAMIN WOODCOCK

Had a shirt & Cap, as per orders of board

Thursday

Sarah Waterton Pauper of Chipping Barnet Admitted in the house this day 13 April by order R[elieving] Officer

Friday

Sarah Camel, Pauper of Shenley, Admitted in Shenley Workhouse this 14 day April, order R[elieving] O[fficer],

Friday

We sent the Girl Eliz[abe]th Williams, to Mrs Coopers at Barnet this morning as per order of Board, but she returned not being Strong enough

Saturday

Mr Goodyear applyd at the new Workhouse Lodge this morning & requested the Porter to let him have 2 of the union Planks, which he accordingly did. I was gone to Shenley

Saturday

The Woman Davison, who came into the house on Wednesday last, being near her Confinement with scarcely any thing for her own use. Would not a box of Childbed Linen be Necessary Kept in the house?

Saturday Shenley

the Women & Children all healthy & orderly, except the Girl Holloway, whoes [who is] still sick

Saturday East Barnet

the inmates all much as usual. Hird no Complaints from the Matron

Saturday

Mr Taplin brought 3 Friends to look over the house on Saturday before 10 Oclock in Morning without any order from Guardians. I was from home

Saturday

The Revd G Mutter, Rector of Whitchurch & one of the Guardians of the Hendon Union applyd for Admission to View the New house, without an order from the Guardians, to which I at first objected, but Subsequently Consented.

The Revd Gent[leman] After going over the Premises gave his name & address & on leaving expressed himself in Writing much gratified

Sunday
Chipping Barnet

nothing Material. The inmates all orderly. No Visitors

Monday
Chipping Barnet

Widow Howard aged 25, the Mother of the 2 Children of the same name in Shenley Workhouse, was admitted In Consequence of Illness by the Visiting Committee. On Monday she Acknowledged to the Medical Officer who Promptly attended, that she had certainly lived a very improper Life

Tuesday
Chipping Barnet

Charles Blackbrow had:

2½ bus[he]l Seed Potatoes 1/6 bu[she]l	3s 9d
paid the same time	
6 bus[he]l d[itt]o D[itt]o 1/6	9s 0d
Recd	12s 9d

Wednesday
East Barnet

Ann Gray, Pauper of Ridge, was removed Yesterday to the Hospital as p[e]r order of Board

Wednesday
Shenley

the Women & Children all same as usual but want Clothing

Chipping Barnet

the Woman Howard much better since she Came into the house but still in a poor way. The other inmates all on the improvement & quite orderly

Thursday 20 April, 1837

Thursday 20

Lord Caledon of Tittenhanger went over the house this Afternoon & Expressed himself much Pleased with the Provisions, Bedding & general arrangements of the Premises

Friday 21

Joseph Hall aged 74 & Sarah his wife aged 54, who where admitted as Casual Paupers by order

R[elieving] O[fficer] on the 23 March in Consequence of Illness, are in a fit State to be removed but he tells me he is not able to walk ½ a mile. He says his Legal Settlement is in Lincolnshire. His examination has not been taken. He still at the old Workhouse

Saturday 22

Elizabeth Williams aged 20 was admitted as Casual Pauper in Chipping Barnet house by order of one of the Guardians this Afternoon. When the Medical Officer attended, he ordered her some hot Brandy & Water after which on a Closer examination he was of opinion that she was nothing but an imposter. I gave her some good soup for Supper & Gruel for breakfast as recommended by the Medical Officer & started her the following morning. She wanted money

Saturday 22

Sarah Granger Widow Aged 79 Pauper of Hadley, Admitted Chipping Barnet house, by order R[elieving] O[fficer] this day 22 Ap[ri]l 1837. Examined by Medical Officer, in good health

Sunday 23
Chipping Barnet

Nothing Material, all orderly

Monday 24
Chipping Barnet

three Gentlemen from the Hendon Union calld on Monday Afternoon to view the New Workhouse but not having A Guardians order I of course refused them Admittance, as p[e]r orders, of Board

Monday 24

Mr Goodyear has returnd the 2 Planks which was borrowd on the 15 Inst[ant]

Received on Saturday Afternoon from Finchley Parish:

8 Wooden Bedsteads
5 Beds
 Some Blankets
5 Chairs
2 forms
& an Old Table

Had rec[eive]d no orders what I was to do with them, so left them at the Old Workhouse

Tuesday

Sarah Camel, one of the Shenley inmates, wishes to Know if the board would allow her 2s a week to go out. This Woman is a Cripple, not able to work, rather weak intellect

Tuesday

The Woman Taylor, One of the inmates at East Barnet, wishes to go out If the board will be pleased to allow her 2s a week & advance he[r] 2 Months Money

Wednesday

John Weedon Chipping Barnet inmate wishes to go out on Monday but he has not a Single garment of his own to Wear. Had we better look him up some old clothes? He also wants shoes

Thursday, 27 April, 1837

Thursday

Thomas Woodwards, belonging to Hadley, received much benefit from the Warm bath on Thursday. A Tin or Wooden Spout would be very usefull to Convey the Water from the Pump to the Copper

Friday

Received on Friday the 28 April from Messrs Road Nightingale & Road:

   36 Mattresses
   36 Bolsters
   30 Beds

Friday

Ann Gilman Pauper of Chipping Barnet Admitted on Friday 28 April by order of Board. Examined same day by Medical Officer

Saturday

Received the Goods from London, as ordered by Mr Franklyn, on Friday Evening

Saturday

Sarah Camel, the imbercile Pauper belonging to Shenley, was permitted to go out of the house by

THE DIARY OF BENJAMIN WOODCOCK

Mrs Rogers the Matron, on Friday, Contrary to the Orders of the board, but was brought back by some Person on the following day together with the enclosed note

Sunday

John Weedon Pauper belong[ing] to South Mims, was discharged from C[hipping] B[arnet] house at his own request, on Sunday 30 inst[ant]. We furnished him entirely with Clothing from the Old Stores as p[er] orders

Monday

A Frenchman of the name of Hubert Perrin, Hadley Casualty Pauper, was admitted C[hipping] B[arnet] house on Friday by order R[elieving] O[fficer] in Consequence of Illness. He has been attended by the Medical Officer but at Present unable to proceed on his way, though some what better

Monday

Mrs Lipscomb of Shenley applyd at the Workhouse for a Servant Girl about 17 or 18. I calld on her the following morning & proposed Betsy Williams.[17] She said she was fearful the Girl was too young but would Consider of it & Let me Know

Tuesday

Eliz[abe]th Bell & Widow Goodall, two of the East Barnet Women whom I removed on Tuesday, came in quite Lousy. We had them Stripd & washed the Same Night

Wednesday

George Jones, Finchley Pauper, wished me to ask If the board would be pleased to allow him 2s Weekly to go out of the house

Wednesday

Eliz[abe]th Sells 89 Widow, Admitted in C[hipping] B[arnet] house on Wednesday the 3rd May, belong[ing] to East Barnet

[17] probably Elizabeth Williams of South Mimms, aged 13 on admission in the Admission and Discharge Register, described as a menial servant who had lost her place

Thursday, 4 May, 1837

Thursday 4 Mr Benj[amin] Clayton, having made application at Chipping Barnet Workhouse for a Servant Girl, the following day I sent him Eliz[abe]th Williams Pauper of South Mimms, as she will not probably be wanted for more than 2 or 3 weeks. May I admit her without the usual order?

Friday 5 Removed this Morning, as p[e]r orders of the board, the Women & Children, together with all the Furniture from Shenley Workhouse, except a 8 day clock & a Night Chair, which Mrs Rogers the Matron says with the approbation of the board, she will pay for at Mr Taplins Valuation. Got them all safe in Chipping Barnet house to Dinner.

Friday 5 The Woman Taylor was discharged from Chipping Barnet house this day as p[e]r orders of the board. We gave her A New Shift for which we have not rec[eive]d the written order

Saturday 6 Fanny Starkins, belon[gin]g to Shenley, applyd and was admitted on Saturday without an order. She was in a very distressed state

Sunday 7 Nothing Material
Read prayers twice to the inmates

Monday Joseph Hall & Sarah his wife, the two South Mims Casualties, was discharged from the Workhouse this Morning, the Medical Officer being of Opinion they where in a fit State to proceed homewards

Wednesday the Medical Officer, recommends two Glasses of Wine & Water to be given Daily to the Woman Howard whoes Sinking very fast, Consumption

Wednesday 10 William Spencer Aged 73 Pauper of Shenley wishes to go out of the house If the board will be pleased to grant him a weekly allowance

Wednesday 10 James Fernell the Sweep at Hadley High Stone, made application on Monday for A Girl. I directed him to call on friday for An Answer. His terms are to board and Lodge her, but not Clothe her

Wednesday 10 Jane Maddams Aged 71, Blind Chipping Barnet Pauper, Admitted in the house on Wednesday the 10 May, by order R[elieving] O[fficer]

The Wife of James Feaman, one of the inmates, being Ill, he wants Permission to go to London to see her. He put the enclosed Letter into my hands Yesterday Wednesday. He has not gone

Wednesday A Patent Mangle was sent in from Mr Bakers Oxford Street this Evening. The Men Want some Leading[learning?] before they can Put it together

Thursday, 11 May, 1837

Thursday 11 James Feaman Aged 37 Pauper of South Mims, discharged from the Workhouse this day, by order

note of the board

Friday 12 George Jones aged 61 Pauper of Finchley was discharged at his own request this Afternoon. Went out with a Union Hat having none of his own

Friday 12 Henry Crew Aged 82 Pauper of Chipping Barnet, was discharged at his own request this afternoon. Had p[ai]r of Shoes New, & P[air] Stocking old, as p[e]r order of Board

Friday 12 Lady Hardwick of Tittenhanger calld & wished to go over the house on Friday Afternoon, but not having A Guardians Order We of Course refused

Saturday 13   Received on Saturday Morning, from Mr Edw[ar]d Marsh

18 MINARIES[18]
18 Skeleton Dresses &
18 Boys Suits
31 P[air] Mens Small cloths

Saturday 13
James & J. Ric[hard]
[crossed through]   Mary Davison Aged 33 Pauper of Hadley, was delivered of two Male infants in Chipping Barnet house about 9 Oclock on Saturday Evening the 13 May 1837. Both of which together with the Mother are doing well but the mother is full of trouble

Sunday 14   Nothing Material

Monday 15   William Camper Aged 30 Supposed Pauper of Finchley, was admitted in the house from, Illness, on Monday 15 May, with the enclosed order from R[elieving] O[fficer]

Tuesday 16   About 4 Oclock this Morning A Man of the name of William Constable Aged 65, belonging to Hemel Hempstead was admitted into the house by order from Mr Coe the Overseer of Chipping Barnet having met with An Accident on Barnet Hill

Tuesday 16   Elizabeth Howard Aged 25 Pauper of South Mims Died of A Consumption this Afternoon. Gave Immediate directions to the Medical Officer Undertaker & Sexton

Tuesday 16
[crossed through]   Having Suspicion that something was going on Wrong when Six of the boys where about to leave the house to go to Work on the ground After dinner on Tuesday, I calld them all back, & on Searching the Leader William Peel, I found Secreted under his waistcoat upwards of one pounds weight of beef, which in fact was & which appeard by their

[18] The address of his London shop?

own Statements to be part of each of their days allowance. One of them Pretended to say it Smelt & that they were going to give it to the Porters dog. But the Meat came in the same Morning & was Perfectly Sweet. They no doubt was going to dispose of it otherwise

On Tuesday afternoon Mr Winter of Shenley with General Mesimin & a Party of Ladies, who had hird a very unfavourable account of the New Workhouse, calld to View the Premises who Acknowledge on leaving they highly approved every thing they saw, see the inclosed

Wednesday 17   Henry Brand Pauper of Finchley, to whom I gave by order a New P[ai]r of 8s 6d Shoes a few days back, as given me Notice to be discharged & wishes me to let him take his new Union shoes with him

Wednesday 17   Miss Hill & Friends calld at the Workhouse on Wednesday by order from Mr Hopewell & was much Pleased

Wednesday 17   The Medical Officer, recommends Hugh Perin, the Frenchman, who is much better in health, 1 Pint of Beer daily

Thursday, 18 May, 1837

Thursday 18   Thomas Foskett Aged 42 Pauper, of Chipping Barnet, was Admitted into the house by Order of the board on thursday 18 May. The Medical Officer orderd him the bath after which, we new Clothed him from head to foot

Friday 19   Henry Brand Pauper of Finchley was discharged from the Workhouse at his own request on Friday 19 day May 1837. Had Union Shoes and an old Smock Frock

THE DIARY OF BENJAMIN WOODCOCK

Saturday 20   Medical Officer recommends John Brill, Pauper of Shenley, to wear a Truss

Saturday 20   Thomas Foskett who was admitted in the house on thursday last, having On Saturday morning shewn Symtoms of unsettled Mind I watchd his Movements during the day but nothing Material appeard in his Conduct after

Sunday 21   Nathaniel Poulton, Chipping Barnet Pauper was discharged from the Workhouse on Sunday 21 May at his own request, Had his Union Shoes & Hat.

Sunday 21   Elizabeth Howard, Pauper of Mims, was Buried on Sunday Afternoon, followed by two of her Kinswomen & about Forty Couple of the inmates with their New Clothing

Monday 22 May   Returned to Mr Marsh, Minories, 1 dozen of the Mens Union Coats being inferior quality as p[er] order of Board.
Same day went to Hoxton Asylum.[19] The Barnet Union inmates all in good health but dirty & very badly Clothed

Tuesday 23   The Rev Mr Newcombe & his two Daughters calld to View the New house on Tuesday & was much Pleased.

Tuesday 23   A Gentleman & 2 Ladies from Totteridge Calld to see the Workhouse this Afternoon by order from the Revd Mr Lendon

Wednesday 24   Mr Weeks sent 2 Men from London to repair the Kitchen Range on tuesday & Wednesday

---

[19] Hoxton Asylum was one of several privately-owned lunatic asylums in the Hoxton district of London. Boards of Guardians had contracts with private asylums for the care of pauper lunatics, and in the case of the Hoxton Asylum the majority of their inmates were paupers; William L. Parry-Jones, *The Trade in Lunacy* (London, 1972), pp 36, 43, 51

Wednesday 24   3 friends of Mr Markwell calld on Wednesday to look over the house by Order from Mr Goodyear

Wednesday 24   Miss Hayward & Friends Came to look Over the house on Wednesday by order from Mr Goodyear

Wednesday 24   Mr Ward & Friends Came on Wednesday Afternoon, to go over the house by order from Mr Hopewell

John Rippon one of the inmates wishes to go out but has not a Single Garment of his own fit to Put on. He came into the house filthy dirty & Ragged

Thursday, 25 May, 1837

Thursday 25   Edward Wells Aged 50 Pauper of Finchley, Admitted in the house by order of board on Thursday 25 May. The Medical Officer recommended the Warm Bath. After which we Clothed him from head to feet, he was in A most filthy dirty Condition Swarmd with Lice

Thursday 25   Ann Grimes Aged 6 Pauper of Chipping Barnet, Admitted in the house on Thursday 25 May by order of board

Friday 26   Mrs Franklyn of Totteridge went over the Premises on Friday 26 May, also Mr Hopewell & Gentleman from London the same Afternoon

Saturday 27   Mrs Adams & 5 friends went over the house this Afternoon by Mr Hopewell Order Saturday 27 May

Sunday 28
Chipping Barnet   Nothing Material the inmates all Orderly to & from Church

Monday 29   Mr Audsley & Daughter from Finchley calld on Monday to View the New house & was quite Pleased with the Bedding & other Comforts of the inmates, by order of Mr Bass

Monday 29	The Medical Officer Mr Morrison found it Necessary this Morning to take from the man Weatherley Upwards of 3 Gallons of Water. This is the third time he as been Tapd
Tuesday 30	On Searching A Casualty Woman, who applyd for Lodging by order R[elieving] O[fficer] we found several Days Provisions of Good Beef & Mutton & Bread, when she acknowledge[d] she was able to pay for Lodging & went Away
	The Medical Officer Certifys that Hubert Perin, the Frenchman, will be quite able in a few days to proceed homeward. All the other Sick inmates going on favourably
Wednesday 31	during the Absence of the Porter on Sunday Morning Thomas Foskett the Idiot got outside the Gate. We Missed him immediately & fetchd him back
Wednesday 31	Laura Cooper having askd the Medical Officer If the Hospital would be any benefit to her complaint, his answer was, it would be useless to send her
Wednesday 31 May	the Inmates all generally healthy & orderly

Thursday, 1 June, 1837

Thursday 1 [crossed through]	The rain in the Wet Weather comes through the Ceiling in the water Closet adjoining the board Room
	Please Notice the floor in the Wash house. The water will not go away
Thursday 1 June	Mr Benj[amin] Clayton has Just sent word he has a woman Servant Coming on Monday and that he will have no further occation for Eliz[abe]th Williams

after that day. This Girl was sent from the Workhouse by order of the board on the 4th May

Thursday 1

Thomas Foskett Aged 12, Pauper of Chipping Barnet, admitted in house 1 June by order of the Board

Thursday 1

Charlotte Seagrave Aged 27, Pauper of Chipping Barnet, Admitted in the house on Thursday 1 June by order of board. On hir examination by the Medical Officer he ordered that her Provision Utensils might be Kept Separate from the other inmates. Shes in a bad State

Thursday 1

As Usual sold her flannel Petticoat & two Shifts given by the Union

Ann Gray Pauper of Ridge, who was sent from East Barnet Workhouse, to the London Hospital by order of board on tuesday 4 March, was discharged on tuesday the 30 May, for the same cause as she was discharged from the Lock [hospital] sometime ago. Namely not willing to submitt to the Operation. Admitted in the house 1 June by order R[elieving] O[fficer] 9 Oclock evening. Placed with the woman Seagrave.

Thursday 1

This man had £2 9s when he came in, which I have in my Possession

George Fisher Aged 52 belonging to the Hitchin Union, having Met with An Accident in the Parish of Hadley on Thursday night 1 June, was Admitted in the Workhouse about 12 Oclock by Order R[elieving] O[fficer]. The Medical Officer Promptly Attended but it was not of any serious nature

Friday 2

Ann Hale Widow, Pauper of Shenley, was discharged from the workhouse at her own request on Thursday 1 June. Gone to live with her Daughter

Friday 2

Thomas Stubbington, Pauper of East Barnet, wishes to try the benfit of the Hospital. Mr Morrisons assistant having told him his Complaint was hopeless

THE DIARY OF BENJAMIN WOODCOCK

Friday 2   Wanted some Children's School books testaments & Prayer books for the Use of the Workhouse

Friday 2   The Revd Mr Thackery & friends Mr Robarts & Daughters, calld to view the house on Friday Afternoon, quite Satisfied. Miss Robarts wished to Know if their would be any objection If she sent the Children some books

Saturday 3   Saturday Eliza Trott Aged 18, Pauper from Elstree
This Girl whoes within two months of her confinement, as not reachd 18 years & brought up to the Methodist Chapel   was Admitted in the house by an Order of removal dated the 9th May, on Saturday the 3 June. The Medical Officer Pronounced her to be in a forward state of Pregnancy

Saturday 3   George Fisher the Casualty, who was Admitted on Thursday night at 12 Oclock, Died in Consequence of An Accident from riding on the Shafts of a wagon Loaded with Straw at 12 Oclock on Friday Night, Just 26 hours After the Accident. Sent notice to the Coroner as p[er] order of Mr Franklyn

Sunday 4   Charles Watson to whom the board gave An Order of Admission in the Workhouse on Thursday, applyd for Admission for himself only, on Sunday, but I refused he not having his wife with him according to the Order

Monday 5   The woman Jiltro, Caroline Montgomery & her three younger Sisters was admitted in the workhouse on Monday Morning by order R[elieving] O[fficer], Paupers of Shenley

Monday 5   William Thursby Aged 50 Pauper of East Barnet, Admitted into the house by order R[elieving] O[ffi-cer} on Monday 5 June, badly ruptured & requires a Truss, See Medical report

Monday 5   George Fisher the Casualty, was Buried this Afternoon 5 Oclock by order of the Coroner

Tuesday 6	Charlotte Seagrave Aged 27, Pauper Chipping Barnet, removed from the Workhouse to the Lock Hospital on Tuesday 6 June by order of board R[elieving] O[fficer]
Wednesday 7	Mr Rogers & friends, P[er] Order of the Revd Mr Elwin, call[d] to View the Workhouse on Wednesday 7 June, highly Satisfied except with the Water
Wednesday 7	James Montgomery his wife & two Children removed to Margate infirmary on tuesday 6 June as p[er] order of board.
Wednesday 7	Col[o]n[el] Dury calld to View the house with a Party of Friends on Wednesday 7 June 1837
Thursday 8	Geo[rg]e Salt Pauper of Finchley who came in the house, a second time but a few weeks back, wished to be discharged this Afternoon. May he take his Union hat
Thursday 8	Hubert Perin the Frenchman is well enough to be discharged but says he has not one Sixpence in his Pocket

Thursday, 8 June, 1837

Thursday 8	Daniel Dolamore Aged 56, Friern Barnet Casualty Pauper bel[ongin]g to Eddlesborough, was Admitted in the Workhouse by order of board, on thursday 8 June 1837. Examined same day by Medical Officer
Friday 9	George Salt bel[ongin]g to Finchley, was Discharged at his own request on Friday 9 June. Had nothing belonging to the Union but an Old Hat
Friday	Susannah Jiltro, Widow belong[ing] to Shenley, was discharged from the Workhouse at her own request on Friday 9 June, going to her Daughter in London.

Begd she might take one of her Union Hand[kerchief]s, not having one of her own

Friday 9

Hadley casualty

Hubert Perin, the Frenchman, was Discharged from the Workhouse this Morning, being Perfectly restored to health. He returnd thanks to the board, for the great benefit he had received I gave him 1s p[e]r order of Capt[ain] Trotter

Friday 9

Eliz[abe]th Williams calld at the Workhouse to say she should leave Mr Benj[amin] Clayton on Monday & was going to London after a situation, but I desired her by all means, not to go, till I had made enquiry where & with whom she was going to live. She's not more than 15 years of age

Saturday 10

Eliza Harris Finchley Casual Pauper Admitted in the house in Consequence of Illness on Saturday 10 June by order R[elieving] O[fficer]
A Sick Casual Ward would be useful this woman having a Slow fever

Saturday 10

Elizabeth Williams Elstree Pauper was Seized with a Lockd Jaw this Afternoon. The Medical officer Promptly Attended an Put right

Saturday 10

The forms belonging the Chapel being sent home this Morn[ing]. The Revd. Mr Winbolt read Prayers to the inmates up Stairs for the first time

Saturday 10

Thomas Lord Pauper of Shenley being absent from his work on Saturday afternoon, I lernt from a question I put to him, he had been to the Beer Shop, when it appear[d] by his own Statement he is in receipt of five pounds p[er] annum left by his Uncle his answer was, the board knows of it

Sunday 11

Nothing Material all orderly

Monday 12   John Brand & Charles Godfrey was punished this Morning, the one for taking some Lead out of the house & selling to to Mr Bennet for one 1d, the other for Wetting the Bed 5 nights

Tuesday 13   Eliz[abe]th Williams, South Mimms orphan aged 15, having been recommended to a Situation in London by A Lady Named Page, I thought it my duty for the satisfaction of the board to make some enquiry, where & with whom she was going to Live before she went. On the receipt of the enclosed & the Address of the Mistress in whoes Service she's going, I gave her Permission to go up the following day, Wednesday, with Proper Advise

        Mrs Reeve
        Wine Merchant
        5 Warwick Lane
        Newgate Street

Wednesday 14   the Woman Davison is quite able to Come Down Stairs but their wants a Cradle for the Children in the day time

Wednesday 14   the Girl from Elstree who is in the family way, has not a Single thing for the use of the Child. Had we better have some Linen made in the house?

Thursday, 15 June, 1837

Thursday 15   Ann Annell Aged 82 Pauper of Hadley, Admitted in the house this day by order of Board

Thursday 15   Thomas Foskett Aged 12 Pauper of Chipping Barnet, discharged from the Workhouse this day P[e]r Order board

Friday 16   the inmates all orderly & doing well except Edward Hull the Elder, whom the Medical officer found Necessary to Bleed this Morning

THE DIARY OF BENJAMIN WOODCOCK

Saturday 17

Several of the inmates took the Sacrament on Saturday Afternoon. Edw[ar]d Hull confined to his Bed, quite unsensible

Admitted in the Workhouse by order R[elieving] O[fficer] on Sunday Afternoon, An Irish Casualty Woman from South Mims. This woman whoes Pregnant and near her Confinement has not an Article of Clothing for the use of the Child. Mr Morrison's Assistant was in the house when she Came in, we put her up in the ward with the other Casualty Woman Harris

Monday 19

Sold John Lemman   19 June
1 bus[he]l ½ Hog Potatoes   1s 4d

Monday evening 19

Mr Morrisons Assistant is of Opinion that Edw[ar]d Hull the elder cannot live many hours.

Tuesday 20

Sarah Delaney the Irish Casualty Woman who came in on Sunday is much better. She's not likely to be Confind at Present but wishes to go on to London in Search of her husband. The Matron gave her 1s that she might git a ride

Wednesday 21

Thomas Lord wishes to go out of the house on Monday & begs the board will be Pleased to give him some Clothing

Wednesday 21

Fredk{Alfred?] Mucham Aged 15 wishes to go out of the house but is entirely without Clothing of his own

Wednesday 21

Rob[er]t Nutkins Pauper of Elstree wishes the board will be Pleased to give him Permission to go out for 2 days

Wednesday 21

Charlotte Tinsley, Pauper from South Mims, Admitted in the house on Wednesday 21 by Order R[elieving] O[fficer]

THE DIARY OF BENJAMIN WOODCOCK

Thursday, 22 June, 1837

Thursday 22
A woman of the name of Brumby calld to see William Tuckfield & askd me If he might go out for 3 or 4 Days. I told her that would be for the Consideration of the board

Friday 23
Charlotte Tinsley, Pauper of South Mims, was discharged from the Workhouse this morning. I left her at Mr Salmon's to be Conveyd to London As P[er] Orders

Saturday 24

Sunday 25
A person calld at the Workhouse this Afternoon, to see the Woman Davison & wished me to let her take the 2 Children out for An hour but I Objected

All orderly Nothing Material

Sunday 25
Hugh Hawkes Pauper of East Barnet was discharged from the Workhouse this day at his own request. We gave him an Old Jacket, Hat, Shirt & one P[air] Stockings beside what was ordered by the board

Sunday 25
Alfred Mucham, Pauper of Chipping Barnet, was discharged at his own request this Morning. Was obliged to look him out some Old Clothing being entirely Naked when he Came in the house

Monday 26
Edward Hull the elder, Pauper of Hadley, Died this Afternoon about 6 oclock, having had a fit of Apoplexy a few days before

Monday 26
Thomas Lord Pauper of Shenley was discharged this Morning at his own request. We also furnishd him with a few old things

John Rippen Pauper of Hadley was discharged at his own request this day. Gave him an Old Suite the whole of what he had when he Came in the house having been burnt

THE DIARY OF BENJAMIN WOODCOCK

Monday 26   Admitted in the Workhouse about 8 Oclock this morning an Irish Casualty Woman & her infant who was delivered a few hours before in a Ditch at East Barnet.
I sent immediately for the Medical Officer who Promptly Attended. They are both in a fair way of doing well. She has nothing for the Child to wear

Monday 26   Please let the Children have some books

the enclosed Letter, was given to the Porter at the Gate, on Sunday afternoon to be deliv[ere]d to me by the Woman Camel on her return from Church. This is the woman who went out of Shenley Workhouse sometime ago, & was sent back in a Cart the following day with a Note saying she was an Idiot & a Cripple & not able to Provide for herself

Tuesday 27   I desired Neben Enever & several of the Other Men who have frequently more Bread than they Can eat themselves, not to waste it but give it to some of the Boys in the house, which they did

Tuesday 27   We have 6 Double & 5 Single Iron Bedsteads without Beds or Mattresses

George Farmer South Mimms Pauper wishes to go out tomorrow, If the board will be pleased to give him a few shillings

Wednesday 28   Thomas Bourne & John Brill, Hadley & Shenley Paupers want to go out but they have Scarcely Any Clothing of their own to put on

Wednesday 28   Edw[ar]d Hull the elder Buried this Afternoon. His Daughter and Several of the inmates followed

All orderly

Widow Maddams Daughter calld at the Workhouse

this Morning to say she would feel Obliged If the board will be pleased to let her Mother go out for 1 day to see a sick Person

Thursday, 29 June, 1837

Thursday 29	Ric[har]d Flint, Casualty Pauper of Finchley Aged 6, Admitted in the house this day by order of board
Thursday 29	Eliza Harris Casualty Pauper of Finchley discharged this Evening by Order of board
Saturday 1 July	George Farmery South Mims Pauper Discharged at his own request on Saturday 1 July
	Susannah Jiltro Pauper Shenley Admitted on Saturday 1 July
Sunday 2	Thomas Baume [Bourne?] Pauper of Hadley was discharged from the Workhouse on Sunday 2nd July. Clothed him as well as I could
Monday 3	Edward Hull Pauper of Hadley was discharged from the Workhouse on Monday 3 July
Monday 3	John Brill, Pauper of Shenley, was discharged from the Workhouse on Monday Morning 3 July
Wednesday 5	Ann Bonnet Widow & her two Children, Mary Ann Aged 3 years & Martha Aged 1 year was Admitted in the Workhouse on Wednesday 5 July from Shenley, with a Magistrates order of Removal from Reading
Wednesday 5	Neben Enever Pauper of Shenley begs the board will be pleased to grant him leave of Absence for 2 days
Wednesday 5	Elizabeth Parkes Pauper of South Mims begs the board will be pleased to grant her leave of Absence for 2 days

| Saturday | Rec[eive]d Mr Bennet 1 July as P[e]r Bill Deliv[ere]d 12s |

Thursday, 5[6] July, 1837

| Thursday 5 [6] | John Burke Aged 30 Casualty Pauper from Elstree, belon[g]ing to Stockport, was Admitted in the Workhouse in Consequence of Illness by order R[elieving] O[fficer] on Thursday 5 [sic] July. Attended by the Medical Officer |

| Thursday 6 | Michael Donavan Aged 48 Cork Casualty Pauper from Totteridge, was Admitted in the Workhouse in Consequence of Illness on Thursday 5 [sic] July by order of Mr White the Guardian. The Medical Officer Promptly Attended & took some blood from him. An Affection of the Chest |

| Friday 7 | Thomas Weatherley Pauper of Hadley whoes been Confined to his bed for Sometime with the Dropsy, was attended by the Medical Officer this Afternoon, & Tapd for the fourth time, took upwards of 3 Gall[o]ns |

| Friday 7 | Received at the Workhouse on Friday the 6th [sic] July 5d weight of oatmeal from the Aberdeen Wharf, London As P[er] Orders |

| Saturday 8 | Bridget Donnally & Catherine McKew two Irish Casualty Women was Admitted in the Workhouse on Saturday Evening with the inclosed, order, from Mr Tatham the Assist[ant] Overseer of Finchley. However the Next day, finding Nothing Material the Matter with them, I filld their belly & sent them Away |

| Sunday 9 | John Bell one of the inmates was bro[ugh]t home by two Men about ½ past 4 Oclock on Sunday Afternoon in a State of intoxication. He went out after Dinner for the rest of the Paupers for the |

Purpose of going to Church instead of which he went to the Black horse Public house, where he remaind till he was unable to walk back by himself. He Swore when the Porter went to fetch him. We have not yet Punished him for it

Mondon 10

Mary Murray thc Irish Casualty who was Admitted in the Workhouse on Monday Morning the 26 June, having been deliverd of A female infant a few hours before at East Barnet, being sufficiently recoverd from her Confinement this Morning, returned thanks for the Attention she received & was discharged at her own request. The Matron gave her a few Necessary things for the Use of the Child

Tuesday

John Burke Aged 30 & Michael Donovan Aged 48, the two Irish Casualtys, who was Admitted in the Workhouse by orders on thursday 6 July in Consequence of Illness, being able to go out, was Discharged on Tuesday 11 Inst[ant].

Tuesday

Mrs Tappin who Keeps Baker's Shop on the Common Applyd at the Workhouse on Tuesday for a Stout Errand Boy
Fred[eric]k Woodhouse, Pauper of Hadley, is desirous of going, but he has none but the Union Clothing

Thursday, 13 July, 1837

Friday 14

Mr Roberts & family Calld to look over the house on friday Afternoon, & was much Pleased with its appearance. Observed they could be very happy in it themselves

Friday 14

Sarah Geer Pauper of Finchley was Admitted in the Workhouse on Friday Evening, the Matron put her in one of the inner Casualty wards the first Night, in Consequence of the dirty Appearance of her Linen

THE DIARY OF BENJAMIN WOODCOCK

Friday 14

The woman Bonnet went out After Breakfast this Morning as p[er] orders of Board & returned to the house about ½ past 7 in the Evening

Saturday 15

William Campen Aged 30 Pauper of Finchley who was Admitted in the House on Monday 15 May in Consequence of Sickness, having recovered, was discharged from the Workhouse this Afternoon at his own request. He expressed his Sincere thanks for the attention he had received.

Sunday 16

The Revd Mr Wood Performd Divine Duty to the inmates in the Workhouse on Sunday Afternoon

Monday 17

Sarah Waterton, Pauper of Chipping Barnet, was discharged from the Workhouse, on Monday 17 July, at her own request

Monday 17

About ½ past 8 Oclock on Monday Morning the Porter informd me their was a Man at the Gate, who wished to see John Bell one of the inmates, but he was intoxicated, Consequently I refused him admittance

Monday 17

Mrs Grimstone of Hadley sent some Tea & Sugar by her footman on Monday evening for Ann Annell, one of the inmates and during their Conversation in the hall I hird her say to the young man she was not well used and wished somebody would take her out of the Workhouse. We are not aware of ever giving her an Angry Word therefore it would be some satisfaction If the board will be pleased to call upon her for an explanation

Tuesday 18

Adam Nixon Aged 18 An Irish Casualty Youth from Shenley was Admitted in the house by order R[elieving] O[fficer] on Tuesday 18 July in Consequence of Sickness

Wednesday 19	Edward Wells Aged 50, Pauper of Finchley Died of Consumption this Morning About 9 Oclock. Gave Immediate Notice to the Medical Officer & others
Wednesday 19	Thomas Stubbington, Pauper of East Barnet, wishes to go out of the house, & begs the board will be Pleased to give him a few shillings
Weddington 19	The Stock of Last years Potatoes will be all gone in a few days. Had we better order some old, or use them on the Ground
Wednesday 19	The Reading Desk in the Chapel was brought home yesterday & fitted up the following day as Order of Clerk

Wednesday 19	Sold Thomas Bennet 2½ bus[he]l Bones 10d bus[he]l	July 19 2s 1d

Wednesday 19	Paid the two Women, Carpenter & Pedley 1s for Laying Out Edw[ar]d Wells, as P[er] order

Thursday, 20 July, 1837

Thursday 20	Mary Satchell Aged 26 & her three Children, Henry Caroline & William Casualty Paupers of Hadley, was Admitted in the house on Thursday 20 July, by order of the board
Thursday 20	James Rice Aged 14, Casualty Pauper of Chipping Barnet, was Admitted in the house on Thursday 20 July, by order of board
Friday 21	Edward Wells Aged 50, Pauper of Finchley, was buried this Afternoon followed by 8 of the inmates
Friday 21	The Woman Satchell & the youth Rice was ordered to be at Mr Franklyn Office at 12 Oclock for examination. They returnd about 3

THE DIARY OF BENJAMIN WOODCOCK

Monday 24 On Monday the 24 July, as p[er] order of Mr Franklyn

Monday 24 William Warren Aged 63, Casualty Pauper from Finchley, was Admitted in the house, by order from Mr Tatham on Monday 24 July. Should not this order, as well as several Others which I have receivd from the same Parish, have come to me, through the hands of the R[elieving] O[fficer]? See the enclosed Order

Monday 24 Received from Mr Marsh on Monday 24 July 10 c weight Potatoes, & carriage £4 7s 0d Had 1 bush[ell] from Mr Cornwalls Same day

Monday 24 Gen[era]l Bunams & two Ladies went over the house on Monday afternoon Said every thing was very Comfortable, order of Mr Hopewell

Monday 24 Mary Pedley & Jane Carpenter, having been called up at one Oclock on Monday morning to attend the cleaning & Laying out of the Man Dolomore, who died about that time, askd the Matron After Breakfast, If they might send one of the boys for a Glass of Gin for each out of the shilling allowd them by the board for Laying out, to which she Consented, Knowing the absolute Necessity for it in such cases but the Porter who was told by the boy that his Mistress desired him to fetch it refused the Admittance without coming to ask the question. This is not the only instance of his Unbecoming treatment which, If suffered to go unnoticed, may tend to Lessen that feeling of due respect & Submission among the inmates, so Necessary to be upheld to Maintain Proper order & Discipline.

Tuesday 25 The woman Satchell, on leaving the Workhouse yesterday, observed to some of the inmates in the event of her husband leaving her again, she would immediately apply for Admission in the house, that herself & family was never so well Provided for at home

Paid Pedley & Carpenter for Laying out Daniel Dolomore 1s as p[er] order of the board

Tuesday 25
James Rice & John Brand was shut up for 2 hours & sent to Bed Supperless for throwing Stones & breaking 2 Squares of Glass

Wednesday 26
Ann Gray & Laura Cooper, 2 of the inmates, made their escape from the Workhouse between 8 Olock on Tuesday evening & 6 the Next Morning. We had no reason to Complain of their Conduct for several days Past. They have both got the Union Clothing on

Wednesday 26
Willis the Porter Came into the Kitchen on Wednesday, while we where serving out Dinner, and abused me & the Matron Shamefully. In fact he disturbed the whole house because the Plate in which I sent his Dinner did not suit him

Wednesday 26
Daniel Dolomore was buried about 6 Oclock this Evening, followed by Several of the inmates, returnd quite orderly

Thursday, 27 July, 1837

Thursday 27
Ann Gray & Laura Cooper was bro[ugh]t back to the Workhouse by three Policemen, between 6 & 7 Oclock on Thursday Evening. We lockd them up separate. Gave them Bread & Water the following day as P[er] orders

Friday 28
The enclosed note from General Dickins was sent to the Workhouse on Friday Morning. I returnd the following Answer

Sir,
I am sorry to say my instructions from the board prevent me from Complying with your request, by Permitting the woman Davison to go out of the house. I have directions to let her husband see her If he calls at the Workhouse

Y[ou]r ob[edien]t Serv[ant]
Woodcock
Barnet Workhouse
28 July 1837

Davisons Sister calld at the Workhouse a second time & wished me to let the Woman Davison go out for the day but I still refused

Friday 28	Flitt the Carrier delivrd at the Workhouse on Friday morning A Small Hamper, Sent from the Peacock Islington
Saturday 29	Thomas Smith the blind Man, & the Boy Salt, went out on Saturday about 2 Oclock, as P[e]r orders of the board
Saturday 29	the Medical Officer visited Ann Gray & Laura Cooper in their refractory wards on Saturday forenoon & askd them, If they would like to have Gruel instead of Water. They said If any one brought them Gruel they would throw it in their face
Saturday 29	William Davison applyd at the house on Saturday Afternoon for Permission to see his Wife. Leave granted as P[e]r orders
Monday 31	Richard Flint, Casualty Pauper from Finchley, was Discharged from the Workhouse on Monday Morning order R[elieving] O[fficer]. Was obliged to send him out in the Union Clothing having no others to put him on
Monday 31	William Davison applyd at the Workhouse on Sunday Afternoon after Divine Service for Permission to see his wife which was granted.

Monday 31 — Thomas Smith the blind Man, & the boy Salt, returned to the Workhouse on Monday Evening in Proper time

Monday 31 — William Dennis Aged 45 Casualty Pauper of South Mimms was Admitted in the house on Monday Evening by order of the R[elieving] O[fficer] in Consequence of Sickness. Burned all his Clothing they were Swarmd with Vermin

Tuesday 1 August — Ann Gray was Committed by the Magistrates to 2 Months hard labour, for going out of the house & selling some of the Union Clothing, by her own Statement this makes the 13th time shes been in Confinement, & only 23 years of age

Tuesday 1 August — William Davison Calld at the Workhouse on Tuesday Afternoon & was in Conversation with his wife some time

Wednesday 2 — It appears Necessary before their can be any further Use made of the Hot Water Furnice, for Mr Weeks or some Person to examine the Pipes for Some of them Leak

Wednesday 2 — John Stops Pauper of Finchley who was Discharged from the Workhouse at his own request on the 31 March, was readmitted this Afternoon by Order R[elieving] O[fficer]

Wednesday 2 — The Woman Davison wishes the board will be Pleased to Notice her Case

Laura Coopers Case

Thursday, 3 August, 1837

Thursday 3 — Isaac Crane Aged 71 Chipping Barnet Pauper was Admitted in the Workhouse by Order of Board on Thursday Aug[us]t 3

THE DIARY OF BENJAMIN WOODCOCK

Thursday 3 the Woman Bonnet went out this Afternoon at 4 Oclock as p[e]r orders of board

Friday 4 George Grubbs Aged 58 Pauper from East Barnet Admitted this day by Order of Board Sent Immediately for the Medical Officer

Saturday 5 William Dennis, the South Mims Casualty Pauper who was Admitted in Consequence of Illness 31 July by order R[elieving] O[fficer], was able to go out. Discharged own request Clothed him with some Old Stores, having burned his own

Saturday 5 Eliza Trott Pauper of Elstree was delivered of a Male infant in the Workhouse on Saturday 5 August about 6 Oclock Evening, both of which are doing well

Saturday 5 The woman Bonnet, returned to the Workhouse about 7 Oclock on Saturday Evening as P[e]r orders of board and askd as a favor If she Might go out with her family on Sunday evening as her Brother would Carry her & children to London free of expense Permission was given

Sunday 6 William Davison calld at the Workhouse to see his Wife About 5 Oclock On Sunday Evening & remained with her till 7 in the Presence of the Porter.

Monday 7 Thomas Stubbington Pauper of East Barnet, was discharged from the Workhouse on Monday 6th Aug[us]t by his own request

Monday 7 Received from Messrs Cook & Son 6 August 2 Pieces Calico 125 yards

Monday 7 Some person from Mr Weeks, should examine the Hot Water Pipes before they are used as some of them Leak

Tuesday 8	The Revd Thomas Blundell & Friends calld to View the Workhouse on tuesday & was much Pleased with the Arrangement Order Revd Mr Lendon
	Mr Goodyear & 2 Friends went over the house on tuesday, was much pleased
Tuesday 8	The men who bring the Coals from London beg they may be allowd a pint of Beer each I gave them 6d the last time out of my Pocket, but nothing this time. May I give them 6d in future?
	Esther Haynes was removed from East Barnet Workhouse yesterday Monday, without the least injury
	Please to say how long we are to send Provisions for Mrs Peat at East Barnet
Wednesday 9	Rob[er]t Briers though not able for hard work I think may be useful in the boys School, If so may he be allowd a pint of Beer daily same as those who work on the Ground?
	We should find A Small Grindstone very useful to Sharpen the Tools
Thursday 10	Thomas Weatherley Pauper of Hadley Died this Morning about ½ past 8 Oclock of the Dropsey

Thursday, 10 August 1837

Thursday 10	Sarah Waterton Aged 50 Pauper of Chipping Barnet was Admitted in the house on Thursday 10 Aug[us]t by order of board
Thursday 10	The Master from the Hendon Workhouse by the recommendation of the Guardians calld & was very desirous to see Chipping Barnet & its Arrangement but not having a Proper order, I refused

Friday 11 August	James Pepper Aged 62 Casualty Pauper from Finchley was Admitted in the house on Friday 11 Aug[us]t by order of the board. Sent Immediately for the medical Officer
Friday 11 August	The Revd & Mr & Mrs Wood the Chaplain Came to the Workhouse on Friday last but to the great Astonishment of the Revd Gen[tlema]n & his Lady she was refused by the Porter at the Gate, who in the Most abrupt manner Observed he had as Much Authority as the Master, and as she had no order for Admission she must go back. But as soon as I herd of it, I sent & requested the Lady to return & insisted upon his Admitting her. Mr & Mrs Wood evidently appeared much hurt at his obnoxious treatment
Saturday 12	Thomas Weatherly Aged 58 was buried this Afternoon 6 Oclock followed by 10 of the inmates
Sunday 13	Miss Montague & friend Visited the Workhouse on Sunday Afternoon, by Order Mr Hopewell & was Much Gratified
Monday 14	The Medical Officer recommends 1 Pint of Beer daily to be given to the Woman Trott for 3 weeks from this date, August 14
Tuesday 15	William Davison on Application at the Workhouse on Tuesday Evening was Permitted to see his wife as P[e]r orders
Wednesday 16	Nothing Material on Wednesday

Thursday, 17 August,1837

Thursday 17	Ann Gillman Aged 71, Pauper of Chipping Barnet was discharged from the Workhouse at her own request on Thursday 17 Aug[us]t, a Discontented Woman

THE DIARY OF BENJAMIN WOODCOCK

Thursday 17   The Woman Davison, after the board on Thursday begd very hard that I would let her go out for ½ an hour only to see her husband & she would be sure to return, but I of Course could not Consent

Friday 18   William Warren, Casualty Pauper from Finchley, who as been very uneasy for some days because he was not discharged, saying he did not want to be Passed home, that his Parish would Pay all his expenses without [outside?] left his bed in the middle of Thursday night saying he was going to the Privy & made his escape over the wall by means of a Piece of rope fastend to a Log of wood

Friday 18   William Green who received Permission from the board on Thursday to go out on Saturday Morning early, wished me to let him go on the Friday Night as he could ride up by Mr Cornwall

Saturday 19   Some Persons got into the Workhouse Garden between Friday night & Saturday morning & Pulld up a quantity of the earliest Potatoes nearest the Porters Lodge

Saturday 19   James Rice, Chipping Barnet Casualty was removed On Saturday the 19th to the Parish of Ealing Near Acton & delivd to the Care of the Master of the Workhouse as P[e]r orders

Saturday 19   The Revd Mr Thackery & Friends went over the house on Saturday Afternoon & was Perfectly Satisfied

Sunday 20   Mrs Marr came with the Revd Mr Wood on Sunday afternoon & attended Divine Service with the inmates

Sunday 20   William Davison Calld at the house on Sunday Afternoon to see his Wife Mary Davison

THE DIARY OF BENJAMIN WOODCOCK

Monday 21   William Waller Chipping Barnet Casualty Admitted in the house on Monday 21 Aug[us]t in Consequence of Illness

Tuesday 22   Esther Bunningham Aged 42 Chipping Barnet Casualty Admitted by order Medical Officer, on Tuesday Morning in Consequence of Illness

Tuesday 22   William Waller who was Admitted on Monday Morning by order R[elieving] O[fficer] in Consequence of Illness having by Proper Attention recovered was discharged the following day. He was very thankful

Tuesday 22   The Man Davison, who calld & saw his wife on Sunday, Came Again on Tuesday & when told it was Contrary to the Orders of the board, said he would Not go Away till he had seen her & Swore he would take her Away in Spite of all the house for two Pins & leave the family

Wednesday 23   The Man Green did not return till Wednesday owing to the Wet Weather

Wednesday 23   the Women Carpenter & Buck begs the board will be Pleased to grant them, leave of Absence for a few days

Wednesday 23   Montgomery & his Wife returned from Margate on Wednesday being discharged from the Infirmary[20] much benefitted

The Painters Carpenters & Lime washers have been at Work in the house all this Week

Wednesday 23   James Pepper the Finchley Casualty want Permission from the board to go to Whetstone on Friday

[20] Margate General Sea-bathing Infirmary was founded in 1791 by Dr John Coakley Lettsom, a Quaker physician, for the benefit of the poor.

THE DIARY OF BENJAMIN WOODCOCK

Thursday, 24 August, 1837

Thursday 24   Montgomerys 4 Children was Discharged from the Workhouse yesterday as P[e]r Orders R[elieving] O[fficer]

Thursday 24   Esther Bunningham, Casualty Woman having recovered, was discharged from the house on Thursday 24 Aug[us]t

Friday 25   Elizabeth Camfield Aged 19 was Admitted in the house by order of board on Friday 25 August, belong[ing] to Chipping Barnet

Mr Goodyear & Friend Visited the house on Friday 25 Aug[us]t, Most Gratified

Mr James Franklyn & friend Visited the Workhouse on Friday, Pleased

Friday 25   The Wesleyan Minister from Whetstone & a Shoe Maker from East Barnet, Calld at the house on Friday Afternoon to see the Man Grubb & wished him to retire to prayers, but he said he was quite satisfied with the house Chaplin

Saturday 26   Henry Crew Pauper of Chipping Barnet Admitted in the Workhouse by order R[eleiving] O[fficer] on Saturday 26 Aug[us]t

Monday 28   Mr Richman & Friend, by Order Mr Hopewell, went over the house Much pleased with its Cleanliness

Monday 28   Mr Sears & Friends,went over part of the house on Monday Ev[en]ing, it being After 6 Oclock

Tuesday 29   May the R[elieving] Officer who is about to leave Hadley, have the use of the Union Truck & the Assistance of one of the Inmates to remove his furniture, If he wishes?

Tuesday 29

the Woman Davison who goes out of the house on Wednesday the 6 Sep[tembe]r wants Permission to take her 2 Children to Church on Sunday next to have them Christend.

Wednesday 30

The Medical Officer recommends 2 Glasses of Gin to be given Daily to the man Constable, instead of the Wine, he having the Dropsy

Wednesday 30

Mary Cox Pauper of Hadley wishes me to Ask the board for Permission to go out for One Day

Thursday, 31 August, 1837

Friday 31
[sic] Thursday

the Woman Carpenter who had leave of Absence from the board returnd in Proper time in the Evening

Friday
1 September

Mr Hall the Commissioner from Totteridge & A Lady calld on Friday Afternoon & went all over the Premises, quite Satisfied.

Saturday
2 September

In Consequence of the enclosed Note from Mr Hawkes of Potters Bar, I permitted the boy Fred[eric]k Woodhouse to go After the Situation on Saturday morning. He did not Suite.

Saturday 2

The Draught from the Kitchen Chimney is so great that the soot Pours out from the Top all over the Premises. A proper Chimney Pot Perhaps might prevent it

Saturday
2 September

The House Water has been so very Indifferent of late we can make no use of it, except for Scouring the house. We have been obliged to fetch water for Cooking & Washing

Saturday 2

Hon[ora]ble Edmund Byng & Gen[era]l Dickins went over the house on Saturday, Much Pleased

Monday 4

the Woman Davison, with 2 of her Children, was discharged from the Workhouse on Sunday 3rd

Sep[tember} having Previously noised to the R[elieving] O[fficer] that I had received no Orders from the board to that effect and that Sunday was a day forbidden for Paupers discharge. Said he Knew that such was the Arrangement by the board on Thursday & that the twins where to be left behind

Monday 4

Five Gent[lemen] from the Maldon Union applyd at the Workhouse for Admission to View the Premises on Monday Morning & was much pleased

Monday 4

Mr Griffin the Survyor lookd over the House on Monday & said the Contractor Could do no more for he had stopd Payment

Tuesday 5

John Stops Pauper of Finchley was taken on tuesday Afternoon with a fit of Apoplexy. The Medical officer Promptly Attended & Bled him, After Which he was better

Tuesday 5

Mr Lucas Overseer Hadley sent one of their Paupers on tuesday Evening, ½ past 9 Oclock, to have the use of the Warm Bath. It was of Some benefit to him

Wednesday 6

The Woman Hedge wished me to ask If she might have Permission to go out for 1 day

Thursday, 7 September, 1837

Thursday 7

Thomas Winterburn Aged 60 Pauper from Finchley, was Admitted in the Workhouse by Order of the board on Thursday 7 Sep[embe]r 1837. Ex[amine]d by Medical Officer

Friday 8

Col[one]l Dury & Friends from Hadley went over the house on friday & was quite Satisfied with all they saw

Mr Goodyear & Friends went over the house on Saturday Morning 9 Sep[tember]

Saturday 9	William Varny Pauper of Friern Barnet was Admitted in the House on Saturday 9 Sep[tembe]r. He was filthy Dirty
Sunday 10 *why enter this there is a book for such purposes*	Mr Goodyear & Friends went over the house on Sunday 10 Sep[tember]
Monday 11	The Water Closet belonging to the Womens Sick Ward, being out of Order, we sent this Afternoon to Mr Cooper to send some one to look to it. On Wednesday Morning 2 Men came and Put it to rights
Wednesday 13	Mr Beattie the Plaisterer is of opinion the Drain leading to the Well should be brickd & Plaisterd before it will be Complete.
Wednesday 13	George Grubb Pauper of East Barnet begs for Permission to go to Whetstone to Morrow or he expects to have his goods Sold
	The Woman Buck & Widow Maddams wants Permission to go out for 1 day

Thursday, 14 September, 1837

Thursday 14 September	Michael Carney Aged 6 years, Admitted in the House by Order of board on Thursday 14 Sep[tember]. The usual order was sent to the Medical Officer but he was from home
	the Medical Officer recommends three instead of two Glasses of Gin to be given daily to the Man Constable
	Laura Cooper, having Positively refused to Scour one of the Women's Sleeping Wards on friday, without any cause, we kept her without her Dinner & Tea
Thursday 14	Widow Collinson Aged 50, Pauper of East Barnet, Admitted in the House this day by Order of board

dated 7 Sep[tember]

Friday 15
The Medical Officer recommends 2 Glasses of Wine to be given daily to the Woman Annell, she having a bowel Complaint

Saturday 16
John Haselgrove Aged 30 Pauper of Friern Barnet, was Admitted in the House on Saturday 16 Sep[tember], Subject to the Approbation of the board.

Saturday 16
Elizabeth Harris Aged 40, Casualty Pauper from Finchley, was Admitted in the house on Saturday in Consequence of Illness, with the enclosed order from the Overseer, Subject to the Approbation of board. This Woman was discharged from the house on the 29 June. The Medical Officer is of the Opinion the Lock Hospital would be the best Place for her

Monday 18
Letter 5d from the Contractor for Coals, he having Omitted Sending the order with the Goods on Monday this should be deducted from his a/c

Sold Thomas Bennet   20 Sep[tember]
3 Bush[e]l Bones   10d   2. 6.

Tuesday 19
The Boy Woodhouse, by Mr Hills request, has gone to his house for a few days upon Trial. If he suits, he will want some clothing, having none but the Union

Wednesday 20
The Blind Woman Maddams begd I would ask If she Might have 1 days holyday & Martha Fox

Wednesday 20
not gravel but some
... ...
Some Gravel wanted for the boys yard

Wednesday 20
John Stops Pauper of Finchley was discharged from the house at his own request on Wednesday 20 Sep[tember]. This Man was Admitted in a filthy dirty State on 2 August

Thursday, 21 September, 1837

1[21] Frederick Woodhouse Pauper of Hadley was discharged from the Workhouse on thursday 21 Sep[tember] Mr Hills

2 John Stops Pauper of Finchley was discharged from the Workhouse at his own request on Wednesday 20 Sep[tember]

3 John Haselgrove Pauper of Friern Barnet was discharged from the house at his own request on friday 22 Sep[tember]

4 The Girl Williams, Pauper of South Mimms, who left Mr Benj[amin] Clayton on the 13 June, & went to London to Live with A Lady in Warwick Lane, having left her Situation on Monday 25 was admitted in the Workhouse the same Evening, subject to the Approbation of the board, she being an Orphan

5 The Medical Officer attended at the Workhouse on tuesday 26 & Vaccinated[22] all the young Children except the infant Trott, whoes Mother Objected.

6 The Revd Mr Wood's Lady attended the Workhouse on tuesday & observed the Children improved in their reading. We want some School Books

[A complete page has either been torn out on purpose or lost at this point. The diary continues on either Tuesday 3 or Wednesday 4 October.]

---

[21] From this point the calendar date previously included in the margin, is replaced by an item number in the original

[22] The mass vaccination of children was precipitated by the very virulent epidemic of smallpox which struck the country between 1837 and 1840; Charles Creighton, *A History of Epidemics in Britain* (Cambridge, 1894), II, pp 604, 614.

8   the woman Harris could not be admitted in the Hospital, Consequently she was oblige to return to the Workhouse

9   Elizabeth Jarvis Aged 46 Chipping Barnet Pauper was Admitted in the House on tuesday 3rd October R[elieving] O[fficer] order

10   George Salt Pauper of Finchley was Admitted in the house on Wednesday 4 Oct[ober] by order Mr Hopewell

Thursday, 5 October, 1837

1   Elizabeth Jarvis, Pauper of Chipping Barnet, was discharged from the Workhouse by order of the board on thursday 5 Oct[ober]

2   the Medical Officer recommends one Pint of Beer to be given to the Woman Ross, having an infant & being weak

3   We expect daily to be obliged to make use of the Strait Waistcoat. The man Foskett, whoes behaviour was allways Strange, evidently gets worse

4   Laura Cooper was Confined in the refractory ward, 4 hours on Saturday, for quarrelling & holding up a Knife to Another inmate

5   It was nearly ½ past 10 Oclock on Monday Morn[ing] before Mr Clayton sent the full Weight of the Legs & Shins for the Soup. We sent them back. This is the 1 week.

6   Mr Clayton sent the Milk this Morning but no Invoice, tuesday 10 Oct[ober]

7   Would it not be Proper in future that the Person who attends the Gate during the Absence of the Porter,

should sleep in the Lodge, the Porter has hitherto lockd up his sleeping Appartment & taken the Key with him to London

8   the Woman Harris was removed from the Workhouse this Morning by Mr Peat, for the Hospital, tuesday 10 Oct[ober]. I wish, with Permission from the board, to go down to Bedfordshire for a few days upon business

9   Thomas Foskett, has been better since he was bled on Monday. The other inmates all as usual

Thursday, 12 October, 1837

1   William Hennessey Aged 8, Pauper of Finchley, was Admitted in the house on thursday 12 Oct[ober] by order board.

2   Thomas Foskett, Pauper Chipping Barnet was removedfrom the Workhouse to the Asylum, 12 Oct[ober] Order board

3   William Varney, Pauper from Finchley, who was admitted in the Workhouse in A Most filthy Dirty Condition on 9 Sep[tember] wished to be discharged on Monday 16 Oct[ober] but his Clothes being entirely rags, we said he had better wait till after the board

4   Thomas Pepper, Pauper from Finchley Died on Wednesday Mor[nin]g 18 Oct[ober], in Consequence of A Cancer. Gave notice of the same to Medical Officer & others

Widow Granger begs Permission to go out for a few hours to see her grand Children who are ill. She has never been out before.

Thursday, 19 October, 1837

1   William Varney, Pauper from Friern Barnet, was discharged from the Workhouse at his own request on friday 20th Oct[ober]

2   the Woman Granger, was Permitted to go out to see One of her Children who was Ill. She returned in a few hours friday Morning 20th Oct[ober]

3   Thomas Pepper, Aged 62, Pauper of Finchley, who Died on Wednesday from a Cancer, was Buried on friday Afternoon, followed by Several of the inmates

4   Mrs Hall of Totteridge & some friends went over the house on Saturday, Pleased.

5   the 4 stone of Beef sent in from Mr Clayton the Butchers on Saturday Afternoon being in 6 Pieces, we took the liberty to send it back. It was also very inferior in quality. He afterwards sent 4 better Pieces. This never happend from the last Contractor [23]

6   Thomas Watts, Aged 12, Pauper from East Barnet, was Admitted in the house, by order of Board, on Monday 23 Oct[ober]. Put him in the School Immediately

7   Louisa Blofield Aged 12 & her 2 Brothers, Charles Aged 11 & Wil[lia]m Aged 8 years, was Admitted in the house on Monday by order R[elieving] O[fficer} from St Lukes London, Paupers from Finchley

[23] The Guardians became so annoyed with Clayton for the poor quality of the meat he delivered to the Workhouse that they ordered him to appear before the Board. When Clayton failed to appear the following week, the Guardians annulled his contract. [HALS BG/BAR 2, 26 October and 2 November, 1837] Bennett, the Barnet butcher, seems to have taken over the contract.

8   Elizabeth Mariah Frilaide Aged 7 years, Chipping Barnet Casualty Pauper, was Admitted in the house by Order of Board on Tuesday 24 Oct[ober]

9   Alexander Galloway & Ann his Wife, Paupers of South Mims, was Admitted in the house with Order of Removal from Woolwich, on tuesday 24 Oct[ober]

10   the Medical Officer is of Opinion that the man Constable May now be removed home to his Parish with safety, at the Pleasure of the board

11   Widow Granger, wanted Permission to go out for A few hours to see her Grand Daughter who lies dangeriously Ill but we refused in Consequence of the Complaint being the Small Pox, Oct[ober] 25

Thursday, 26 October 1837

1   James Brown Aged 68 Pauper of Totteridge was Admitted in the house this day by Order of Board

2   Alfred Mercham Aged 17 Pauper from Chipping Barnet was Admitted in the house on thursday 26 Oct[ober] Obliged to Burn all his Old Rags, being in a filthy dirty State

3   the Clerk of the Watford Union & the Master of the Workhouse Calld on friday Evening to look Over Barnet house but it was After the hour. They only saw the lower part

4   Nathaniel Poulton Aged 49, Pauper from Chipping Barnet, was Admitted in the house by order of Board on Saturday 28 Oct[ober]. He was set to work immediately

5   the Woman Hall's 3 Children was sent to the house on Saturday Afternoon for Admission as p[e]r orders

of Board but having lernt they had not recoverd from the Smallpox we sent them back, as p[er] orders of the Medical Officer

6 Rob[er]t Nutkins, who attends the Furnace, being told that the Fire was unnecessary large on Monday began to Swear & was Abusive, when I sent him out of the Celler & said the Board should Know of it

7 Geo[rge] Salt Aged 60 Pauper, from Finchley, who was Discharged from the Hospital a short time back, Died on Saturday Night About 10 Oclock The usual Notices was sent to all the Officers, 28 Oct[ober]

8 Laura Cooper having gone into the Laundry on tues-day Afternoon got fighting one of the inmates. The woman Collinson mearly told her she must not be there, as the Order of the Matron. She used the most Horrible threatening Language when I was taking her away

9 The Man Galloway & his wife who was Admitted in the house on tuesday 24 Inst[ant] by An Order of Removal from Woolwich, wished me to give them A p[ai]r Shoes each & their Discharge on Monday but I of course refused

10 Geo[rge] Salt was Buried this After[noo]n Tuesday, about 4 Oclock, followd by Several of the inmates

11 Widow Annell Aged 82 Pauper from Hadley Died on Wednesday [Tuesday inserted] Evening 8 Oclock Gave Proper Notice to the Medical Officer & Others

12 A Weather board, to each of the outside Doors, would be quite Necessary, as the rain in Wet Weather comes into the house

Thursday, 2 November, 1837

1   Jean [Jane?] Brandon, Aged 7, Pauper from Finchley, was Admitted in the house by Order of board on thursday Nov[ember] 2nd

2   Alex[ande]r Galloway & his Wife Ann was Discharged from the house by order of the board on friday 3 Nov[embe]r

3   Widow Annell Aged 82 Pauper of Hadley was buried on friday, followed by her Son & Daughter

4   William Constable, Chipping Barnet Casualty Pauper, was removed home by Order of the board on Saturday 4 Nov[embe]r to Hemel Hempstead Union

5   William Bennet   4 Nov[embe]r

         2 bush[he]l Bones   10d   1. 8.
         Paid the same time

6   Paul Peart has been Confind to the Sick Ward Since Saturday with the Smallpox. Charles Lambert, Another inmate as attended the Gate

7   Margaret Galloway, Mother to Susannah Galloway, Aged 5 years, now in the house, Calld on Monday & wished to take the Child Out, when I wished her to apply to the board on thursday, which she said she would do

8   Mr Samuels, Farmer Potters bar wants A Servant Girl. His Daughter Calld at the Workhouse on Monday & saw Martha Fox & said she would attend the board on Thursday about her

9   Its quite evident the Privys in the Mens Yard drains itself into the well, the soil having sunk upwards of 2

inches after the man had been Pumping a few hours

10   Mr Wager the Carpenter has taken down the Great Bell. It being entirely useless

Thursday, 9 November, 1837[24]

1   Thomas Bourne, Aged 57, Pauper of Hadley, was admitted in the House by Order of the Board on Thursday 9 Nov[ember] 1837

2   Sarah Goodale, Aged 88, Pauper belonging to Finchley, Died on Friday 10 Nov[embe]r gave the usual Notice to Medical Officer & others

3   Susannah Galloway, Aged 5 years, Pauper of South Mims, was Discharged from the Workhouse by Order of board on thursday 9 Nov[embe]r, at the request of her Mother

4   William Smith, aged 50 & his wife Hannah aged 43 & five Children

>   Moses 12
>   Jane   12
>   James   9
>   Ann   7 &
>   Emma   9 months

belonging to Ridge was Admitted in the house by Order of board on friday 10 Nov[embe]r. They all had the Itch. We kept them Separate

5   If one of the Outhouses in the Girls or womens yard had a Fire Place, we should find it very useful in Such Cases as the Smith family. They are now obliged to be in the house

6   the Woman Carpenter, who had Permission from the board, to go to Whetstone on Sunday to see her

---

[24] A Change in the handwriting for this week only can be noted.

Daughter, returnd in Proper time

7   Paul Peart whoes been laid up more than a week with the Smallpox is going on exceedingly well

8   there wants A New Sucker to the Pump. I sent the order to Mr Coopers

9   Sarah Goodale Buried this afte[rnoo]n, Monday 13

10   Eliza Wilding Aged 10 years, has been Kept in A Separate apartment for the last few days, having Symptoms of the Typhus fever

11   The Matron used the Birch rod to one of the Children on tuesday for breaking one of the Chamber utensils

12   James Basterfield calld at the Workhouse on Wednesday Evening, to shew me 3 Letters he had received R Post from Ann Hipgrave one of the inmates. It appears she's some Kin to him, but its not in his Power to do any thing for her. They was sent unknown to me

Thursday, 16 November, 1837

1   James Kelly Aged 16, Casualty Pauper from Friern Barnet, was Admitted on friday 17th Nov[embe]r. This youth in Addition to the Smallpox, was in A most filthy Lousy Condition. We had him Stripd & Washed & Put him in one of the Out houses. He tells me he never was inside A Church or Chapel, in his life. He was born at Gurnsey

2   Miss Samuels of Potters bar will attend the board on thursday Next, respecting taking the Girl, Martha Fox, out of the house

3

Wandsworth

Anne Brown Aged 27, Pauper of Totteridge, was Admitted in the house with An Order of Removal, on friday 17 Nov[embe]r, Subject to Fits

4

Georgiana Hawkins, Aged 15, Illegitimate, Pauper of Ridge, was Admitted in the House on Saturday 18 Nov[embe]r, order Mr F for Approval of board.

5

Charlotte Brandon, Aged 45 Pauper of Finchley, was Admitted in the house on Saturday 18 Nov[embe]r, p[e]r Order of the board

6

A Small Cupboard in the Mens & Womens Sick Wards would be very useful

7

Thomas Stubbington, Aged 45, Pauper of East Barnet was Admitted in the house on Wednesday 22 Nov[embe]r by Order R[elieving] O[fficer]

Thursday, 23 November, 1837

1

William Smith, his wife Hannah, and their five Children was Discharged from the Workhouse at their own request on thursday 23 Nov[embe]r

2

Charlotte Hall Aged 9 years, William Hall Aged 6 years & John Hall Aged 4 years, Paupers of Chipping Barnet, was Admitted in the house on Saturday 25 Nov[ember], Order R[elieving] O[fficer]

3

Mr Wright, 10 Giltspur St[reet], Made Application to the house on friday, for A healthy young Woman, As Wet Nurse, see the enclosed Letter

4

the Medical Officer, Having Certifyd that the boy Kelly who was Admitted in the house in Consequence of Illness on the 17 Nov[ember] was now able to go out, we lookd him up some Old

Clothing and Discharged him on Monday 27 Nov[ember]

5   One of the Guardians of the Watford Union calld at the house on Monday to look at the Cooking Apparatus

6   the Medical Officer wishes two Glasses of Wine to be given daily to the Girl Wilding till further Orders

7   Eliza Trott went up to London early on Monday Morning After the Situation as Wet Nurse but the Lady had engaged with A person, on Saturday. She paid her expenses

Martha Fox, who was engaged by Mr Samuels of Potters bar, having been clothed as p[e]r orders of board, was Discharged from the house on tuesday 28 Nov[ember]

Thursday, 30 November, 1837

1   Daniel Connel Aged 45, Casualty Pauper from South Mims, was Admitted in the house on Consequence of Illness on thursday 30 Nov[embe]r, order Medical

Granted   Officer. This man belongs to Hulbech, Lincolnshire, he was going to work on the Western Rail Road, he dropd Mims side [of] Barnet

2   Henry James Aged 30, Pauper of Shenley, was Admitted in the house by order of board on thursday 30 Nov[embe]r. The next Morning he askd to go home to fetch some things, but I of course refused

3   Ann Boman Aged 35 Pauper of Hadley, was Admitted in the house on friday Dec[ember] 1 1837, quite An Idiot

THE DIARY OF BENJAMIN WOODCOCK

4

the Man Eames, who was Admitted in the house by order of the board on thursday Just before Bedtime Absconded this Evening friday Just before Bedtime. He told the Other inmates he was going to the Privy. He had observed to me in the Afternoon he did not want to be in the house. He applyd to the board for out relief. He Appear An Idiot

5

Mrs Baker of the Swan Inn Finchley having made the application at the workhouse for a Servant Girl, I calld on Saturday and Ascertaind we had not One in the house likely to suit her

6

Daniel Connel the South Mims Casualty who was Admitted in the house by Medical Order in Consequence of Illness on the 29 Nov[ember], having recoverd was Discharged on Monday 4 Dec[embe]r. He appeared very thankful

7

Eliza Trott went out

Francis Young from Hadley, calld at the Workhouse on Monday to see Eliza Trott And Persuaded her to go out of the house. The following morning Eliza Trott gave the usual Notice & was discharged

8

Jane Bishop Aged 18, Friern Barnet Casualty, was Admitted in the house on tuesday 5 Dec[ember] by Order Mr Franklyn, Subject to the approbation of the board

9

Jane De Cardac wants A New Wooden Leg, the Old One being so short, she has some difficulty to walk. The Carpenter can make one

10

We shall want 2 doz[en] P[air] More Blankets to finnish all the Beds, Linsey [coarse wool on cotton warp] for Gowns, Calico flannel & check

11

Recd from Mr Bowers on Wednesday Dec[ember] 1 doz Wine

4 Gent[leme]n Guardians of the Amersham Union went entirely over the house on Wednesday and was much Satisfied

Thursday, 7 December 1837

1   Eliz[abe]th Salt Aged 54 Pauper, of Finchley was
Admitted in the house on thursday 7th Dec[embe]r,
Order R[elieving] O[fficer]

2   Jane Salt Aged 6 Pauper of Finchley was Admitted
in the house on thursday 7 Dec[embe]r, Order
R[elieving] O[fficer].

3   Received from Mr Bowers on Wednesday 6
December 1 dozen of Port Wine for the Sick
inmates

4   Sophia Anderson Aged 28 and her 6 Children, was
Admitted in the house by order of the board on
thursday 7th Dec[embe]r. They were in the Most
Miserable Condition.

         Emily aged 11
         John 9
         George 4
         Charles 3
         Caroline 2
         Henry 1

William the Father did not come with them
Paupers of Hadley.

5   Received of Mr Tho[ma]s Bennet
for 1 & ½ bush[el] Bones 10d   1s 3d
8 Dec[ember] 1837

6   John Fowler Aged 66, Barnet Casualty Pauper, was
Admitted in the house Order R[elieving] O[fficer]
on friday 8 Dec[ember], in a most filthy State

7   The Medical Officer recommends ½ Pint of Beer
daily, to be given to Elizabeth Sell, Pauper of East
Barnet

8   Michael Carney Aged 6, Pauper of Finchley, is
       removed to the Sick Ward, he having the Smallpox

9   William Anderson Aged 40 Pauper of Hadley was
       Admitted in the house by Order R[elieving] O[fficer]
       on Monday 11 Dec[embe]r, filthy Dirty

10   In Consequence of the refractory Conduct of the
       Woman Pedley on Monday, we orderd her out of the
       Kitchen and put the Woman Brandon in her place

11   Jane Bishop, Friern Barnet Casualty was discharged
       from the house on tuesday for the Purpose of being
       removed to Enfield, Order R[elieving] O[fficer]

12   Eliza Wilding aged 10 years, who has been Ill
       Sometime, Died about 6 Oclock on Tuesday Evening
       12 Dec[embe]r. Let her Mother Know the following
       Morning

Thursday, 14 December 1837

1   Esther Sygrave, Aged 20, Pauper of Chipping Barnet
       was Admitted in the house on thursday 14
       Dec[embe]r by Order R[elieving] O[fficer]. Sent for
       the Medical Officer the following Morning, Illness

2   Eliz[abe]th Williams Aged 78 Pauper of Finchley,
       Died from decay of Nature on thursday Evening 14
       Dec[embe]r. Sent the Usual Notice to Medical Officer
       & Others

3   James Bell, Aged 22, Pauper of Chipping Barnet, was
       Admitted in the house in consequence of Illness, on
       friday 15 Dec[embe]r by order R[elieving] O[fficer].
       We put him in the Warm Bath by order Medical
       Officer

4	Eliza Wilding Aged 10 years was buried on friday afternoon, followed by her Mother & several of the inmates
5	Mr Hewitt, Master of St Andrews Holborn Workhouse, calld to look over the Barnet house on Saturday. Said he never saw any Workhouse before he was so much pleased with
6	Eliz[abe]th Williams, aged 78, Pauper of Finchley, was buried on Sunday
7	the Man Anderson askd permission on Monday afternoon to go out for ½ an hour to see his Sister who was dying. Leave granted. Returned in time.
8	Elizabeth Williams askd If she might go out to spend a few hours with her Sister on Sunday afternoon but I objected.
9	Paid to Mr Buckland, The Treasurer for the Barnet Union, fifteen & nine pence, for Bones & Ashes, as per order of board, this 19 Dec[embe]r 1837 15s 9d
10	the Pump in the back Kitchen wants a new Sucker. Shall we apply to Mr Cooper?
11	Eliz[abe]th Mariah Fulade aged 7, Chipping Barnet Casualty, was discharged on Wednesday 20th December by order R[elieving] O[fficer] for the Purpose of being removed to her proper Settlement
12 *Allowed* *T.H.E[lwin]*	The Medical Officer recommends a new truss for Benj[amin] Skipsey, his old one being broke, & useless.
13	We are much in want of Linsey, flannel & Calico not having a sufficient change for the inmates

THE DIARY OF BENJAMIN WOODCOCK

Thursday, 21 December 1837

1   James Sanders Aged 57 Pauper of Chipping Barnet, was Admitted in the house by order of board on Thursday 21 Dec[ember] 1837

2   Hannah Sanders Aged 16 Pauper of Chipping Barnet was Admitted in the house on Thursday 21 Dec[ember] 1837

3   Georgiana Hawkins Aged 15 Pauper of Ridge was removed to the Sick Ward with Symptoms of Typhus, this day, Medical report

4   the man Sanders went to Mr Hammonds on Friday Morning as p[er] orders of board. He returned in proper time

5   Received on Monday 25 Dec[embe]r a New Bible & Prayer book for the Chapl[a]in.

6   The inmates had all plenty of Roast Beef & Plumb Pudding on Christmas day & was very Comfortable except the Cook who got intoxicated soon after Dinner. We sent her to Bed

7   Received from Messrs Cook & Co on 25 Dec[embe]r some Calico, flannel & Linsey

8   Elizabeth Williams went out on Tuesday to see her sister as p[er] order of the board

9   Mr Nicholls calld at the Workhouse on Tuesday Afternoon with an Order for James Sanders Admission into St Bartholomews Hospital on Thursday 28 Dec[ember]

10   Edw[ar]d Hull askd Permission on Wednesday Afternoon to go out for 2 hours to see his Mother, who
leave granted   lies dangerously ill

The Man Sanders went out of the house this M[orn]ing to go to St Bartholomews Hospital. We gave him 3s. as p[er] Orders

Thursday, 28 December, 1837

1

William Cogdale Aged 19 Pauper of Chipping Barnet was Admitted in the house on Thursday 28 Dec[embe]r by Order of board

2

Moses Smith	Aged 12 years
Jane Smith	aged 12 years
James Smith	aged 8 years
& Ann Smith	aged 6 years

was admitted in the house by order of board on Thursday 28 Dec[embe]r

3

the Man Brown went to Totteridge on Friday M[orn]ing to see his Daughter. He returned in Proper time

4

James Bell, who was Admitted in the house in Consequence of Illness on Friday 15 Dec[embe]r, Died this afternoon Saturday 30, Affection of the Lungs

5

Mr Lawrance of Hadley, calld at the Workhouse on Saturday Afternoon to say he had Work for William Anderson, one of the inmates and wished to Know what Weekly allowance it would be Necessary for him to pay for the Maintenance of his wife & family till he had an opportunity of taking them out of the house

6

John Tomkins Aged 45 Pauper of Elstree was Admitted in the house by order R[elieving] O[fficer] on Saturday 30 Dec[embe]r, from Watford Union

7   Thomas Clark, Aged 60 Pauper of Chipping Barnet, was Admitted in the house in Consequence of Illness, on Sunday 31 December by order R[elieving] O[fficer]. Sent to the Medical Officer

8   John Fowler Barnet Casualty Pauper was discharged from the house on Monday 1 Jan[uar]y 1838, by order Mr Franklyn for removal

9   The Medical Officer recommends one Glass of wine daily to be given to Georgiana Hawkins in the Sick Ward

10   James Bell Chipping Barnet Pauper, was Buried this Afternoon followd by his Sister & Some of the inmates

11   The Medical Officer recommends one Glass of wine to be given daily to Jacob Robinson, in the Sick Ward

12   Joseph Ellis Aged 60, Pauper of Friern Barnet, was Admitted in the house by order R[elieving] O[fficer] on Wednesday 3rd Jan[uar]y 1838

13   the Man Enever begs Permission for leave of Absence for two days to see his brother

Thursday, 4 January, 1838

1   Joseph Ellis Pauper of Friern Barnet, Admitted on Thursday 4 Jan[uar]y, R[elieving] O[fficer]

2   The Man with his wife & family belonging to Ridge, for whom I had An Order of Admission on Thursday, left the following Morning After Breakfast

3   Henry Brand, Aged 61, Pauper of Finchley, was Admitted in the house, by order of board on Thursday, 4 Jan[uar]y. He was in A Most filthy State

4   William Smith Pauper of Ridge, applyd on Friday to be admitted in the house, but not having his wife & child with him as p[e]r order we refused him Admission

5   The Medical Officer wishes the Sick Man Thomas Clark to be allowed ½ Pint of Beer daily

6   The following Copy was sent to Mr Weeks on Friday

Sir,
I am directed by the Guardians of the Barnet Union to require your early examination of the Hot Water Apparatus in the Barnet Union Workhouse, which as not acted properly for some time, being out of order

7   William Smith, Hannah his wife & 1 Child Was Admitted in the house on Saturday 5 Jan[uar]y by Order of board

8   The Revd Mr Thrackey [Thackery] calld at the house on Saturday to say he would take the Man William Anderson into his Employ on Monday morning but it being Contrary to the General rule for the Husband to go out without taking his wife & family Mr Thrackey said it had better stand over for the Consideration of the board on Thursday

9   The Medical Officer wished us to allow the young Woman Brown, who is subject to fits, to go to Barnet once a day for the relief of her mind, but we objected. We let her go out in the garden for an hour daily

10   We have not been able, to warm the Children's School Rooms, all the week. The Medical Officer wishes the Chapel to be used as a School till something be done to the pipes

11   I understand from Mr Buckland, he sent the Knitting Needles to the Workhouse some time back. We have not seen anything of them

12   We have about 38 Bushel of small potatoes. Had we better sell them and buy some onions

13   Mr Allen has been at work at the hot water pipes all day but cannot make them to act properly. We are sadley Pledyd [Plagued?] with them

Thursday, 11 January, 1838

1   Thomas Clark Aged 65 Chipping Barnet Pauper, died yesterday Wednesday 10 Jan[uar]y, Affection of the Lungs

2   Thomas Huntly the Elder aged 70, Pauper of South Mims, wasAdmitted in the house by order of board on Thursday 11 Jan[uar]y

3   Thomas Huntly the younger, Aged 25, Pauper of South Mims, was Admitted in the house by order of board on Thursday 11 Jan[uar]y, quite Blind

4   John Tomkins Aged 45, Pauper of Elstree, was the discharged from the house by order of board on Friday 12 Jan[uar]y. He had a New P[ai]r of Shoes

5   We permitted the Girl Sanders to go after a situation on Friday afternoon p[er] order from Mr Hopewell but the person was suited with a Servant.

6   I wrote to the Matron of Wandsworth Workhouse on friday Morning for the Box of Clothing belonging to Ann Brown. See the enclosed answer

7   The Revd Mr Nichols & the Revd Mr Trinders has performd Divine Service during the Absence of Mr Wood

8

Maria Hilsden Aged 12 years, Pauper of Shenley, was admitted in the house by order of board on Friday 12 Jan[uar]y 1838

9

Paupers of Friern Barnet

Phoebe Smith Widow aged 35, & her 4 Children was admitted in the house on Friday 12 January 1838.

Sarah Smith   aged 9 years,
George Smith   aged 7
Elizabeth Smith aged 1
Harriet Smith   aged 3 Months

By order of Board.

10

Ann Gillman, Pauper of Chipping Barnet, was admitted in the house by order R[elieving] O[ffi-cer] on Saturday 13 Jan[uar]y 1838

11

Mr Benjamin Smith calld at the house on Saturday & lookd at the hot water pipes but could not find out the Cause of them not Acting properly

12

Mr Lawrance & his Son calld at the Workhouse on Saturday to see the man Anderson and his wife, when the woman at the request of Mr Lawrance signd to become a member of the Tea Total Society

13

Thomas Clark Pauper of Chipping Barnet, was Buried on Sunday Afternoon followd by two of his sons from London & Several inmates

14

E Williams gone to Service

Mrs Tilley, Ivy Cottage, Barnet Hill, having engaged Elizabeth Williams aged 15, Pauper of South Mims as Menial Servant. I took her on Monday. Should she not suite I am to know one month before she leaves. 2 shifts & 1 flannel Petticoat is what she stands most in need of. Please to say if we shall make them for her. Her Shoes & Stockings are very indifferent.

15   John Underwood 22 Pauper of Shenley was Admitted in the house in Consequence of Illness on Monday 15 January 1838 order of Mr Freeman. See the enclosed Letter

16   Anne Hale, Mays Lane Barnet Gate, was brought to the Workhouse on Monday Night by, Mr Coe the Overseer. She had Several Strong fits caused, we think, by too much Drink. We put her on the Strait Waistcoat and laid her before the fire. She soon recovered. She was quite able to go home the following Morning

17   Mr Goodyear calld at the Workhouse on Monday to engage with the woman Brandon one of the inmates but he considered she was not Strong enough for the Situation

18   The Womens Black Stockings sent from Mr Cha[rle]s Smith'son Tuesday, was 1 Pair Short. I sent the boy up, he sent another p[ai]r back

19   Ann Child's Aged 16, Pauper of Ridge, was Admitted in the house by order R[elieving] O[fficer] on Tuesday 16 Jan[uar]y 1838

20   A Man of the Name of Larman Applyd at the Workhouse on Wednesday for Admission, but the order being in a very dirty Condition and without date or Signature, I refused him admission without a proper order

21   The man Anderson Pauper of Hadley, wishes to take his family out of the house as soon as the frost goes. He wishes to see the board, I believe, to ask for further assistance.

Thursday, 18 January, 1838

1   Charles Harrard Aged 70 Pauper of Finchley was Admitted in the house on Thursday 18 Jan[uar]y by order Mr Ray, deceased [diseased] Leg,

2   John Tomkins Aged 45 Pauper of E[l]stree was Admitted in the house by Order of board on Thursday 18 Jan[uar]y 1838

3   George Harris Aged 15 Pauper of Shenley was Admitted in the house by order of board on Thursday 15 Jan[uar]y 1838

4   Mr & Miss Hall of Totteridge went over the work-house on Friday 19 Jan[uar]y

5   Mr Nichollas, Barnet, calld at the house by order Mr Franklyn to look at the Hot Water Pipes on Friday. He said he could do Nothing with them unless he took them all down

6   About 12 Oclock on Saturday we was suddenly Alarmd by the Bursting of the Hot Water Pipes. We was obliged to pull the furnice entirely down before they could be repaird. Fortunately their was no one Burnt

7   Mr Buckland's Men was at work at the pipes all day on Sunday

8   Phoebe Smith Pauper of Friern Barnet and her four Children was discharged from the Workhouse at her own request on Monday 22nd Jan[uar]y 1838

John Underwood Aged 22 Pauper of Shenley, Who was Admitted in the house in Consequence of Illness on Monday 15 Jan[uar]y, was discharged at his own request on Monday 22nd

Ann Brown Pauper of Totteridge, Not having he[a]rd any thing of her Box of Clothes, wants Permission from the board to go to London After them

Thursday, 25 January, 1838

1

William Lawrance Aged 57, Pauper of Chippiing Barnet, was Admitted in the house by order of board on Thursday 25 Jan[uar]y 1838

the first since Paid to treasurer

Thomas Bennet   Jan[uar]y 26 1838
had 2½ bush[e]l Bones at 10d bus[he]l 2s

We had the Hot Water Pipes at Work on Saturday, they act better than before

Received from Mr Cha[rle]s Smith
24 p[ai]r Blankets   Jan[uar] 29 1838

The Woman Smith, askd permission on Monday, to go out for 1 hour to see her Daughter whoes been confind to her Bed for A Week

The Medical Officer recommends, two Glasses of Wine to be given daily, to the Woman Sell. She is Confined to the Sick Ward

Susan Thomas, Aged 52 Pauper of Hadley was admitted in the House by Order R[elieving] O[fficer] on Tuesday 30 Jan[uar]y, from Marylebone work house

Ann Brown Pauper of Totteridge wants Permission from the Board to go & see her Sister

Thursday, 1 February, 1838

Elizabeth Sell Aged 88, Pauper of East Barnet Died, yesterday Wednesday, 31 Jan[uar]y 1838, decay of Nature

Thomas Slade Aged 13 Pauper of Finchley was Admitted in the house by order of board on Thursday 1 Febr[uar]y 1838

Ann Lenman Aged 47 and her 4 Children, was admitted in the house by order of board on Thursday 1 February 1838.

Joseph	Aged 13}	
Lawson	9}	all in a very
Sarah	7}	distressed State
James	4}	

James Sanders Aged 29, Pauper of Chipping Barnet, was Admitted in the house by order of board on Friday 2nd Feb[ruar]y 1838

Mrs & Miss Hays Hadley calld at the house to see Ann Bowman on Friday. Said they never Saw her look So Clean & Well

Paid Mr George Harvey	Feb[ruar]y 3 1838
100 Faggots 35s	£1 15s 0d

Eliza Smallbones Aged 25 Pauper of Hadley was Admitted in the house by order R[elievin]g O[fficer] on Saturday Feb[ruar]y 1838, Pregnant

A woman from Whetstone, applyd at the Workhouse Monday Morning and wished to take Sarah Godfrey, A Girl about 15 years of Age, out of the house, but we objected to her discharge, without an order from her Guardian Mr Bass having complaind that the Bread on Monday was heavy, Mr Rayner said it was almost impossible to avoid it this weather

Mr Bass, having sent an order for Sarah Godfrey to go out of the house on Tuesday Morning She was discharged According. Her Petticoat, Shift & Shoes was the Unions

William Anderson Pauper of Hadley, wishes to Know If the board will be pleased to give him Some Wearing Apparel for his wife & Children and Advance them £2, As he would like to take them all out on Friday Next

Mr Buckland's 2 men where at work all night on Tuesday at the Hot Water Pipes.

Mrs Newman at the Green Man, Barnet, applyd at the Workhouse on Wednesday for strong Servant Girl. We sent the Girl Sanders & Mrs N engaged her at five pounds p[er] annum from Monday next.

Joseph Fisher Dodson Aged 15 Pauper of Chipping Barnet was admitted in the house by order R[eliev-ing] O[fficer] on Wednesday 7 Feb[ruar]y from Walton Workhouse Surrey

James Sanders Pauper of Chipping Barnet, who was Admitted on the 2 Feb[ruar]y, wishes to go out If the board will give him A New P[ai]r Shoes. He was he[a]rd to say when he came in, he should only Stop, till he got some shoes. Not allowd

Granted

Hannah Sanders, Pauper of Chipping Barnet, wishes the Board will be pleased to give her a few things before she goes to Mrs Newman's.

Thursday, 8 February, 1838

Fisher Dodson Aged 15, Pauper of Chipping Barnet, was Admitted in the house by order R[elieving] O[fficer] yesterday Wednesday 7th Feb[ruar]y from Walton Union, Surrey

THE DIARY OF BENJAMIN WOODCOCK

James Sanders Aged 29, Pauper of C[hipping] B[arnet], was discharged from the workhouse at his own request on Friday 9 Feb[ruar]y 1838

Hannah Sanders, Pauper of Chipping Barnet, was discharged from the house on Friday 9th Feb[ruar]y. Had clothing to the amount 13s by the order of board. Gone to Mrs Newman's, Green Man

William Anderson, Sophia his wife, & Six Children, was discharged from the workhouse at their own request on Saturday 10 Feb[ruar]y 1838. The Children was obliged to go out with Some of the Union Clothing, some being without shoes & stockings & some Almost naked, when they came in the house

Mrs Dixon, Barnet made application at the Workhouse on Saturday, for A Strong Servant Girl. None Suited

Mr Hammond of Whetstone calld at the workhouse on Saturday by the request of the Revd Mr Elwin, to see Esther Haynes & recommended her to use P[ai]r crutches

Sarah Hedge, one of the inmates, was Permitted to go out for 2 hours on Monday to take tea with her Daughter at the request of Mr Goodyear

Mrs Cottle from the Green Man Tap, Barnet Calld at the Workhouse on Monday Afternoon to say she wanted A Servant Girl. She engaged with Esther Sygrave, Pauper of Chipping Barnet at five Pounds P[e]r Annum to go in about A fortnight should the board have no objection

Mrs Melville, Boreham Wood, Applyd at the Workhouse on Monday Afternoon for a Servant Girl. She saw Georgiana Hawkins, Pauper of Ridge

& engaged with her to go on Wednesday

Capt[ain] Seaton & Miss Hays from Hadley was much pleased with the house on Wednesday

Ann Brown Pauper of Totteridge begs the Board will grant her Permission to go to see her Sister living at Totteridge on friday

Thursday, 15 February, 1838

Joseph Cogdale Aged 18, Pauper of South Mims, was admitted in the house by order of board on Thursday 15 feb[ruar]y

John Brill Aged 32, Pauper of Shenley, was Admitted in the house by order of board on thursday 15 feb[ruar]y

William Marlborough Aged 18, Pauper of Ridge, was Admitted in the house by order of the board on thursday 15 febr[uary]. He was in a most filthy dirty state

Joseph Marlborough Aged 59, Pauper of Ridge was Admitted in the house by order of board on thursday 15 Feb[ruar]y. He was Covered with Vermin

Georgiana Hawkins Aged 16 Pauper of Ridge was discharged from the house on thursday 15 Feb[ruar]y. Gone as Menial Servant to Mrs Melville Boreham Wood

Ann Brown Pauper of Totteridge, was Permitted to go out on friday to see her Sister at Totteridge as p[e]r order of board

Neben Enever Pauper of Shenley was Permitted to go out on friday to see his Brother as p[e]r order of board

THE DIARY OF BENJAMIN WOODCOCK

Maria Potter Aged 22 Pauper of Shenley was
Admitted in the house on Saturday 17 feb[ruar]y
1838 in A forward State of Pregnantcy [pregnancy]

The Revd Mr Lendon, having written to the
Workhouse requesting the Woman Brandon one of
the inmates to apply to him for a Situation, she was
Permitted to go out on Monday Morning According

William Cogdale aged 21 Pauper of Chipping Barnet,
A very Troublesome young man, was locked up for 4
hours on Tuesday Afternoon, for having Struck &
Knocked down George Harris, Another inmate

George Tomson Aged 18, Pauper of South Mims,
was Admitted in the house by order R[elieving]
O[fficer] on tuesday 20 feb[ruar]y, Deceased feet

Jane Thorndike Aged 61, South Mims Casualty
Pauper,was Admitted in the house by order R[eliev-
ing] O[fficer] in Consequence of Illness on tuesday 20
feb[ruar]y. She belongs to Yeoval [Yeovil, Somerset]

Mrs Cottle at the Green Man Tap, Barnet calld to say
she wishes Esther Sygrave, one of the inmates, to go
on Monday week, as Menial Serv[an]t. Is it the
Pleasure of the board for her to go

William Smith, Pauper of Ridge wishes to take his
Wife & family out of the house on friday & begs the
board will be pleased to grant his wife A p[ai]r
shoes, Gown & Petticoat & some under clothing for
the children

Goods wanted for the use of the house0
22 February

1 Piece check for aprons
1 Piece Blue Print for Pinafores
1 Piece Cambrick Muslin for Caps

1 Piece Thin Calico for Baby Linen
2 Pieces Common Diaper
3 Yards Mull Muslin Cap Borders
3 dozen Mens Neck Handkerchiefs

Thursday, 22 February, 1838

William Burton Aged 47, Pauper of Finchley, was Admitted in the house by order of board on friday 23 feb[ruar]y.

Henry Burton Aged 14, Pauper from Finchley, was admitted in the house by order of board on friday 23 feb[ruar]y

Eliz[abe]th Fitch Aged 14, Casualty Pauper of South Mims was Admitted in the house in consequence of Illness on friday 23 feb[ruar]y order R[elieving] O[fficer] belong to St Peters Norwich

Eliza Crew Aged 20, Casualty Pauper from South Mims was Admitted in the house in Consequence of Illness on friday 23 feb[ruar]y order R[elieving] O[fficer] belong to St Peters Norwich

One of the Sacks of Coals sent from Mr Wingrave on thursday, was 10 pounds short weight. I wrote to him to that effect

Nathaniel Poulton, one of the inmates askd Permission to go out to see his sick father on Saturday. He returned in ½ an hour

John Tompkins Aged 45 Pauper of Elstree was Discharged from the house at his own request on Monday 26 Feb[ruar]y

William Field Aged 18 Pauper of South Mims was Admitted in the house by order R[elieving] O[fficer] on Monday 26 Feb[ruar]y

Charity Freeman Aged 42, & her Daughter Harriet
Aged 17, Paupers of South Mims was Admitted in
the house by order R[elieving] O[fficer] on Monday
26 feb[ruar]y

Jane Thorndike Aged 61, South Mims Casualty
Pauper, was discharged from the house on
Wednesday 28 feb[ruar] y   better

Elizabeth Fitch Aged 14, S[outh] Mims Casualty
Pauper, was discharged from the house on
Wednesday 28 Feb[ruar]y

Eliz[abeth] Crew Aged 20, S[outh] Mims Casualty
Pauper, was Discharged from the house on
Wednesday 28 feb[ruar]y

Ann Lenman Pauper of Chipping Barnet, requested
me to say she wishes to speak to the board

Thursday, 1 March, 1838

Jacob Robinson, Aged 68 Pauper of Friern Barnet
died yesterday Evening about 10 Oclock 28
feb[ruar]y

Joseph Childs Aged 21 Pauper of Ridge was
Admitted in the house by order of board on thursday
1 March in Consequence of Illness

The Woman Lenman went out after Breakfast on
friday & returned as per orders of board

Jane Thorndyke Aged 61, Casualty Pauper of Elstree,
was Admitted in the house by order of board, on
Thursday 1 March in Consequence of Illness

Mary Webster Aged 71, Pauper of Shenley, was
Admitted in the house by order R[elieving] O[fficer
on friday 2 March, dirty State,

Joseph Marlborough Pauper of Ridge was discharged from the house at his own request on friday 2 March. Bought him a Jacket & Trowsers 4s as per orders of board

William Smith, Hannah his wife & five children, was discharged from the house at their own request on friday 2 March. Gave her new shoes & other necessary clothing for the Children as per orders of board, for which she was very thankful

William Anderson Pauper of Hadley applyd at the Workhouse on Saturday evening with A Note from the Revd Mr Thackery for a p[ai]r of Union shoes. When I wrote to the Revd Gent[lema]n to say that not having had orders from the board I was sorry to say I must not send them

William Lawrance, Pauper of Chipping Barnet, was Discharged from the house at his own request on Monday 5 March

Esther Sygrave aged 21 Pauper, of Chipping Barnet, was discharged from the house on Monday 5 March. Gone to A Situation at the Green Man Tap, Barnet. 1 p[ai]r New Stockings, 1 p[ai]r Shoes

Jacob Robinson Pauper of Friern Barnet was Buried on Saturday Afternoon. He was followd by two of his Kinswomen & several of the inmates

Mr & Mrs Rouse from Finchley went over the house on Tuesday. Was much pleased & observed the man Harrard, was much improved since he had been in the Workhouse.

Eliz[abe]th Signall aged 46, & her 7 Children was admitted in the house by order of Removal and R[elieving] O[fficer] on Wednesday 6 March. Paupers of South Mims

George aged 13
Eliz[abe]th 11
Mary 7
Diana 5

& the Mother Stopd, the other three went back to London all having Situations to go to. They where in a Most Wretched Condition Naked & Starved

William Field Pauper of South Mims was Discharged from the house at his own request on Wednesday 7 March

Thursday, 8 March, 1838

Joseph Cogdale Aged 18, Pauper of South Mims, was discharged from the house by order of board on friday 9 March. Gave him a p[air] old Shoes, Waistcoat & Stockings, as P[er] orders

Eliz[abe]th Parkes, Pauper of south Mims, went out after Breakfast on friday as p[er] orders of board & returned

William Cogdale, Pauper of Chipping Barnet, was discharged on Monday 12 March. We bought him Suite of clothes 3s 6d & Shoes out of Store 9s 6d as P[er] order of board

A Casualty Woman, to whom the R[elieving] O[ffi-cer], on Sunday gave an order to the Workhouse for some food refused A Good Dinner, because We objected to her coming into the house to eat it

Widow Freeman & her Daughter Harriet, Paupers of South Mims, was Discharged from the house at their own request on Friday 13 March

The Medical Officer recommends 1 Glass of Gin to be given daily to Ann Sears Pauper of South Mims. She has the Dropsy

William Burton, Pauper of Finchley, wishes to see the board Previous to his going Out, to ask for a p[ai]r shoes for his Son Henry 14 whoes going out with him

Sarah Geer, Pauper of Finchley, begs for leave of Absence for 2 or 3 days

The Woman Lenman wishes to see the board about going out of the house

Thursday, 15 March, 1838

William Burton, Pauper of Finchley, was discharged from the house by Order of board on Friday 16 March

Sarah Geer, Pauper of Finchley, went out on Friday 16 March for 3 days on leave of Absence by the board

Ann Lenman Pauper of Chipping Barnet, was Discharged from the house without her family on Friday 16 March as p[er[orders of board

Thomas Huntley Aged 70, Pauper of south Mims, died about 11 Oclock onSaturday Evening 17 March. He was confind to his Bed but A few days. Sent the usual Notice to Medical Officer & others

John Allen, Labourer of South Mims, having met with An Accident & broke his Thigh on Saturday Evening, was sent to the Workhouse for Admission, the following Evening by Order R[elieving] O[fficer]. Observing to the Medical Officers in attendance the

Orders of the board, that such Cases was to be sent forthwith to the Hospital they Admitted it was Certainly the fittest place but Mr Morrison looking at the time elapsed since the Accident & the Night air it would not be prudent. We at once admitted him in the house

The Medical Officer recommends 1 Pint of Beer to be Given daily to the man, Thomas Smith, Pauper of Finchley

Thomas Huntly, Pauper of South Mims, was Buried on Tuesday Afternoon, followed by his son & several of the inmates

Mr Humphreys calld at the house on tuesday to see the man with the Accident & was Glad to find him going on so well

Mr Ward of Wood Street calld at the house on tuesday to Know If we wanted to buy any Potatoes for the use of the house, as he had a quantity to sell at 2s P[e]r bushel

Widow Maddams Pauper of Chipping Barnet, begs the board will grant her leave of absence for 1 day. She had leave from the board about 4 months back

The Woman Buck also wants leave to go out for a day

The Woman Geer to whom the board gave leave of Absence on Thursday last, deserves A severe reprimand from the board for Loitering about Barnet all friday with William Cogdale, late inmate, and not returning till Wednesday Night & then very troublesome & drunk

Thursday, 22 March, 1838

Samuel Eastwell Aged 9 years, Bastard belonging
Finchley, was Admitted in the house by order of
board on Thursday 22 March

Mary Millington Aged 72, Chipping Barnet Casualty
Pauper, was Admitted in the house by order of
board on Thursday 22 March. She dont Know to
what Parish she belongs

The man Lenman's 4 children was discharged from the
house by order of board on thursday 22 March,
Joseph, Lawson, Sarah, & James, Paupers of
Chipping Barnet

allowed

The Medical Officer recommends ½ Pint of Beer to
be given daily to Ann Gray Pauper of Ridge

Allowed

Mr Morrison recommends a high heel shoe for
Esther Haynes, Pauper of Hadley.

Mary King aged 21, Single Woman, & Emmanuel
King aged three months, Bastard was admitted in the
house by order of board on Friday 23 March 1838,
Paupers of East Barnet.

The Medical Officer recommends 1 Pint of Beer to be
given daily to Mary King, Pauper of East Barnet, she
having an Infant at the Breast.

*Boy taken out by his
mother*

James Waters, the man who brought the boy
Eastwell to the workhouse for admission on
Thursday, called on Monday & wanted to take him
out, but I of course refused without orders from the
board

A Labouring Man namd Stratton applyd at the
Workhouse on tuesday for a house keeper but from

what I could learn from his conversation Perhaps it would not be Prudent to send one

The Blind Woman Maddams wants a Holiday

Mary King, one of the inmates, having complaind to the Matron that she had lost some of her child's linen upon enquiry Suspicion fell upon Fanny Starkins, when we found 2 of the childs Napkins sewn inside her Stays. We always found her disposed to Pilfer. Some little Punishment from the board might do her good

Charles Hanard Pauper of Finchley wishes to go out on friday. He also wishes the board grant him some clothing

Joseph Childs, Pauper of Ridge, begs the board will grant him a p[air] shoes. He wishes to go out on friday

The Woman Buck wished me to ask the board to grant her a Holiday

Margaret Webster Pauper of Shenley, An Old Travelling Woman upwards of 70, wishes to go out of the house. She has no Means of Getting her Living but by Tramping about the Country

William Marlborough aged 18, Pauper of Ridge wishes to go out on friday If the board will provide him some clothing. He was admitted on 15 February so filthy dirty we was obliged to Burn all his rags

Thursday, 29 March, 1838

Charles Harrard aged 71 Pauper of Finchley was discharged from the house by order of board on friday 30 March, Loaf & waistcoat as p[er] orders

THE DIARY OF BENJAMIN WOODCOCK

Margaret Webster Aged 71, Pauper of Shenley, was discharged as p[e]r orders Friday 30

Joseph Childs aged 21, Pauper of Ridge, was discharged by order of board Friday 30

William Malborough Aged 18, Pauper of Ridge, was discharged from the house on friday 30 March

Widow Granger, Pauper of Hadley, begs the board will grant her a holiday

Mary Millington, Chipping Barnet Casualty Pauper was discharged of [*sic*] friday 30 March

Samuel Eastwell, Aged 9 years, was discharged from the house by order of board on thursday 29 March Pauper Finchley

Jane Thorndike, Casualty Pauper of Elstree, was discharged from the house at her own request on Thursday 29 March

The Rev Mr Thackery sent a quantity of Toys & Dolls to the Workhouse on Saturday for the use of the Boys & Girls

Mary Fisher, Pauper of Codicot[e], & Mary Rolfe & her three children was removed home on Monday, to Kimpton[25]

James Perkins aged 67, Pauper of Friern Barnet, was admitted in the house by order of removal from Oxford on tuesday 3 April

[25] The parishes of Codicote and Kimpton were both in the Hitchin Poor Law Union.

Admitted Monday 2
April Totteridge
Casualtys

Sarah Bunce Aged 24 & her female infant 3 Months, Paupers of Hatfield, was detaind in the Workhouse till Board day, under Particular Circumstances

Sarah Geer, Pauper of Finchley to whom the board gave leave of absence last week, was discharged from the house at her own request on Monday 2 April

The Revd Mr Wood being unable to attend Divine Service at the Workhouse on Sunday, The Revd Mr Wimbolt sent a Gentleman in his Place

The woman Buck begs the board to grant her leave of absence for 1 day. She wants to go to Ridge

Joseph Ellis, Pauper of Friern Barnet, who was admitted by order on 4 Jan[uar]y, wishes to go out on friday, begs the board will give him a p[ai]r shoes

Thursday, 5 April, 1838

John Hills Aged 10 years, Pauper of South Mims, was admitted in the house by order of board on 5 April

William Hennessey Aged 9 Pauper of Finchley, was Discharged from the house by order of board on thursday 5 April

Henry Bick Aged 41, Pauper of Ridge, was admitted in the house by removal order from London on thursday 5 April

William Peel aged 17 Pauper of Friern Barnet was discharged from the house by order of board on friday 6 April. To go to the Green Man Tap, Barnet. He was clothed by order of the board at Miss Shuttleworth's, amount £1 7s 7d.

James Perkins Aged 67 Pauper of Friern Barnet was discharged from the house at his own request on friday 6 April

Sophia Seagrave Aged 18 Pauper of Chipping Barnet was Admitted in the house in Consequence of Illness on friday 6 April, order R[elieving] O[fficer]

John Allen, Pauper of South Mims, to have 1 pint of Beer daily, recommended by Medical Officer

Benjamin Bourne Aged 46 & Ann Bourne his wife Aged 46, Paupers of Hadley was Admitted in the house by order of board on Saturday 7 April

Thomas Smith, One of the inmates on Sunday Morning having found fault with the weight of his Bread, I took the Scales into the Men's Hall & weighd it before them. It proved to be Correct. This Man, though the most discontented in the house, has generally more Bread than he can eat. We stoppd his allowance of Bread for the day for Abuseing & Swearing at the Cook

The Medical Officer recommends 1 Pint of Beer to be given daily to Benjamin Bourne 46, Pauper of Hadley

The mother of the Boy Harris, Pauper of Shenley, applyd at the house on Monday & wished to take him out, but he having none but the Union shoes, & being under Age, I desired him to stop till board day

The Revd Mr Barnard of Colney, after going over the house Odbserved that the inmates here had more comforts than at St Albans [workhouse] of which he was a Guardian

The Medical Officer, recommends ½ pint of Gin & Water, to be given daily to Ann Gregory, Pauper of Ridge, till further orders

Edw[ar]d Hull Pauper of Hadley to have 1 Pint of Beer daily by Order of Medical Officer

Thursday, 12 April, 1838

Widow Grainger Pauper of Hadley had Permission from the board to go out for the day on Good friday

The son of Widow Cox, Pauper of Hadley, calld to see his Mother on Friday & begged I would let her go to Barnet for 2 hours with him as he had not seen her from some years & was going away directly

granted Jos[eph] Ellis Pauper of Friern Barnet was discharged from the house at his own request on Saturday 14 April

Mrs Coe, the landlady of the Castle, Barnet, applyd at the Workhouse on Saturday Afternoon for A Servant girl and having fixed upon Ann Childs, Pauper of Ridge, left it for the approbation of the board to send her as soon as convenient. She wants some Clothing

Mariah Potter aged 22, Pauper of Shenley, was delivered of a female infant at the Workhouse on Wednesday 18 Ap[ri]l at 3 Oclock morning

The Medical Officer recommends ½ Gill of Gin, to be given daily to the Woman Gregory, 18 April

Ann Buck, Pauper Ridge, begs for leave of absence 1 day, to see her friends

Ann Brown, Pauper of Totteridge, wants Permission from the board to go to Finchley. She says after a Situation

THE DIARY OF BENJAMIN WOODCOCK

Thursday, 19 April, 1838

John Archbold Aged 20, single casualty Pauper of Finchley, was admitted in the house by order of board, on Thursday 19 Ap[ri]l

Frederick Woodhouse, aged 17 Pauper of Hadley was Admitted in the house by order R[elieving] O[fficer] on Sunday 22 Ap[ri]l

An Irish Woman namd Callagan Aged 38, with 2 children was Admitted in the house on Sunday afternoon 22 April. This Woman came to the Workhouse about 4 Oclock on Sunday Afternoon with an infant female 19 Months old in her arms quite dead. It appears she had walkd from St Albans Workhouse, where she had slepd the night before & the Child died in her arms on the road. Immediate information was given to the overseer

Ann Childs Aged 18, Pauper of Ridge, was clothed as p[er] orders of board, & discharged on Monday 23 April. Gone to Service Mrs Coe the Castle Barnet

William Varney Aged 58 Pauper of Friern Barnet was Admitted in the house by order R[elieving] O[fficer] on Monday 23 April. Sent him to the Sick Ward Immediately

The Coroners Jury met at the Workhouse on Tuesday at 11 Oclock to View the Body of the female infant Sarah Callaghan. After which directions was given for its interment as P[er] orders of the Coroner

allowed Elizabeth Salt, one of the washerwomen, begs the board will be pleased to grant her leave of Absence on Saturday & Sunday to go to see her Brother

Laura Cooper, Pauper of Hadley, has behaved so Disorderly this last week, we dont know what to do with her

William Leighton Pauper of Shenley wants leave of Absence to go to Mims

Allowed

Thomas Winterbourn, Pauper of Finchley, wants leave of Absence for 3 days to go to Chelsea, on Wednesday

Our Potatoes will be all Gone by to Morrow except a few we left for Seed 26 Ap[ri]l

Thursday, 26 April, 1838

Catherine Callaghan & Michael her son, was discharged from the house at their own request on thursday 26 April

David Freeman, Aged 40, Pauper of Friern Barnet was Admitted in the house by order of board on thursday 26 April. He was well Purifyd before Admitted as P[er] orders of board

William Bowman, Aged 40, Single, Pauper of Chipping Barnet wasAdmitted in the house in Consequence of Accident by order of board, on Friday 27 Ap[ri]l

Made enquiry at the Green Man Tap of the behaviour of William Peel, no complaints, also about Esther Sygrave, Hannah Sanders, Ann Childs & Eliz[abe]th Williams. All from the house, Living in Barnet

Benjamin Alison Aged 35 Pauper of East Barnet, was Admitted in the in Consequence of Illness on Saturday 28 April, by order of R[elieving] O[fficer]. Mr Morrison Considers this Man, a subject for the Hospital

The Medical Officer, recommends 1 Pint of Good Beer to be Given daily to the Man Bowman

THE DIARY OF BENJAMIN WOODCOCK

Allowed

William Layton, Pauper of Shenley, begs Permission from the board for 1 days leave of Absence to go to see A sick Person at South Mims

Thomas Stubbington, East Barnet inmate, died About 5 Oclock on tuesday Morning, 1 May, An inward Complaint

John Allen, South Mimms inmate, to have 2 Glasses of Port Wine daily as P[e]r Medical order

Widow Ansell Friern Barnet inmate to have ½ Pint of Beer daily, Medical Officer

Laura Cooper An inmate, whoes case was briefly stated before the Bench of Magistrates on tuesday, as P[e]r orders of board, was orderd to stand over till the Next Meeting & If found Necessary they would certainly Commit her. Being askd If she had any Complaint or defence to make [she] mearly observed in an indifferent tone that she should not mind being sent to St Albans [gaol]

The Revd Mr Thackery Attended the inmates in the Chapel on Wednesday Afternoon, for Mr Wood

Sophia Sygrave Aged 18, C[hipping] B[arnet] underwent An operation on Saturday. Mr Morison the Medical Officer, recollects but one Similar Case during.the whole of his Practice

Thursday, 3 May, 1838

The Man Winterbourn & the Woman Buck, who had leave of absence, returned according to the orders of the board.

Sarah Cole, 70 Shenley inmate, was Admitted in the house by order R[elieving] O[fficer] on friday 4 May in Consequence of Illness, filthy State

THE DIARY OF BENJAMIN WOODCOCK

Thomas Stubbington E[ast] B[arnet] inmate, was
Buried on Friday 4 May, the inmates followed

Geo[rg]e Harris about 16 years, Pauper of Shenley,
wished to be discharged from the house on Saturday
but his Mother not making the application, I requested him to wait till Board day

Mr Bennet	3rd May 1838

2½ Bus[hel]l Bones	10 @	2s 1d
2½ ditto ditto	10 @	<u>2s 1d</u>
		4s 2d

Rec[eive]d B[arnet] W[orkhouse]

This Am[oun]t by order of Board was paid to
Treasurer on the 7 May

to Church

Mariah Potters female infant has not been Babtized.
Should we name it to the Chaplin or will it be
Necessary to send her to Church

Admonished

Alfred Mercham Aged 19, Chipping Barnet inmate
was put in the refractory ward on Sunday, & Kept
without his Dinner for quareling & Striking another
inmate,

George Harris, Shenley inmate, was discharged from
the house on Monday 7 May. His mother having
made application for him, and given the usual Notice

Permission given

Widow Collinson, E[ast]] B[arnet, inmate an
Industrious woman begs the board will be pleased to
grant her leave of Absence for A few days to go to
London

Widow Signall, with a family of 4 children & unable
to work wants to go out of the house. This Woman &
her family has been 3 times Passed home to Mims

from different Parishes in the most distressed state Possible

Henry Brand upwards of 60 years of Age, Finchley inmate, wants to go out. This man has been discharged from the house 2 or 3 times & returned shortly afterwards in the most filthy Condition, being obliged to Burn his rags.

Assented to

Thursday, 10 May, 1838

Sarah Woodby Aged 20, Single, Pauper of Totteridge, was Admitted in the house by order R[elieving] O[fficer] on friday 11 May

Henry Brand, Finchley inmate, was discharged from the house at his own request on friday 11 May

Mrs Cotterell at the Green Man Tap, Barnet, will not keep the Girl Esther Sygrave longer then [sic] Thursday 17 May, in Consequence of her misconduct.

A woman from Shenley named Vyse applyd at the workhouse on Saturday and wanted to take the girl Hilsden aged 13 out of the house, I desired her to apply to the board

[crossed through]
The Secretary of the Margate infirmary, inform[ed] me on tuesday it was contrary to the rules of the establishment to grant a Ticket of Admission as an indoor Patient to An inmate of A Workhouse

Thursday 26 Oct[ober] 4 doz Wine

The labour master's rules were pasted onto a piece of board
[Barnet Museum]

Appendix I

Barnet Union
Rules for the guidance of the labour master
[Barnet Museum]

He shall assist the Master and Matron in maintaining order and obey all their lawful orders, and immediately report to the Master, or in his absence the Matron, any irregularity, and inform him of all things affecting the security of the house and welfare of the inmates.

He shall never absent himself from his duties without the sanction and permission of the master, or in his absence the sanction of the Matron.

He shall, during the Porter's absence or inability to act, perform the duties of the Porter.

He shall wear the complete uniform provided by the Guardians at all times when on duty.

He shall not entrust his pass keys to inmates for any purpose.

He shall place his pass keys in the basket provided for them in the Porter's Lodge and receive them in the morning from the Master's office.

He shall unlock the Yard Gates, see the Inmates to and from work, and immediately afterwards carefully lock all Yard Gates and Divisional Doors.

He shall, under the directions of the Master, enforce the employment of able-bodied Male Adult Inmates during the hours of labour, and keep the partially disabled occupied to the extent of their ability, and allow none of this class who are capable of employment to be idle at any time.

He shall in accordance with the time table, punctually set to work the Male Inmates of the Workhouse, also the Male and Female inmates of the Casual Wards.

He shall strictly carry out the regulations for the detention and discharge of Casual Paupers, copies of which regulations are suspended in each room and compartment of the Casual Wards; he shall also see that all the casuals are punctually and regularly supplied with their proper dietary.

On the admission of the male casuals, he shall see that each is properly bathed and supplied with a night shirt, their own clothing disinfected, and if wet thoroughly dried. He shall see that the lavatories and bathrooms are kept clean and tidy, and the towels changed daily.

He shall give special attention to enforcing a task of work for Casuals.

He shall give out the farm implements and tools every morning, and see that they are brought back clean, placed in the tool-house, and the door locked every night.

He shall superintend the delivery of coals, carefully count all the sacks, see that at least three in each load are weighed, and immediately report to the Master any defect or deficiency as to weight or quality he may observe, and he shall sign each delivery note, stating the number of sacks he saw weighed.

He shall see that all coals for consumption in the house and infirmary are served out before 10:30 a.m.

He shall superintend the delivery of firewood to the house and infirmary every Saturday, at 3 p.m., and prevent it being taken from the wood shed at any other times unless by order of the Master or Matron.

The Labour Master shall not visit the infirmary unless ordered to do so by either the Master or Matron, nor the kitchen when performing the Porter's duty.

Rules as to leave of absence:

- One day a month till 10 p.m.
- Every alternate Sunday from 2 till 10 p.m.
- Once a week from 2 to 10 p.m.
- Two evenings a week from 6:30 to 10 p.m.
- Fourteen days annually

The above leave will be granted except when the Master considers the Labour Master's services are required.

Appendix II

Workhouse Accounts

Held at Barnet Museum under reference WE/04/2003.A.001, is a set of accounts that covers the period from March 1835 to March 1838. The accounts show the names of those paying poor rates and the sums paid out by the Board of Guardians.

The editor has transcribed them below but would mention that the faded nature of the volume and the quality of the handwriting has meant that some errors may have been inadvertently included and she would advise checking material with the original, when readers are in doubt. To assist the reader the editor has completed abbreviations where space permits and modernised the punctuation and spelling. She has also italicised headings for lists of categories of paupers.

Please note that in the original accounts all income is shown on the left hand page and expenditure on the right hand page. This is repeated in the transcript up to December 1837. Thereafter the original accounts include a number of blank pages because while entries showing income for 1838 continue to occur in the original on the left hand side spread over six pages, the corresponding entries for expenditure are all included on one right hand page. Subsequent right hand pages are therefore blank. The editor has therefore set the last pages consecutively leaving out the blank pages.

Inside Benjamin Woodcock's Diary appears an account for 1837–8, included at the end of this Appendix, that shows expenses received.

Workhouse Accounts 25 November 1835 to February 1838 (Barnet Museum)

1835	Debit Cash		£ s d
March 26	Received of Mr Strong (his balance)		59.07.04.
27	Beach John on a/c of Poors Rate		1.00.
April4	Ditto		1.00.
10	Kightley Mr Poors Rate		13.06.
	Benwell Josh his moiety of J.Beach's wages for 1 month		12.00.
	Ditto first month's rent of workhouse		2.06.08.
	Royer G. Mr Poors Rate		1.01.00.
	Milson Mrs ditto		15.00.
	Logsdon John Mr ditto		1.14.06.
	Secret R Mr Junr		1.04.00.
	Beach John	on a/c	1.00.
11	Parker Mr		16.06.
	Sheffield S Mr		16.06.
	Jennings John Mr ditto		13.06.
	Millar John Mr		7.06.
	Ditto for flour		5.00.
	Tooth Rd Mr Poors Rate		13.06.
	Wood Mrs ditto		1. 07.00.
13	Batt Miss		12.00.
14	Burrows F. Mrs		1.01.00.
	Buckell James Mr		15.06.
	(Ditto as for land		3.07.06.
15	Tuley Mr		15.00.
	Sharp John Mr		12.00.
	Pooley Mrs		2.00.06.
	Pooley John Mr		1.14.06.
17	Beach John	on a/c	1. 00.
20	Doughlass Mrs		1.10.00.
	Crawley Mr Jas		16.06.
	Halsey Mr		10.06.
	Wells William G Mr		16.06.
			£87.10.00.

1835	Cash Credit	£	s	d

1835	Cash Credit	£ s d
March 26	Bill for Magistrates' Meetings	1.03.00.
27	Beach John (Beaches 1 weeks wage	8.00.
April 3	Ditto	8.00.
6	Letter from Mr Adey St Albans	.05.
	Ditto from Hanwell Asylum	.03.
	Benwell Josh for balance acc. up to the 7th Instant for maintenance of Poor etc.	31.16.00.
10	Beach for 1 weeks wage	8.00.
11	Constable's Bill for Jennings John up to the 27th March last inclusive	6.10.10.
11	Headborough's Bill for Millar John up to the 19th January last	2.12.00.
13	One yrs rent of Workhouse up to Lady day	7.00.00.
17	Beach John 1 weeks wage	8.00.
		£50.14.06.

Entered Received

1935	Brought over		£87.10.00.
Apr 20	Cook Mr, Poor's Rate		13.06.
	Hall & Cannon Misses		13.06.
	Leathers Josh Mr		13.06.
	Ditto for Woodwards		7.06.
	Ditto for Goby Mrs		7.06.
	Randall Mrs		12.00.
	Bailey Mr		1.07.00.
	Lawrence Josh Esq		2.14.00.
24	Harrington B. Mr		19.06.
	Cox James Mr		9.00.
	Lawrence Josh Mr		7.06.
	Beach John	on a/c	1.00.
28	Evens William Mr		13.06.
29	Hunts Mr		13.06.
	Flecknoe Mr		12.00.
	Provach O Mr		12.00.
	Lucas Mr		13.06.
	Goodwyn Mr		13.06.
30	Finney Thomas Mr		1.08.06.
	Ditto for Miss Finney		19.06.
	Ditto for		7.06.
	Knight Thomas Mr		13.06.
May 1	Hawkes Mr		10.06.
	Beach John	on a/c	1.00.
5	Paris A. Esq		1.08.06.
8	Beach John	on a/c	1.00.
11	Clarkson Mr		13.06.
	Benwell Josh 1 month's rent of workhouse		2.06.08.
	Ditto as 1 month's wage to Beach John		12.00.
	Houseley Mr rate		1.01.00.
	Harris William Mr		1.04.00.
			£112.00.08.

APPENDIX II

1935	**Brought over**		£50.14.06.

April 24	Beach for 1 weeks wage		8.00.
May 1	Ditto		8.00.
	Exd Dd	First a/c	£51.10.06.

8	Beach for 1 weeks wage		8.00.
9	Benwell Josh for one Month's maintainance		
	of the Poor up to the 7th Inst		10.00.00.
15	Beach John 1 weeks wages		8.00.
20	Apprenticing Sarah Cooper	£5}	
	deduct Mr Benwells proportion	£2}	3.00.00.
22	Beach John 1 wks wage		8.00.
25 {	County Rate assessed 16th April		6.09.04.
{	Houseley, Mr for paying the Farm		1.00.
29	Beach John 1 wks wages		
8.00.			
	Entd D	2nd A/c	£51.02.04.
	Entd Rec.		

June 6	Beach John 1 weeks wage		8.00.
	Paupers in the House		
	William	2.00.	
	Dellar		4.00.
	Hull Edw - Senr		4.00.
	Bourne John		4.00.
	Cox Mary		4.00.
	Bourne Ann		4.00.
	Carpenter Jane		4.00.
	Thomas Wm & Wife		10.00.
	Woodhouse Frederick		4.00.
	Woodhouse Charles		4.00.
	Laura Cooper		4.00.
	Kit House		4.00.
	Temporary Relief to Thomas Larman		2.60.
			£3.02.06.

1835	Brought over		£112.00.08.
May 11	Kemp G Mr rate		1.13.00.
	Dimsdale T Esq		1.17.06.
	Willey William		15.00.
	Millar Josh		12.00.
	Nicholas, Alfred		1.05.06.
	Carter for Sears		7.06.
15	Beach, John	on a/c	1.00.
19	Anderson James		10.06.
	Nicholas Mr for cottages		1.10.00.
	Millar George Mr		16.06.
	Goldsmith Mrs		10.00.
	Secret Mr Snr		12.00.
	Insell John		7.06.
22	Beach John	on a/c	1.00.
29	ditto ditto down		1.00.
	Stannett		10.06.
	Harris Edward for Cottages		18.00.
	Tibbett Mr		10.06.
30	Attfield Wal		2.02.00.
	Pepper Mr		2.17.00.
	Goldsmith Mr	on a/c	3.06.
	Carter for Royer		7.06.
	Hawthorn	on a/c	5.00.
	Andrews	on a/c	1.06.
	Jennings George Mr		16.06.
	Buckle Richard Mr		12.00.
	Lampkin Mr		10.06.
	O'Neil Mr		13.06.
	Davison Miss		15.00.
June 6	Beach John on a/c of rate		
1.00.			
	Andrews,	on a/c	4.06.
	Nash James		2.18.06.
			£137. 07.08.

APPENDIX II

1835	**Brought over**	**£3.02.06.**

June 13	*Paupers in the House*	
	Green William	2.00.
	Hull Edward Senior	4.00.
	Bourne John	4.00.
	Cox Mary	4.00.
	Bourne Ann	4.00.
	Carpenter, Jane	4.00.
	Kit House	4.00.
	Thomas, Wm & wife	10.00.
	Cooper Laura	4.00.
	Cooper Mary	4.00.
	Woodhouse Frederick	4.00.
	Woodhouse Charles	4.00.
	Dellar	4.00.
	Out Pensioners	
	Widow Granger	2.00.
	Bourne	.2.00.
	Gobby	.2.00.
	Rolf Richard	2.06.
	Dove Senr	2.06.
	Widow Scott	2.00.
	Stannett	2.00.
	Bibby	1.06.
	North	1.06.
	Annell	1.06.
	Ansell	1.06.
	Shuttleworth's child	1.06.
	Fisher's child	1.06.
	Maria Shuttleworth	1.06.
	Elizabeth Jones	1.06.
Beach John 1 week's wage		8.00.
Fetching Dove from Hertford Infirmary for J W		8.00.
		£8.01.06.

Crossed through – Larman Thomas Snr temporary relief 2s6d
[Excluded from total]

THE DIARY OF BENJAMIN WOODCOCK

1835 June	Brought over	£137.07.08.
13 June	Williams John Poors Rate for January	16.06.
	Beach John on a/c	1.00.
20	Two days Hay making for Charles Woodhouse	1.00.
	Beach John on a/c	1.00.
	Nisbet John Poors Rate	2.00.06.
	Ditto for Cottages	1.04.00.
	Hawthorn Mr residue of rate	5.06.
	Hill Mr for Read	7.06.
	Cornwell Wm	2.15.06.
	Payne B. Mr (June rate)	1.07.00.
25	Newman Mr for land	4.17.00.
	Ditto for House	2.00.00.
	Quilter Miss	1.03.00.
	Wilson Miss	18.00.
	Strong S Esq	2.00.00.
	Nutting J Esq	4.10.00.
	Haye R Esq	1.12.00.
	Aiken Mrs	2.04.00.
	Dury A Esq	3.00.00.
	Harvey Revd	1.16.00.
	Dickins F Esq	1.16.00.
	Winbolt Revd	2.04.00.
	Johnson Miss	1.10.00.
	Darby I Esq	18.00.
	Child Mrs	3.09.00.
	Williams Richard for January rate	15.00.
	Ditto for June rate	10.00.
	Ditto for Ditto cottages	12.00.
	Hudson Mr	1.01.00.
	Ditto for Purkiss	5.00.
	Thorp William	1.12.00.
	Compton Mrs	10.00.
		£185.09.02.

APPENDIX II

1835	**Brought forward**	**£8.01.06.**
10	Essendon Parish for 2 wks support of Wm Scotton	9.00.
17	Whitehead for Fox's child	2.00.
	Postage of Papers from Poor Law Commissioners	1.
	Beer Tap (for Workhouse)	2.00.

Paupers in the House

	Scotton William 3 days	2.00.
20	Green William	2.00.
	Hull Edward	4.00.
	Bourne John	4.00.
	Cox Mary	4.00.
	Bourne Ann	4.00.
	Carpenter Jane	4.00.
	House Christopher	4.00.
	Thomas William & wife	10.00.
	Cooper Laura	4.00.
	Cooper Mary	4.00.
	Woodhouse Frederick	4.00.
	Woodhouse Charles	4.00.
	Dellar	2.00.
	Scotton William	4.00.

Out Pensioners

Widow Granger		2.00.
	Bourne	2.00.
	Gobby	2.00.
	Scott	2.00.
	Stannitt	2.00.
	Bibby	1.06
	Annell	1.06.
	Ansell	1.06.
Richard Rolf		2.06.
Dove, Senr		2.06.
Shuttleworth's child		1.06.
Fisher's child		1.06.
		£12.17.01.

THE DIARY OF BENJAMIN WOODCOCK

1835	**Brought over**		**£185.09.02.**
June 26	Monro T Mrs June rate		1.06.00.
	Cottrell Mrs		3.00.00.
	Ditto for Cottages		8.00.
	Beach John on a/c		1.00.
27	Andrews on a/c of January rate (all one)		1.06.
	Wills John ditto		13.06.
	Propstring F ditto		7.06
July 4	Beach John	on a/c	1.00.
	Two Woodhouses 4 days haymaking		4.00.
11	Beach John on a/c of rate		1.00.
13	Hopegood A. Esq (June rate)		8.11.00.
14	Lucas Mr		9.00.
	Lawrence J Esq		1.16.00.
	Wells John		9.00.
	Tuely Mr		10.00.
	Sharp John		8.00.
	Pooley John		1.03.00.
	Pooley Mrs		1.07.00.
	Secret, M. Thomas		16.00.
	Hill Henry		9.00.
	Houseley James		14.00.
	Goodwyn Richard		9.00.
	Courtnall Mr		1.16.00.
	Turner Charles		1.00.00.
	Cotton Miss		1.15.00.
	Crop of Grass for Cox James		3.10.00.
	Harris Edward		1.06.00.
	Ditto as for Cottages		12.00.
18	Beach John on a/c		1.00.
	Browning T Esq		7.08.00.
20	16 Registries for the County		16.00.
22	Harman Mrs (June rate)		1.02.00.
			£227.19.08.

APPENDIX II

1835	**Brought over**	**£12.17.01.**

June 20	*Out Pensioners*	
	Maria Shuttleworth	1.06.
	Elizabeth Jones	1.06.
	William Monk & wife 2 weeks	8.00.
	Kingston's child 2 weeks	3.00.
	Two garden brooms	6.
	Beach John 1 week's wages	8.00.
	Williams Richard Mr, Vestry Clerk, salary	
	From Easter 1834 to Easter 1835	12.12.00.
27	Beach John 1 weeks wage	8.00.
	Out Pensioners	
	Widow Granger	2.00.
	Bourne	2.00.
	Gobbey	2.00.
	Scott	2.00.
	Stannitt	2.00
	Bibby	1.06.
	Smart (3 weeks)	4.06.
	Ansell	1.06.
	Annell	1.06.
	Kingston's child	1.06
	Rolf Richard	2.06.
	Dove Senior	2.06.
	Shuttleworth's child	1.06
	Fisher's child	1.06.
	Maria Shuttleworth	1.06.
	Paupers in the House	
	Green William (not at work)	4.00.
	Dellar	2.00.
	Hull Edward Senior	4.00.
	Cox Mary	4.00.
	Bourne Ann	4.00.
	Bourne John	4.00.
	Carpenter Jane	4.00.
	House Christopher	4.00.
		£29.19.07.

153

1835	Brought forward	£227.19.08.
July 22	Horton Mrs June rate	1.03.00.
	Dimsdale Thomas Esq	1.05.00.
24	Neale Mrs	1.00.00.
	Quilter Mrs	18.00.
	Royer George	14.00.
	Hurts	9.00.
	Byford Mr	9.00.
	Propstring F	5.00.
	Randall Mr	8.00.
	Hawkes Mr	7.00.
	Harris William Mr	10.00.
	Logsdon John Mr	1.03.00.
	Kemp G Mr	1.02.00.
	Secret Mr Senior	8.00.
	Lawrence Josh Mr	5.00.
	Knight Thomas Mr	9.00.
	Batt Miss	8.00.
	Insell John	5.00.
	Harrington Benjamin	13.00.
25	Beach John on a/c	01.00
	Bailey Mr	18.00.
	Evens William	9.00.
	Parker Mr	11.00.
27	Hoddesdon William	5. 00.
	Milson Mrs	10.00.
29	Harden N. Esq	7.10.00.
	Benwell Josh for 1 months rent of workhouse up to the 6th June last	2.06.08.
	Ditto for 1 month's wage for Beach John	12.00.
	Lowen James Poors Rate	1.04.00.
30	Briers B Mr	6.00.00.
August 1	Attfield W P Mr	1.08.00.
		£262.01.04.

APPENDIX II

1835	**Brought over**	**£29.19.07.**

June 27   *Paupers in the House*

Thomas William & Wife	10.00.
Two Coopers	8.00.
Two Woodhouses	8.00.
Scotton William	4.00.

Out Pensioners

Nash's children	6.00.
Madgley's child	6.00.
Temporary Relief to Watson Charles	1.06.

July 4   *Paupers in the House*

Green Wm	2.00.
Dellar	2.00.
Hull Edward Senior	4.00.
Bourne John	4.00.
Cox Mary	4.00.
Bourne Ann	4.00.
Carpenter Jane	4.00.
House Christopher	4.00.
Thomas William & wife	10.00.
Two Coopers	8.00.
Two Woodhouses	8.00.
Scotton William	4.00.

Out Pensioners

Widow Ansell	1.06.
Granger	2.00.
Bourne	2.00.
Gobby	2.00.
Scott	2.00.
Stannett	2.00.
Bibby	1.06.
Annell	1.06.
Shuttleworth's child	1.06.
Fisher's child	1.06.
Maria Shuttleworth	1.06
Rolf Richard	2.06.
Dove Senior	2.06.
	£36.05.01.

1835	**Brought over**		**£262.01.04.**
August 1	Beach John on a/c for Poor's rate		1.00.
	Thackeray J R Revd		1.03.00.
	Ditto for house		3.07.00.
			£266.12.04.
	Hall & Cannon		9.00.
			£267.01.04.
	Millar George Mr		11.00.
2 {	Cox Lowther for the support of his child		
{	for 7 weeks ending July 25th		10.06.
			£268.02.10.
3	Magdon Mr June rate		09.00.
5	Sheffield S Mr		11.00.
	Burrows F Mrs		14.00.
	Finney Thomas Mr		2.02.00.
	Tootle Mr		9.00.
	Buckell James Mr		11.00.
	Ditto for Land		2.05.00.
	Jennings Mr baker		11.00.
	Nicholas Mr		17.00.
	Ditto ditto for Cottages		1.00.00.
	Cornwall William Mr		1.17.00.
	Halsey Mr		7.00.
8	Beach John on a/c		1.00.
	O'Neil Mr		9.00.
12	Bevan D Esq for Leifchild Mr		9.01.00.
15	Beach John		01.00.
	Straw for Cox James		1.17.06.
17	7 Bushel Potatoes	18.02.	
	3 Bushel Chat ditto	2.03.	
		1.00.05.	
	Deduction		
	Quartern Measure	1.02.	
	Hull Edward 5 bags @ 4d	1.08	
		2.10.	17.07.
			£292.02.11.

APPENDIX II

1835	**Brought over**	**£36.05. 01.**
July 6th	Monk William 2 weeks	8.00.
	Beach John 1 weeks wage	8.00.
	Morison Doctor as per bill ending 6th June	5.11.06.
	Third a/c	£42.12.07.
	Rolf Richard extra for last week	2.06.
	Third a/c ...cont	£42. 15.01.
6	Larman Thomas Senior	2.06.
9	Hall Edward Junior	1.06.
11	Beach John 1 weeks wage	8.00.
	Paupers in the House, (1 weeks pension)	3.06.00.
	Out Pensioners	
	5 widows @ 2s per week	10.00.
	3 ditto @ 1s 6d	4.06.
	Shuttleworth's child	1.06.
	Maria Shuttleworth's child	1.06.
	Fisher's child	1.06.
	Rolf Richard	5.00.
	Dove Senior	2.06.
	Jones Elizabeth 3 weeks	4.06.
	Ditto 1 wk in advance	1.06.
	Coach hire for Houseley taking Hull E Jun to the Hospital	2.00.
	Receipt stamps	9.
18	*Out Pensioners*	
	5 widows @ 2s	10.00.
	3 ditto @ 1s 6d	4.06.
	Widow Nash 5 weeks	7.06.
	Kingston's child 3 weeks	4.06.
	Shuttleworth's ditto	1.06.
	Maria Shuttleworth's ditto	1.06.
	Fisher's child	1.06.
	Rolf Richard	5.00.
	Dove Senior	2.06.
		£7.11.09.

1835	**Brought over**			**£292.02.11.**
August 21	Barnes Sir E			19.00.
22	Beach John	on a/c		1.00.
24	Davison Mr			10.00.
	7 bushell potatoes			14. 00.
	Hull E 5 days	1.08. }		
	Measuring of	2. } 1.10.		12. 02.
29	Beach John	on a/c		1.00.
	1 Bushell Onions			2.60.
	Leather Mr			9.00.
	Ditto for cottages			10.00.
	Millar Josh			8.00.
	Wells G W			8.00.
	Crawley James			11.00.
	Carter James			10.00.
	Hawthorn on a/c			5.00.
	Flecknoe Mr			8.00.
	Cox James			6.00.
	Cooke Mr			9.00.
	Provart Mr C			8.00.
	Goldsmith Mrs			9.00.
5	Beach John	on a/c		1.00.
	Harrisson Benjamin (2 rates)			1.15.00.
	Williams John			11.00.
				£301.16.07.

1835	**Brought forward**	**£7.11.09.**

July 18	*Out Pensioners*	
	Monk William 2 weeks	8.00.
	Beach John 1 week's wage	8.00.
	Paupers in the House 1 week's Pension	2.18.00.
	Hanwell Asylum 25 days up to 30th June }	
	for Samuel Smith 24s & postage 1s 3d	1.05.03.
	Housely Mr for paying the above	1.00.
	Journey to St Albans per Messrs Royers	
	Willliam to meet Commissioners	1.01.00.
	Hawkes Mr as per Bill for Dellar's shoes	12.00
	Ansell John as per ditto for Green's ditto	12.08
24	Postage from Mr Franklyn Barnet	01.
25	Beach John 1 week's wage	8.00.
	Paupers in the House, 1 week's Pension 2.18.00.	
	Out Pensions	
	5 Widows 2s	10.00.
	3 ditto 1s 6d	4.06.
	Kingston's child	1.06.
	Shuttleworth's ditto	1.06.
	Fisher's child	1.06.
	Madgley's child	8.00.
	Maria Shuttleworth	1.06.
	Richard Rolf	5.00.
	Dove Snr	2.06.
	Mr Monk	4.00.
	Myers Mrs for Cox's child (7 weeks)	10.06.
	{Benwell Josh for 1 month's maintenance of the	
	{Poor up to June 7th	40.00.00.
	Receipt stamp	03.
Aug 1	Beach John 1 week's wages	8.00.
	Paupers in the House	3.00.00.
	Out Pensioners	
	5 widows @ 2s per week	10.00.
	3 ditto @ 1s 6d	4.06.
	Widow Smart (5 weeks)	7.06.
		£65.04.06.

THE DIARY OF BENJAMIN WOODCOCK

[Blank in the original]

APPENDIX II

1835	**Brought over**	**£65.04.06.**

Aug 1		
	Kingston's child	1.06.
	Shuttleworth's ditto	1.06.
	Fisher's ditto	1.06.
	Whitehead Mr ditto (7 weeks)	14.00.
	Maria Shuttleworth	1.06.
	Richard Rolf	5.00.
	Dove Snr	2.06.
	William Monk	4.00.
	Gadsbury's child (8 weeks)	12.00.
	Casual poor from 29th May to 29th July	8.00.
	Hall & Cannon as per Bill for Hall's … clothes	8.00.
	4th a/c	£68.04.00.

Ent'd Received

3	William Nash's children (5 weeks)	10.00.
8	Beach John	8.00.
	Paupers in the House	2.16.00.
	Out Pensioners	
	5 widows @ 2s	10.00.
	3 ditto @ 1s 6d	4.06.
	Kingston's child	1.06.
	Shuttleworth's child	1.06.
	Fisher's child	1.06.
	Madgley's child 2 weeks	4.00.
	Maria Shuttleworth	1.06.
	Richard Rolf	5.00.
	Dove Senr	2.06.
	William Monk	4.00.
	Widow Nash	4.06.
	Myers Mrs for Cox's child	3.00
	Elizabeth Jones 3 weeks	4.06.
	Widow Smart	1.06.
	William Nash's children	2.00.
	Gadsbury's child	1.06.
		£6.07.00

1835

Brought forward   <u>£301.16.07.</u>

APPENDIX II

1835	Brought over	£6.07.00.
Aug 8	Whitehead for Fox's child	2.00.
	Casual relief	1.00.
	Barnet Union as per Receipt from	
	Mr James Buckland, Treasurer	43.16.08.
13	County rate assessed 9th July	19.08.00.
	Houseley Mr for paying the above	1.00.
15	Beach John 1 week	8.00.
22	Ditto	8.00.
29	ditto	8.00.
	Insell Mr shoemaker, as per Bill	10.
	Hunt Mr draper as per Bill	1.04.00.
	Thimbleby Mr as per Bill	3.03.
	Courtnall Mr as per Bill	1.02.
	Postage from Edmonton (Lunatic List)	06.
	Late Hammond's child 9 weeks ending 8th Nov	13.06.
	Williams Richard Mr as per Bill	1.10.10.
Sept 3	Washing 11 pair sheets	3.08.
	Harrington B as per bill for funeral etc of Alfred	
	Brewer June 28th	15.00.
5	Beach John 1 weeks wage	8.00.
	5th a/c	£76.00.05.
	Journey to Edmonton with list of bokes	10.00.
		£76.10.05.

Entd Recd

1st a/c	51.10.06.
2nd a/c	51.02.04.
3rd a/c	42.15.01.
4th a/c	68.04.00.
5th a/c	76.10.05.
	£290.02.04.
In hand	11.14.03.
	£301.16 07.

1835	**Debit Cash Brought over**		**£301.16.07.**
Sept 11 7.00.	Tibbert Mr Poors Rate		
	Hawthorne Josh ditto balance		2.00.
	Willey Mr		10. 00.
14	Buckle Mr		8.00.
	Paine Mr	(Sept rate)	1.07.00.
23	Pepper Jas	(June rate)	1.18.00.
28	Hopegood A Esq	(Sept rate)	8.11.00.
	Nash James	(June rate)	1.19.00.
	Newman Mr	(Sept rate)	6.17.00.
	Strong Mr	ditto	2. 00.00.
	Harvey H Revd	ditto	1.16.00.
	Darby Mr	ditto	18.00.
	Harman Mrs	ditto	1.02.00.
	Bailey Mr	ditto	18.00.
	Jennings John Mr	(June rate)	9.00.
	Ditto	(Sept rate)	9.00.
29	Dickins James Esq	ditto	1.16.00.
	Williams Richard Mr	ditto	10.00.
	Ditto for cottages		12.00.
	Monro T Mrs		1.06.00.
	Quilter Miss		1 03.00.
	Grimstone Honorable Miss		3.08.00.
	Wilson Miss		18.00.
	Sheffield S Mr		11.00.
	Dury A Esqr		3.00.00.
	Johnson Miss		1.10.00.
	Winbolt Revd		2.04.00.
	Compton Mrs		10.00.
	Horton Mrs		1.03.00.
	Thorpe William		1.12.00.
	Hay R Esq		1.12.00.
	Nisbet John	(June rate)	2.03.00.
			£355.05.07.

APPENDIX II

1835	**Cash Credit**	
Sept 11	Postage from registering Barristers	1.
	Ditto to & from Hanwell Asylum	6.
	Journey to Edmonton with lunatic list for	
	G. Royer	10.00.
	Fees on ditto	4.00.
25	Journey to Edmonton with Jury List for	
	G. Royer	7.00.
	Fees on ditto	4.00.
	Journey to Enfield with list of Voters	7.00.
	Constables Bill ending Aug 24	3.16.11.
29	Williams Richard Mr (Vestry Clerk) half years	
	salary ending Michaelmas	6.06.00.
	Half years rent of workhouse up to Michaelmas	
	from C H Cottrell Esq as per receipt	14.00.00.
	Hedges [...] round workhouse Field & Garden	
	2 men 3 days each	9.00.
	6th A/c	£26.07.06.

Ent Rec

First 5 A/c	290.02.04.
6th A/c	26.07.06.
In hand	38.15.09.
	£355.05.07.

1835   **Debit Cash**

Oct 5	Child Mrs	(Sept rate)	3.09.00.
	Harris Edward Mr		1.06.00.
	Ditto for Cottages		12.00.
	Cotton Miss		1.15.00.
	Turner Mr		1.00.00.
	Anderson James	(June rate)	7.00.
12	Browning Thomas Esq,(Sept rate)		7.08.00.
	Nutting Josh Esq		3.10.00.
	Ditto for Cottages		1.00.00.
Nov 5	Furniture etc for Barnet Union	35.11.06.	
	Deduct Stamp 1s	1.00.	35.10.06.
12	Page S Esq	(Sept rate)	7.10.00.
	Neate Mrs Executors of		1.00.00.
	Smith C Mr		18.00.
	Hurt Mr		9.00.
	Sharp John Mr		8.00.
	Dimsdale Thomas Esq		1.05.00.
	Lawrence Josh Esq		1.16.00.
	Milson Mrs		10.00.
	Tueley Mr		10.00.
	Finney Mr		19.00.
	Ditto for Miss Finney		13.00.
	Ditto for Cornwell & Mawby		10.00.
	Logsdon John Mr		1.03.00.
	Millar George Mr		11.00.
	Crawley James Mr		11.00.
	Hudson Mr		1.06.00.
16	Beach John	(all one)	4.00.
	Hall & Carmon		9.00.
23	Douglass Mrs	(June rate)	1.00.00.
	Halsey Mr	(Sept rate)	7.00.
			£77.16.06.

1835   **Cash Credit**

Oct 3	Postage from Hanwell asylum	3.
10	Barnet Union (paid to Mr James Buckland Treasurer)	43.16.08.
20	Hanwell asylum for 13 weeks and 1 day maintenance of Samuel Smith	4.04.04.
	Journey to Clerkenwell Sessions House with return of rental of Parish	10. 00.
13	County rate	8.15.04.
30	Barnet Union	43.16.08.
	Letter from Hanwell	3.
24	Voting Papers as per Bill	13.00.
		£101.16.06.

1835	Debit Cash	Brought over		£77.16.06.
December 11	Barnes S. Edward	(Sept rate)		19.00.
	Burrows Mrs			14.00.
	Aikin Mrs			2.04.00.
	Quilter H Mrs			18.00.
	Harrington Mr B			13.00.
	Hill Henry Mr			9.00.
19	Hoddesdon William			5.00.
24	Courtnall Mr			1.16.00.
	Byford Mr			9.00.
	Randall Mr			8.00.
	Goodwyn Mr			9.00.
	Jennings Mr baker			11.00.
	Harris Mr butcher			16.00.
	Secret Mr Junr			16.00.
	Toothe Mr			9.00.
	Secret Mr Senior			8.00.
	Kemp G. Mr			1.02.00.
	Houseley Mr			14.00.
	Pepper Mr			1.18.00.
	Buckell James Mr			11.00.
	Ditto for Land			2.05.00.
	Provart O Mr			8.00.
				96.18.06.
		To cash		38.15.09.
				£135.14.03.
	Credit Cash			£33.17.09.

APPENDIX II

1835	Cash credit	Brought forward	**£101.16.06.**

.   In hand   <u>33.17.09.</u>

£135.14.03.

1836	Debit Cash		
January 12	Evens William Mr		9.00.
13	Leather Mr		9.00.
	Ditto for Woodward		5.00.
	Ditto for Crane		5.00.
14	Nisbett John Mr		1.07.00.
	Ditto for Cottages		12.00.
	Parker Mr		11.00.
	O'Neil Mr		9.00.
	Lampkin Mr	(June rate)	7.00.
	Harrisson Benjamin	(Sept rate)	14.00.
	Lawrence Josh		5.00.
	Thackary Revd		1.03.00.
	Ditto & Thorp for land		3.07.00.
	Royer G Mr		14.00.
	Knight Thomas Mr		9.00.
	Ball Miss		8.00.
19	Anderson James		7.00.
20	Briers Benjamin Mr		6.00.00.
22	Propstring F		5.00.
	Flecknoe Mr		8.00.
	Davison Mr		10.00.
	Wells G W Mr		11.00.
	Sears Thomas Mr		
18.00.			
February 1	Leifchild Mr		9.01.00.
	Nash Mr		1.19.00.
	Lowen Mr		1.04.00.
	Maydon Mr		9.00.
	Lucas Mr		9.00.
	Cooper Josh	(January rate 1835)	13.06.
	Insell John		5.00.
	Pooley Mrs		1.07.00.
	Pooley John		1.03.00.
			£37.03.06.

APPENDIX II

1836　　　　　**Cash Credit**

January 1	Barnet Union paid to the Treasurer	£30.00.00.
2	Postage from Hanwell Assylum	3.
15	Duckworth & Taplin as per Bill	
	for valueing furniture etc to the Union	1.02.03½
February 5	County Rate dated 14th January 1836	13.03.00.
8	Barnet Union	29.19.10.
		£74.05.04½

1836 Debit Cash Brought forward		£37.03.06.
February 1 Buckell Richard Mr		8.00.
Scarfe Mr		7.00.
Cornwell William		1.17.00.
Cook Mr		9.00.
Kingstone Mrs		5.00.
Carter Mr		5.00.
Ditto for Sears Mr		5.00.
Goldsmith Mrs		9.00.
Harden Mr		1.00.00.
Hawkes Mr		7.00.
Trickett Mr		7.00.
Attfield W P		1.08.00.
Tibbert Mr		7.00.
Cox James Mr		6.00.
Wells John Mr		9.00.
Hawthorn		7.00.
Millar Josh		8.00.
Nicholas A		1.00.
Ditto for cottages		17.00.
Aut[horit]y Mark on a/c January rate		3.00.
Ditto for Expences of Summons etc		2.00.
21 Williams John	(Sept rate)	11.00.
Cooper Josh	ditto	9.00.
ditto per	(June rate)	9.00.
Expences for ditto for Summons & Warrants		4.00.
Willey William	(Sept rate)	10.00.
Anderson William	(January rate)	12.00.
Ditto	(June rate)	8.00.
Ditto for expences of Summons & Warrants 4.00		
Constable serving ditto	1.00.	3.00.
Thorp William advanced to the Parish		1.13.08½
		53.09.02½
		33.17.09.
To Cash		£87.06.11½

1836	Cash Credit Brought forward	£74.05.04½
February 22	Two postages from Hanwell Assylum	6.
	Postage from Mile End, removal order	3.
	Two Postages from Clerkenwell Sessions House	6.
March 9	Two Postages from Poor Law Commissioners	2.
10	Barnet Union as per order for Balance due to Xmas	7.03.02.
24	Hill James Mr magistrates clerk as per Bill	1.10.06.
	Cowing Mr stationer as per Bill	4.06.06.
		£87.06.11½

1836	Debit Cash	£ s d
April 11	Strong Mr	£4.17.00.
	Newman Esq	2.00.00.
7	Hopegood Esq	8.11.00.
	Monro Mrs	1.06.00.
	Quilter Miss	1.03.00.
6	Trolop Mrs and the Revd Harvey	1.16.00.
	Wilson Miss	18.00.
	Cottrell Mrs on Cottage	8.00.
	Ditto ditto House	2.02.00.
	Ditto ditto Land	18.00.
	Browning Esq	7.08.00.
	Quilter Miss [crossed through]	0.00.00.
8	Thackeray Revd	1.15.00.
	Aitken Mrs	2.04.00.
	Dury Esq	3.00.00.
	Dickens, Esq	1.16.00.
	Page Esq	7.10.00.
	Darbey, Esq	18.00.
	Seers Mr	18.00.
	Lawrence Mr	1.16.00.
	Sheffield Mr	11.00.
9	Tapster Miss	9.00.
	Dimsdale Esq	1.05.00.
	Tuley Mr	10.00.
	Crawley Mr	11.00.
	Horton Miss	1.03.00.
	Child Mrs	3.09.00.
	Harman Mrs	1.02.00.
	Wimbolt Revd	2.04.00.
	Quilter Mrs H	18.00.
	Knight	9.00.
	Payne	1.07.00.
		£65.02.00.

1836	April	Cash Credit	£ s d
April 1		paid Mr Thorp balance	1.13.08½
12		Barnet Union as per receipt from	
		Mr James Buckland treasurer	80.02.08.
			£81.16.04½

1836	Debit cash	brought forward	£65.02.00.
April 9	Harrington Mr		13.00.
	Cox Mr		6.00.
	Hudson Mr		6.00.
	Burrows Mrs		1.06.
	Nutting Esq		14.00.
11	Logsdon Mr		4.10.00.
	Sharp Mr		1.03.00.
	Toon [Tooth?] Mr		8.00.
	Milson Mrs		9.00.
	Provart Mr		10.00.
	Miller G		8.00.
	Compton Mrs		11.00.
	Pooley Mr		18.00.
	Hodson Mr		1.03.00.
	Thorp Mr		5.00.
	Smith Mr		2.17.00.
	Buckle Mr		18.00.
	Pooley Mrs		2.16.00.
	Johnson Miss		1.07.00.
22	Beach John		1.10.00.
25	Howell Mr		8.00.
	Batt Miss		5.00.
28	Courtnall Mr		8.00.
	Randal Mr		1.16.00.
	Secrett Johnr		8.00.
	Bones Mr		16.00.
	Lewcas Mr		9.00.
May 2	Byford Mr		9.00.
	Housley Mr		14.00.
	Jennings Mr baker		11.00.
	Tricket Mr		7.00.
	Bailey		18.00.
			£95.14.00.

APPENDIX II

1836 April 11	**Cash Credit**	**Brought forward**	**£81.16.04½**
23	Mr Cowing as per Bill		6.00.
May 9	County Rate dated April 14th		6.11.08.
			£88.14.00½

1836	Cash Brought over	£95.14.00.
May 2	Flecknoe Mr	8.00.
	Cornwell Mr W	5.00.
	Finney Miss	13.00.
	Finney Mr Thomas	19.00.
	Mawbey	5.00.
6	Parker Mr	11.00.
11	Williams Richard 4 cottages	12.00.
	Williams ditto Mr	10.00.
27	Leather Mr	9.00.
	Crane	5.00.
	Woodwards	5.00.
June 6	Alsey Mr	7.00.
	Secrett Mr	8.00.
	Negus	9.00.
	Goodwin Mr	9.00.
	Shirt Mr	18.00.
	Royer Mr	14.00.
7	Anderson Old rate with 2 expence	10.00.
9	Insell Mr	5.00.
	Lawrence Mr carpenter	5.00.
10	Baldock Mr	9.00.
	Wells William	11.00.
13	Maiden Mr	9.00.
15	Richards Mr	1.10.
17	Williams Mr Enfield	9.01.
18	Harison Mr	14.00.
	Dyson George William for list to vote	1.00.
21	Cook Mr	9.00.
	Turner Mr	1.00.00.
	Loden Mr for land	17.00.
	Ditto for House	7.00.
July 17	Williams Mr [crossed through]	
		£120.09.00.

APPENDIX II

1836	Cash credit	Brot forward	£88.14.00½
June 17	Stamp for Mr Williams		3.
20	postage voters list		1.
			£88.14.04½

1836	**Debit Cash**	**Brought over**		**£120.09.00.**
June 20	Barnes Sir Edward			19.00.
	Cotton Miss			1.15.00.
	Briars Mr			6.00.00.
	Harris Mr			1.06.00.
	Nash Mr			1.19.00.
	Clark Mr			6.00.
	Smith Mr	audited		6.00.
25	Carter Mr			5.00.
	Carter Mr			5.00.
	Evans Mr			9.00.
	Harris Mr			16.00.
30	Cornwell Mr			18.00.
	Cornwell Mr			19.00.
	Tibbet Mr			7.00.
	Nicholas Mr			17.00.
	Nicholas Mr			1.00.00.
	Pepper Mr			1.18.00.
July 5	Popstring Mr			5.00.
5	Scarf Mr			7.00.
	Williams J			11.00.
11	Atfield Mr			1.08.00.
	Blackwell			10.00.
	Miller John			5.00.
	Cook Mr			5.00.
	Miller Jos			8.00.
	Nisbet John			1.07.00.
	Ditto			12.00.
	Hawthorn			7.00.
	O'Neil			9.00.
	Anderson James			7.00.
14	Williams Richard for list to vote			1.00.
	Williams Gilbert for list to vote			1.00.
				£147.17.00.

APPENDIX II

1836	**Cash Credit brought forward**	**£88.14. 04½**
July 11	Barnet Union as per Receipt	96.04.02.
		£184.18.06½

1836	Debit Cash brought over	£147.17.00.
July	Kemp Mr	1.02.00.
	Hay Capt. for Tod Mr	1.12.00.
19	Strong Capt Registered	1.00.
	Sears Mr ditto	1.00.
20	Nisbet John ditto	1.00.
30	Courtnall Mr	1.16.00.
	Smith Mr	18.00.
	Royer Mr	14.00.
	Randal Mr	8.00.
	Secrett Junior	16.00.
	Pooley Mr	1.07.00.
	Bailey	18.00.
	Tapster Miss	9.00.
	Sharp Mr	8.00.
	Logsdon Mr	1.03.00.
	Flecknoe Mr	8.00.
	Dimsdale Mr	1.05.00.
	Melson Mrs	10.00.
	Tuley Mr	10.00.
	Probart Mr	8.00.
	Crawley Mr	11.00.
	Harman Mrs	1.02.00.
	Hopegood Esq	4.08.00.
	Ditto	4.03.00.
	Monro Mrs	1.06.00.
	Strong Capt	4.17.00.
	Browning Esq	2.08.00.
	Ditto	3.10.00.
	Ditto	1.10.00.
	Dury Esq	12.00.
	Ditto	2.08.00.
	Aitken Mrs	2.04.00.
		£191.11.00.

APPENDIX II

1836	Cash Credit	Brought forward	£184.18.06½
July 16	Letter		2.05.
			£185.00.11½

THE DIARY OF BENJAMIN WOODCOCK

1836	Debit Cash Brought over	£191.11.00.
July 30	Thackeray Revd J R	1.15.00.
	Nutting Esqr	3.10.00.
	Ditto	15.00.
August 5	Buckle Mr	2.05.00.
	Ditto	11.00.
	Newman Esqr	2.00.00.
	Atwood Mr	7.00.
	Child Mrs	2.14.00.
	Ditto	15.00.
	Sears	18.00.
	Page Esqr	4.00.00.
	Ditto	1.10.00.
	Burrows Mrs	14.00.
	Hudson Mr	1.01.00.
	Purkis	5.00.
	Harington	13.00.
	Knight	9.00.
	Dickens Esqr	1.16.00.
	Pain Esqr	1.07.00.
	Noles 2 rates	10.00.
	Wells Jos 2 rates	18.00.
11	Darbey Capt	18.00.
	Compton Mrs	18.00.
	Leather Mr	9.00.
	Woodward Mr	5.00.
	Crane Mr	5.00.
	Byford Mr	9.00.
	Housley Mr	14.00.
	Kemp Mr	1.02.00.
13	Thorp Mr	1.05.00.
	Ditto	1.12.00.
	R Harvey	1.16.00.
		£229.17.00.

APPENDIX II

1836   Cash Credit   Brought forward   £185.00.11½.

1836	Debit Cash	Brought Over	£229.17.00.
August 12	Quilter Miss		1.03.00.
	Grimston		2.02.00.
	Ditto		18.00.
	Ditto		8.00.
19	Wilson Miss		18.00.
	Hart Mr		1.03.00.
	Pepper Mr		1.18.00.
	Shirt Mr		18.00.
	Goodwin Mr		9.00.
	Buck Mr		8.00.
25	Secrit Mr		8.00.
	Halsey Mr		7.00.
	Lucas Mr		9.00.
27	Finney Mr		13.00.
	Ditto ditto		19.00.
	Ditto late Thomas		5.00.
	Mawbey Ditto		5.00.
	Tooth Mr		9.00.
30	Anderson back rate		5.00.
	Anderson		5.00.
31	Reed back rate		5.00.
	Reed Mr		5.00.
	Buckle back rate		8.00.
Sept 1st	Miller George		11.00.
	Wells Postman		11.00.
10	Popstring Mr		5.00.
	Nicholas Mr 2		1.17.00.
	Nisbet John 2		1.19.00.
	Baldock Mr		9.00.
	Jennings baker		11.00.
	Cornwell Mr 2		1.17.00.
	Scarf Mr		7.00.
			£253.12.00.

APPENDIX II

1836	**Cash Credit** **brought forward**	**£185.00.11½**
August 23	County rate assessed 14th July Mr H	13.03.04.
Sept 10	Paid Mr Jessop (Lunatic)	4.00.
		£198.08.03½

1836	Debit Cash	Brought forward	£253.12.00.
September 10	Bonus Mr		11.00.
	Lawrence Mr		1.16.00.
	Sheffield Mr		11.00.
	Richards Mr		1.10.00.
	Lawrence Mr		5.00.
	Negus Mr		9.00.
14	Maden Mr		9.00.
	O'Neil Mr		9.00.
	Miller Joseph		8.00.
16	Quilter Mrs H		18.00.
19	Jennings John bricklayer	(April Rate)	9.00.
	Ditto ditto	(July rate)	9.00.
	Ditto Expenses of Summons & Warrants		5.06.
	Moles's Summons omitted		2.06.
	Anderson's Ditto Ditto		2.00.
24	Williams Esq		7.13.
	Horton Miss		1.03.
27	Johnson Miss		1.10.
29	Wimbolt Revd		2.04.
	Turner Mr		1.00.00.
	Spranger Mr		17.00.
	Ditto Ditto		7.00.
	Briars Mr		6.00.00.
	Harris Edward		1.06.00.
	Nash Mr		1.19.00.
	Clark Mr		6.00.
	Smith Mr		6.00.
	Parker Mr		11.00.
	Davinson Mr		10.00.
	Williams John		11.00.
	Cooper Mr		9.00.
			£288.18.00.

APPENDIX II

1837	Cash Credit Brought forward	£	s	d
January 1	Paid Mr Williams for letters		1.	03.
12	Paid letter			3.
			1.	06.

1837 January 7 Debit Cash   Brought forward   **£70.10.00.**

13	Sears Mr	1.07.00.
	Buckle R	12.00.
19	Winbolt	3.06.00.
	Sheffield Mr	16.06.
	Hudson Mr	1.11.06.
	Purkis Mr	7.06.
	Batt Miss	12.00.
	Harrington Mr	19.06.
	Hart Mr	1.14.06.
	Lawrence Mr	2.14.00.
	Courtnall Mr	2.14.00.
20	Popstring Mr	7.06.
	Maiden Mr	13.06.
	Secrett T Mr	1.04.00.
	Child Mrs	5.03.06.
	Payne Esq	2.00.06.
21	Shirts Mr	1.07.00.
	Leather Mr	13.06.
	Randal Mr	12.00.
	Page S Esq	8.05.00.
	Browning Esq	11.02.00.
	Flecknoe Mr	12.00.
	Newman Esq	3.00.00.
23	Goodwin Mr	13.06.
25	Thorp Mrs	1.10.00.
	Thorp Mr	1.17.06.
	Thorp Mr	2.08.00.
27	Richards Mr	2.05.00.
30	Dimsdale Esq	1.17.06.
Feb 18	Attfield Mr	2.02.00.
	Wren Mr	10.06.
	Housley Mr	1.01.00.
		£136.10.00.

APPENDIX II

1837	Cash Credit Brought forward	£	1.06.

January 13	Barnet Union per receipt from Mr James Buckland Treasurer	3.11.08½
25	Ditto as per receipt from Mr James Buckland Treasurer	105.04.00.
February 13	County rate assessed 19 January 1837	14.09.03.
		£123.06.05½

1837 February 7 Cash Brought forward   **£136.10.00.**

20	Buckle Mr	16.06.
	Ditto land	3. 07.06.
	Scarf Mr	10.06.
	Lodgsdon	1.14.06.
23	Thackary Rev T R	1.14.06.
	Ditto land	18.00.
27	Williams R	15.00.
	Ditto ditto	18.00.
	Lewcas Mr [Lucas?]	13.06.
	Halsey Mr	10.06.
	Nicholas Mr	1 05.06.
	Ditto ditto	1. 10.00.
	Holden Mr gas company	15.00.
	Finney Miss }	19.06.
	Finney Mr }	1. 08.06.
	Mawbey Mr }	7.06.
	Late Cornwell }	7.06.
	Hawkes	10.06.
	Bonu1s	16.06.
March 3	Johnson Miss	2.05.00.
	Anderson James	10.06.
	Probart	12.00.
	Miller George	16.06.
	Lawrence Mr	7.06.
	Pepper Mr	2.17.00.
	Baldock Mr	13.06.
	Knight Mr	13.06.
	Moles Mr	7.06.
	Brittleston Mr	15.00.
	Nisbett Mr 2.00.06	2.06.00.
	Ditto	18.00.
	Beech	12.00.
		£170. 03.00.

APPENDIX II

1837 February Cash Credit   Brought forward   £123.06.05½

1837 March	Cash Brought forward	£170.03.00.
13	Hodson Mr	7.06.
	Bourne Mr [crossed through]	16.06.
18	Cox Mr	9.00.
	Harding Esq	1.10.
	Insell	7.06.
	Blackwell	15.00.
25	Harriss Mr B	1.04.00.
	Turner Mr	1.10.00.
	Spranger Mr	1.05.06.
	Ditto	10.06.
	Williams Mr	11.09.06.
	Sir E Barnes	1.08.06.
	Cotton Miss	1.13.00.
	Ditto ditto	2.12.06.
	Bryars Mr	9.00.00.
	Harriss Mr	1.19.00.
	Parker Mr	16.06.
	Atwood Mr	10.06.
	Davison Mr	15.00.
	Tibbett Mr	10.06.
	Negus Mr	13.06.
	Jennings baker	16.06.
	Jennings	13.06.
27	Williams J	16.06.
	Cook Late Thomas	7.06.
	Cooper	13.06.
	Miller John	7.06.
	Wells	13.06.
April	Miller Jos	2.00.
3	Crane	7.06.
	Woodward	7.06.
	Evans	13.06.
		£215.19.06.

APPENDIX II

1837 March	Cash credit	brought forward	£123.06.05½
16		Letter for Guardians	05.
25		Mr Hill's bill	18.06.
		Mr Buckell's bill	11.00.
		Mr Cowen ditto	5.00.
			£125.01.04½

1837 April	Debit Cash Brought forward	£215.19.06.
3	Cornwell Mr	1.08.06.
	Ditto	1.07.00.
	Cook Mr	13.06.
	Carter Mr	7.06.
	Ditto ditto	7.06.
	Clark Mr	9.00.
		£220.12.06.
	Error in Nisbet's rate	5.06.
		£220.07.00.

APPENDIX II

1837 April	**Cash Credit**	£125.01.04½

3	Paid Mr Williams for letters	09.
	Journey to Enfield Mr Harris omitted	7.00.
		£125.09.01½

	Cash in hand	94.17.10½
		£220.07.00.

[Crossed through]

Balance in hand	£94.17.10 ½}	
Ditto from old rate	22.03.08 }	117.01.06½
Rates remaining due	4.13.00.	
Empty houses	2.18.06.	
Balance corresponding	}	
With Auditors account	}	£124.13.00½

Omited magistrate excess	2.18.06.

1837 April	Debit Cash	Balance in hand	£117.01.06½
4	Anderson Mr }		7.06.
14	Nash Mr }	rate made Nov 36s	2.18.06.
	O'Neil Mr) }		13.06.
			£121.01.00.

APPENDIX II

1837	**Cash Credit**	£ s d
April 4	Affidavit	02.00.
	Barnet Union as per receipt from	
	Mr Jas Buckland treasurer	£78.18.00.
		£42.01.00½
		£121.01.00½

1837		£ s d
May 1	Received of Mr Buckland	8.02.00.
19	Ditto of Mr Page	42.01.00½
August 17	Ditto Registering Voters	11.00.
	Rate Granted 12th of June	£153.12.00.
		204.06.00½
Rate Made 25th November		255.09.00.
		£459.15.00½

1837	Debit Cash	
June 21	Mr Turner	£1.00.00.
	Spranger Esq	17.00.
	Ditto	7.00.
	Mr Scholoker	7.13.00.
	Sir Edward Barnes	19.00.
	Miss Cotton	1.15.00.
	Ditto	1.02.00.
	Mr Briars	6.00.00.
	Mr Edward	1.06.00.
	Samuel Strong Esq	4.17.00.
	Thomas Newman Esq	2.00.00.
	Andrew Hopegood Esq	4.08.00.
	Ditto	4.03.00.
	Mrs T Monro	1.06.00.
	Miss Quilter	1.03.00.
July 10	Thomas Browning Esq	3.10.00.
	Ditto	2.08.00.
	Ditto	1.10.00.
	Miss Wilson	18.00.
	Honorable Miss Grimstone	2.02.00.
	Ditto	18.00.
	Pestel	4.00.
	Revd J R Thackeray	1.03.00.
	Ditto	12.00.
	Mr William Thorp	1.05.00.
	Mr Richards	1.10.00.
	Josh Nutting Esq	3.10.00.
	Ditto	15.00.
	Mr R Williams	12.00.
	Mrs F Burrows	14.00.
	Late Ditto	1.12.00.
		£61.19.00.

APPENDIX II

1837

May 20	County Rate	£14.09.03.
	Carriage to Ditto	1.00.
24	Barnet Union as per receipt from	
	Mr James Buckland Treasurer	39.18.07.
July 12	Ditto	<u>78.18.00.</u>
		£133.06.10.

1837	Debit Cash	Brought forward	£61.19.00.
August	Mrs Aitkin		2.04.00.
	A Dury Esq		2.08.00.
	Ditto		12.00.
	Mr Hudson		1.01.00.
	Mr Parkes		5.00.
	Mr William Hodson		5.00.
	Mr Harrington		13.00.
	Mr Mallett		1.03.00.
	Mr William Thorp		1.12.00.
	Mr B. Payne		1.07.00.
	Mr N. Thorp		1.00.00.
	Mr Evans		9.00.
	Mrs Trollope		1.16.00.
	James Dickens Esq		1.16.00.
	Mrs Wood		18.00.
	Mrs Simpson		18.00.
	Revd J H. Winbolt		2.04.00.
	Late Mr Harden		1.00.00.
	Miss Johnson		1.10.00.
	Samuel Page Esq		4.00.00.
	Ditto		1.10.00.
	Mr Acason		18.00.
	Lawrance Esq		1.16.00.
	Mrs Harman		1.02.00.
	Mrs Childs		2.14.00.
	Ditto		15.00.
	Mr R. Williams		10.00.
	Mr Bittlestone		10.00.
	Mrs Horton		1.03.00.
	Mr Parker		11.00.
	Mr Robert Lucas		9.00.
			£100.18.00.

APPENDIX II

1837	**Cash Credit**	**£133.06.10.**

August 5	County rate	14.09.03.
	Carriage to ditto	1.00.
	Letters	06.
	Paid Buckell for Overseers precepts	6.00.
Sept 1	Paid Thomas Austin for apprehension etc of	
	Abraham Tinsley	2.00.00.
15	Paid for Lunatic papers	3.00.
	Journey to Edmonton	10.00.
21	Letters from Revising Barristers	06.
24	Ditto for Lunatic Papers letter	03.
27	Journey to Enfield with Notice papers	7.00.
29	Jury List to Edmonton Paid Fees	3.00.
	Journey to Edmonton	10.00.
		£151.17.04.

1837	Debit Cash	Brought forward	£100.18.00.
August	Mr Tuely		10.00.
	Mrs Millson		10.00.
	Mr Flecknoe		8.00.
	Mr Beach		8.00.
	Mr Sharp		8.00.
	Thomas Dimsdale Esq		1.05.00.
	Miss Tapster		9.00.
	Mr Logsdon		1.03.00.
	Mr Bailey		18.00.
	Mrs Pooley		1.07.00.
	Mr Tilbury		9.00.
	Mr Buckell		11.00.
	Ditto		2.05.00.
	Mr Propstring		5.00.
	Mr Leather		9.00.
	Mr Walker		17.00.
	Mr C Smith		18.00.
	Mr Courtnall		1.16.00.
Oct 4	Mr Insell		5.00.
	Mr Knight		9.00.
	Mr Crawley		11.00.
	Mr Cooper		9.00.
	Mr Finney		19.00.
	Mr Chater		5.00.
	Mr Willey		5.00.
	Miss Finney		13.00.
	Mr Provart		8.00.
	Mr Tooth		9.00.
	Mr Scarf		7.00.
	Mr Kemp		1.02.16.
	Mr		16.00.
	Mr Negus		9.00.
			£123.01.00.

APPENDIX II

| 1837 | **Cash Credit** | **£151.17.04.** |

Oct 17	Journey to Clerkenwell Sessions House with	
	returns of Rentall of Parish	10.00.
23	Ditto as per Receipt from Mr James Buckland	78.18.00.
Nov 11	2 letters from Coroner	06.
16	Paid George Wardle for apprehension of	
	James Williams	18.00.
		£232.03.10.

1837	Debit Cash	Brought Forward	£123.01.00.
	Mr John Jennings		9.00.
	Mr Randell		8.00.
	Mr Byford		9.00.
	Mr Thurts		18.00.
	Mr Royer		14.00.
Oct 5	Mr Clark		6.00.
	Mr Smith		6.00.
	Mr Baldock		9.00.
	Mr Carter		5.00.
	Ditto Sears		5.00.
	Mr Goodwin		9.00.
	Mr Wren late Hawthorn		7.00.
	Mr Jennings baker		11.00.
16	Mr Halsey		7.00.
	Mr Nisbet		1.07.00.
	Ditto		12.00.
	Mr Housley		14.00.
	Mr Nicholas		1.00.00.
	Mr Secret		16.00.
	Mr Wells		9.00.
	Mr Attfield		1.08.00.
18	Mr Cox		6.00.
	Mr Lawrence		5.00.
	Mr Wigley		11.00.
	Mr William Anderson		5.00.
	Mr Cook		9.00.
	Mr Davison		10.00.
Nov	Miss Batt		8.00.
	Mr Blackwell		10.00.
	Gas Company		10.00.
	Mr G Miller		11.00.
	Mr O'Neil		9.00.
			£140.04.00.

1837	**Cash Credit**	£232.03.10.

Dec 6	County Rate	8.10.08.
	Carriage of ditto	1.00.
8	Barnet Union as per receipt from Mr James }	
	Buckland treasurer }	34.03.04½
20	Barnet Union as per receipt from Mr James }	
	Buckland treasurer }	30.08.05.
		£305.07.03½

1837	Cash Brought forward	£140.04.00.
December	Mr Tibbert	7.00.
	Mr Sheffield	11.00.
	Mr F Cornwell	5.00.
	Mr Joseph Miller	8.00.
	Mr John Williams	11.00.
	Mr Richard Buckell	8.00.
	Mr Pepper	1.18.00.
	Mr Nash	1.19.00.
	Mr Hawkes	7.00.
	Mr Attwood	7.00.
	Mr Cornwell	1.17.00.
	Mr Woodward	5.00.
	Mr Crane	5.00.
	Mr James Anderson	7.00.
	Mr John Miller	8.00.
		£150.07.00.

1838   Cash Credit   **£305.07.03½**

Jan 19	Letter from Mr Jessop, ditto from Mr Franklin	06.
	Ditto from Sessions House Clerkenwell	03.
Feb 9	Barnet Union as per receipt from	
	Mr James Buckland Treasurer	106.00.00.
19	County Rate	12.16.00.
	Carriage of ditto	1.00.
March 15	Letter from Hanwell	03.
23	Journey to Edmonton Lucas & Flecknoe	
	appeal day	1.10.00.
	Letter from Hanwell	03.
30	Journey to Edmonton Lucas & Flecknoe	
	appeal day	1.00.00.
	Paid Jessop for fees	3.00.
	Richard Buckell Constable Bill	5.05.06.
	Ditto Anderson Headborough Bill	2.15.00.
		£434.19.00½
	Overseers Expences to Edmonton with	
	Jury List omitted 16 September	10.00.
		24.06.00.
		£459.15.00½

Empty Houses	4.08.06
Error in ditto	5.03.06
Rates Remaining due	5.03.00.
Cash in hand	9.11.00.
	£24.06.00.

1837	Cash Brought forward	£150.07.00.
December 4	Mr Charles Turner	1.10.00.
	Spranger Esq	1.05.06.
	Late Lowen	10.06.
	Sir E. Barnes	1.08.06.
	Miss Cotten	2.14.00.
	Ditto	1.13.00.
	Mr Briars	9.00.00.
	Mr E. Harris	1.19.00
	Mr J Nash	2.18.06
	Strong Esq	7.05.06.
	Mr Newman	3.07.06.
	A. Hopegood Esq	7.19.00.
	Ditto	6.04.06.
	Mrs T. Monro	2.05.00.
	Miss Quilter	1.17.06.
	Mr Browning	6.06.00.
	Ditto	3.12.00.
	Ditto	2.05.00.
	Miss Willson	1.07.00.
	Honourable Miss Grimstone	3.16.06.
	Ditto	1.07.00.
	Pestel &	12.00.
	Revd J R Thackeray	2.00.00.
	Ditto	18.00.
	Mr Thorp	1.17.06.
	Mr Richards	2.05.00.
	Robert Hay Esq	6.06.00.
	Ditto	1.02.06.
	Mr Sheffield	18.00.
	Mr Richard Williams	18.00.
	Mrs E. Mackenzie	3.00.00.
	Mrs Burrows	1.07.00.
		£242.13.06.

APPENDIX II

1837/38?	**Brought forward**	**£242.13.06.**
30	Mrs Burrows for Mrs Monro	2.00.00.
	Mrs Atkins	3.19.06.
	A Dury Esq	4.07.00.
	Ditto	18.00.
	Mr Hudson	1.17.06.
	Mr Purkes	7.06.
	Mr J Lawrance	10.06.
	Mr William Hodson	7.06.
	Miss Batt	12.00.
	Mr Harrington	1.00.00.
	Mr Insell	7.06.
	Mr Mallet	1.17.06.
	Mr William Thorp	2.17.00.
	Mr Payne	2.05.00.
	Mrs R Thorp	1.16.00.
	Mr T Knight	13.06.
	Mr Evans	13.06.
	Mrs Trollope	3.07.06.
	James Dickens Esq	3.12.00.
	Mrs Wood	1.13.00.
	Mrs Simpson	1.13.00.
	Revd J H Winbolt	3.15.00.
	Mr Howden	1.16.00.
	Miss Johnson	2.05.00.
	S Page Esq	7.04.00.
	Ditto	2.05.00.
	Mr Lawrence	3.03.00.
	Mrs Harman	1.13.00.
	Mrs Childs	4.17.06.
	Ditto	1.02.06.
	Mr Richard Williams	18.00.
	Mr Bittlestone	18.00.
		£309.17.06.

1838	**Brought forward**	**£309.17.06.**
	Mr Attfield	2.05.00.
February 7	Mrs Horton	2.02.00.
	Mr Bunnage	10.06.
	Mr Crawley	16.06.
	Mr Parker	19.06.
	Mr Lucas	16.06.
	Mr Halsey	10.06.
	Mr G Miller	1.01.00.
	Mr Wells	16.06.
	Mr Bartlet	7.06.
	Mr F Cornwell	7.06.
	Mr Finney	1.13.00.
	Mr Chater	9.00.
	Mr Willey	9.00.
	Miss Finney	1.01.00.
	Mr Childs	16.06.
	Mr Joseph Miller	13.06.
	Mr Provart	15.00.
	Mr Tuely	18.00.
	Mr Davison	15.00.
	Mrs Nillson	18.00.
	Mr Tooth	13.06.
	Mr Flecknoe	13.06.
	Mr Beech	12.00.
	Mr Buckel	12.00.
	Mr Sharp	16.06.
	Mr Scarf	12.00.
	T Dimsdale Esq	2.05.00.
	Miss Tapster	15.00.
	Mr William Cornwell	1.10.00.
	Ditto	1.08.06.
	Mr Logsdon	2.05.00.
		£341.01.06.

APPENDIX II

1838	Brought forward	**£341.01.06.**

Mr Henry	1.16.00.
Mr Bailey	1.10.00.
Mrs Pooley	2.05.00.
Mr Secret	1.07.00.
Mr William Harris	1.07.00.
Mr Attwood	10.06.
Mr Tilbury	13.06.
Mr Negus	13.06.
Mr Jennings baker	16.06.
Miss Johnson	10.06.
Mr Hawkes	10.06.
Mr Baldock	13.06.
Mr Buckel	1.01.00.
Ditto	3.07.06.
Mr J Jennings	13.06.
Mr Clark	09.00.
Mr Baker	09.00.
Mr Carter	07.06.
Ditto for Sears	07.06.
Mr Woodward	07.06.
Mr Crane	07.06.
Mr Nisbet	2.02.00.
Ditto	18.00.
Mrs Housley	1.01.00.
Mr Randall	12.00.
Mr Propstring	07.06.
Mr Nicholas	1.10.00.
Mr	13.06.
Mr O'Neil	13.06.
Mr Byford	15.00.
Mr Leather	15.00.
Mr Sharp	1.08.06.
	£372.01.00.

1838	**Brought forward**	**£372.01.00.**
	Mr Walker	1.10.00.
	Mr Royer	1.05.06.
	Gas Company	18.00.
	Mr James Anderson	10.06.
	Mr Wren	10.06.
	Mr Courtnall	2.17.00.
	Mr Pepper	3.09.00.
	Mr Blackwell	18.00.
	Mr Cox	9.00.
	Mr Schlencker	7.14.06.
	Mr Cook	13.06.
	Mr Wigley	16.06.
		£393.13.00.

APPENDIX II

Account taken from inside front cover
Benjamin Woodcock's Diary

1837-8

11 December Received of Mr Higgs on a/c as Per Expenses
the Sum of £2.00.00.

11 January 1838	£2.00.00.
11 February ditto	£2.00 00.
26 March	£2.00.00.
- April -	£2.00.00.
11 July -	£2.00.00.
13 August	£2.00.00.
10 Sept	£2.00.00.
16 Oct	£1.10.00.
13 Nov	£2.10.00.
	£20.00.00.

*The cartouche from the front cover of the
Admission and Discharge Register [Barnet Museum]*

Appendix III

Extract of first 450 entries in
Admission and Discharge Register

The information provided below is taken from the first 450 entries of the first Admission and Discharge Register, one of two held at the Barnet Museum. These entries include paupers who had been admitted prior to August 1835 as well as those admitted up to mid-1837.

Each entry runs across two pages in the original register. The left hand page includes the information included here but additional information such as subsequent discharge, religious denomination etc is shown on the right hand page in the original. A full database of the register is being set up and the latest version can be seen at Barnet Museum.

Each entry represents one admission not one person. The entries have been sorted alphabetically and as a result often show more than one entry for each person. The reference number included in the first column on the left is made up from the book number, the page number and the position on the page. This enables readers to locate the original entry and establish the date order of admission.

In order to maximise the amout of information provided in this Appendix place names have been abbreviated and some details reduced. Where entries have been crossed through in the original this is shown by [XX].

Ref no	House	Age	Surname	First name	Born	Parish
1.43.04	Hadley	82	Annell	Ann	1755	Hadley
1.17.03	F Barnet	73	Ansell	Elizabeth	1764	F Barnet
1.32.02	F Barnet	73	Ansell	Elizabeth	1764	F Barnet
1.47.01	F Barnet	73	Ansell	Elizabeth	1764	F Barnet
1.5.04	E Barnet	72	Ansell	Elizabeth	1764	F Barnet
1.26.03	S Mims	20	Barnes	William	1817	S Mims
1.14.09	C Barnet	7	Barnet	John	1830	C Barnet
1.29.09	C Barnet	7	Barnet	John	1830	C Barnet
1.44.07	C Barnet	7	Barnet	John	1830	C Barnet
1.7.01	Shenley	6	Barnet	John	1830	C Barnet
1.13.01	C Barnet	46	Bartlett	Elizabeth	1790	Totteridge
1.20.04	Totteridge	47	Bartlett	Elizabeth	1790	Totteridge
1.1.05	C Barnet	54	Bell	John	1782	C Barnet
1.12.02	E Barnet	61	Bell	Elizabeth	1775	Totteridge
1.14.05	C Barnet	56	Bell	John	1781	C Barnet
1.20.03	Totteridge	62	Bell	Elizabeth	1775	Totteridge
1.29.05	C Barnet	56	Bell	John	1781	C Barnet
1.35.03	Totteridge	62	Bell	Elizabeth	1775	Totteridge
1.44.04	C Barnet	56	Bell	John	1781	C Barnet
1.50.03	Totteridge	62	Bell	Elizabeth	1775	Totteridge
1.5.08	E Barnet	61	Bell [XX]	Elizabeth	1775	Totteridge
1.22.06	Shenley	82	Blake	Hannah	1755	Shenley
1.37.05	Shenley	82	Blake	Hannah	1755	Shenley
1.52.05	Shenley	82	Blake	Hannah	1755	Shenley
1.6.03	E Barnet	81	Blake	Hannah	1755	Shenley
1.8.02	Shenley	13	Bone	William	1823	Finchley
1.52.17	Shenley	35	Bonnet	Mary Ann	1802	Shenley
1.52.18	Shenley	3	Bonnet	Mary Ann	1834	Shenley
1.53.01	Shenley	1	Bonnet	Martha	1836	Shenley

Calling	State	Disability?	Cause	Condition
menial servant	widow	aged	infirm	not any
washerwoman	single	infirm	aged	not any
washerwoman	single	aged	infirm	not any
washerwoman	single	aged	infirm	
washerwoman	single	infirm	aged	not any
labourer	single	illness	accident	
	orphan		deserted	
	orphan		deserted	
	orphan			
	orphan		deserted	
menial servant	single	able	out of place	mother able to provide
menial servant	single	able	out of place	not any
bricklayer	single	lost use right side	past work	
needlewoman	widow	infirm	nervious	all poor
bricklayer	single		infirm	
needlewoman	widow	nervious	infirm	not any
bricklayer	single	lost use right side	not able	none
needlewoman	widow	nervous	infirm	none
bricklayer	single	lost use of right side		
menial servant	widow	nervious	not able to work	
needlewoman	widow	infirm	not able to work	
nail maker	widow	blind	infirm	not any
nail maker	widow	aged blind	infirm	none
nail marker	widow	blind	infirm	none
nail maker	widow	blind	unable to work	not known
errand boy	deserted		fatherless	
menial servant	widow	able to work	2 children to keep	
	fatherless			
	fatherless			

Ref no	House	Age	Surname	First name	Born	Parish
1.27.07	Hadley	54	Bourne	Thomas	1783	Hadley
1.4.10	C Barnet	53	Bourne	Thomas	1783	Hadley
1.42.06	Hadley	54	Bourne	Thomas	1783	Hadley
1.18.06	Finchley	12	Brand	John	1825	Finchley
1.19.07	Finchley	62	Brand	Henry	1775	Finchley
1.33.06	Finchley	12	Brand	John	1825	Finchley
1.33.16	Finchley	62	Brand	Henry	1775	Finchley
1.48.06	Finchley	12	Brand	John	1825	Finchley
1.8.04	Shenley	11	Brand	John	1825	Finchley
1.1.07	C Barnet	66	Briers	Robert	1770	Totteridge
1.20.01	Totteridge	67	Briers	Robert	1770	Totteridge
1.35.01	Totteridge	67	Briers	Robert	1770	Totteridge
1.50.01	Totteridge	67	Briers	Robert	1770	Totteridge
1.23.03	Shenley	31	Brill	John	1806	Shenley
1.37.12	Shenley	31	Brill	John	1806	Shenley
1.4.09	C Barnet	30	Brill	John	1806	Shenley
1.52.09	Shenley	31	Brill	John	1806	Shenley
1.12.04	E Barnet	70	Buck	Ann	1766	Ridge
1.24.01	Ridge	71	Buck	Ann	1766	Ridge
1.39.01	Ridge	71	Buck	Ann	1766	Ridge
1.54.01	Ridge	71	Buck	Ann	1766	Ridge
1.45.03	C Barnet	42	Bunningham	Esther	1795	CB Casualty
1.33.14	Finchley	6	Bunyan	Mary Ann	1831	Finchley
1.48.14	Finchley	6	Bunyan	Mary Ann	1831	Finchley
1.19.05	Finchley	6	Bunyan	Mary Ann	1831	Finchley
1.9.03	Shenley	5	Bunyan	Mary Ann	1831	Finchley
1.51.06	Elstree	30	Burke	John	1807	Elstree Casualty
1.19.07	Finchley	35	Burton	Thomas	1802	Finchley
1.25.05	S Mims	52	Burton	Frances	1785	S Mims
1.6.06	E Barnet	51	Burton	Frances	1785	S Mims

Calling	State	Disability?	Cause	Condition
labourer	single	infirm	out work	not any
sailor	single	infirm	starving	all poor
labourer	single	aged	infirm	none
labourer	orphan		no home	
labourer	widower	infirm	out work	not any
labourer	orphan		no home	not any
labourer	widower	infirm	out work	not any
labourer	orphan		out place	
errand boy	orphan		no home	
gardener	single	lame		
gardener	single	lame	unable to work	not any
gardener	single	lame	not able to work	none
gardener	single	lame	not able to work	not any
labourer	single	weak intellect	out work	not any
labourer	single	aged	out work	not any
labourer	single		out of work	no home
labourer	single	illness	out of work	none
charwoman	widow	infirm	illness	all poor
charwoman	widow	infirm	aged	not any
charwoman	widow	infirm	aged	not any
charwoman	widow	aged	infirm	not any
traveller	married	illness	not able to work	not any
labourer	orphan		no home	not any
	orphan			
	orphan		no home	not any
	orphan		no home	
haymaker	married	fever	illness	belong to Stockport
labourer	married	illness	no home	not any
charwoman	widow	illness	out place	not any
charwoman		Cancer	not able	

225

Ref no	House	Age	Surname	First name	Born	Parish
1.37.14	Shenley	33	Camel	Sarah	1804	Shenley
1.52.10	Shenley	33	Camel	Sarah	1804	Shenley
1.24.03	Ridge	76	Camfield	Thomas	1761	Ridge
1.45.04	C Barnet	19	Camfield	Elizabeth	1818	C Barnet
1.34.01	Finchley	30	Campen	William	1807	Finchley
1.48.15	Finchley	30	Campen	William	1807	Finchley
1.49.06	Finchley	6	Carney	Michael	1831	Finchley
1.12.05	E Barnet	67	Carpenter	Jane	1769	Hadley
1.28.04	Hadley	68	Carpenter	Jane	1769	Hadley
1.42.13	Hadley	68	Carpenter	Jane	1769	Hadley
1.10.08	Shenley		Chambers	Walter [XX]		not known
1.4.07	C Barnet	14	Collins	Joseph	1822	Shenley
1.9.05	Shenley	14	Collins	Joseph	1822	Shenley
1.16.03	E Barnet	13	Collinson	William	1824	E Barnet
1.46.02	E Barnet	13	Collinson	William	1824	E Barnet
1.46.10	E Barnet	50	Collinson	Olivia	1787	E Barnet
1.7.06	Shenley	8	Collinson	William	1828	E Barnet
1.31.02	E Barnet	13	Collinson	William	1824	E Barnet
1.30.01	C Barnet	65	Constable	William	1772	CB casualty HH'sted
1.44.14	C Barnet	65	Constable	William	1772	CB casualty H H'sted
1.27.05	Hadley	20	Cooper	Mary	1817	Hadley
1.27.09	Hadley	23	Cooper	A Laura	1814	Hadley
1.28.05	Hadley	53	Cooper	Thomas	1784	Hadley
1.4.02	C Barnet	19	Cooper	Mary	1817	Hadley
1.42.08	Hadley	23	Cooper	A Laura	1814	Hadley
1.6.08	E Barnet	22	Cooper	Amelia Laura	1814	Hadley
1.25.03	S Mims	77	Cox	Ann	1760	S Mims
1.27.08	Hadley	70	Cox	Mary	1767	Hadley
1.42.07	Hadley	70	Cox	Mary	1767	Hadley
1.6.04	E Barnet	76	Cox	Ann	1760	S Mims

APPENDIX III

Calling	State	Disability?	Cause	Condition
staw plait	single	cripple	not able to work	not any
straw plaiter	single	cripple	not able to work	
labourer	married	infirm	blind	not any
menial servant	single	idiot	not able to work	not any
groom	single	illness	accident	none
groom	single	illness	out work	
not been out	deserted		no home	
washerwoman	widow	infirm	past work	illness
washerwoman	widow	infirm	aged	not any
washerwoman	widow	aged	infirm	none
beadle	married	able to work		
	orphan		left employment	pretended being ill
	orphan		no home	
	orphan			
labourer	fatherless	idiot	infirm	
menial servant	widow	infirm	out of place	
	orphan			
	orphan	weak intellect		
labourer	widower	illness	accident	
labourer	widower	illness	accident	
menial servant	single	able	out place	not any
menial servant	single	illness	subject to fits	not any
shoemaker	widower	illness	out work	none
menial servant	single		lost place	no home
menial servant	single	illness	subject to fits	none
menial servant	single	weak intellect	out of place	
poulterer	widow	infirm	aged	not any
needlework	widow	bad eyes	aged	not any
needlewoman	widow	bad legs	infirm	none
poulterer	widow	infirm	unable to work	

227

Ref no	House	Age	Surname	First name	Born	Parish
1.6.07	E Barnet	69	Cox	Mary	1767	S Mims
1.14.07	C Barnet	71	Crane	Isaac	1766	C Barnet
1.29.07	C Barnet	71	Crane	Isaac	1766	C Barnet
1.4.08	C Barnet	70	Crane	Isaac	1766	C Barnet
1.44.18	C Barnet	61	Crane	Isaac	1776	C Barnet
1.1.01	C Barnet	81	Crew	Henry	1755	C Barnet
1.14.01	C Barnet	82	Crew	Henry	1755	C Barnet
1.45.05	C Barnet	82	Crew	Henry	1755	C Barnet
1.29.01	C Barnet	82	Crew	Henry	1755	C Barnet
1.19.04	Finchley	8	Davis	Elizabeth	1829	Finchley
1.33.13	Finchley	8	Davis	Elizabeth	1829	Finchley
1.48.13	Finchley	8	Davis	Elizabeth	1829	Finchley
1.9.02	Shenley	8	Davis	Elizabeth	1828	Finchley
1.42.15	Hadley	33	Davison	Mary	1804	Hadley
1.42.16	Hadley	9	Davison	Mary Elizabeth	1828	Hadley
1.42.17	Hadley	2	Davison	Robert	1835	Hadley
1.43.02	Hadley	0	Davison	bastard children	1837	Hadley
1.43.03	Hadley	0	Davison	bastard children	1837	Hadley
1.1.04	C Barnet	34	De Fardac	Jane	1802	C Barnet
1.29.04	C Barnet	35	De Fardac	Jane	1802	C Barnet
1.44.03	C Barnet	35	De Fardac	Jane	1802	C Barnet
1.14.04	C Barnet	35	De Vardac	Jane	1802	C Barnet
1.15.02	C Barnet	7	Dean	John	1830	C Barnet
1.29.12	C Barnet	7	Dean	John	1830	C Barnet
1.44.10	C Barnet	7	Dean	John	1830	C Barnet
1.7.04	Shenley	8	Dean	John	1828	C Barnet
1.41.01	S Mims	23	Delaney	Sarah	1814	Ireland EBarnet casualty
1.26.05	S Mims	50	Dickins	John	1787	S Mims
1.48.08	Finchley	9	DocKerry	James	1828	Finchley
1.18.08	Finchley	9	Dockery	James	1828	Finchley

APPENDIX III

Calling	State	Disability?	Cause	Condition
needlework	widow	bad legs	infirm	
brickmaker	single	aged	infirm	
brickmaker	single	aged	infirm	none
brickmaker	single	infirm	out of work	naked & hungry
brickmaker	single	aged	infirm	not any
gardener	widower	lame		
gardener	widower	lame	infirm	
gardener	widower	lame	aged	none
gardener	widower	lame	infirm	none
	deserted	motherless	cripple	not any
	deserted		cripple	not any
	deserted			
	deserted	cripple	motherless	
menial servant	married	pregnant	deserted	none
			deserted	none
			deserted	none
knitter	widow	idiot		
knitter	widow	idiot	not able	none
knitter	widow	idiot		
knitter	widow	Idiot	not able to work	
	bastard			
	bastard			
	bastard			
	bastard			
tramp	married	pregnant	illness	removed Mims to w'khouse
sailor	single	lame	out work	
labourer	orphan		out place	
	orphan		no home	

Ref no	House	Age	Surname	First name	Born	Parish
1.33.08	Finchley	9	Dockery	James	1828	Finchley
1.8.06	Shenley	8	Dockery	James	1828	Finchley
1.32.07	F Barnet	57	Dolomore	Daniel	1780	F Barnet casualty
1.47.01	F Barnet	57	Dolomore	Daniel	1780	Casualty F B
1.50.04	Totteridge	48	Donovan	Michael	1789	Totteridge Casualty
1.16.04	E Barnet	1	Ebbs	William	1836	E Barnet
1.31.03	E Barnet	1	Ebbs	William	1836	E Barnet
1.46.03	E Barnet	1	Ebbs	William	1836	E Barnet
1.7.07	Shenley	0	Ebbs	William	1836	E Barnet
1.22.04	Shenley	75	Enever	Neben	1762	Shenley
1.3.03	C Barnet	75	Enever	Neben	1761	Shenley
1.37.04	Shenley	76	Enever	Neben	1761	Shenley
1.52.04	Shenley	76	Enever	Neben	1761	Shenley
1.26.04	S Mims	66	Farmery	George	1771	S Mims
1.40.11	S Mims	66	Farmery	George	1771	S Mims
1.40.13	S Mims	37	Feaman	James	1800	S Mims
1.26.07	S Mims	37	Fearman	James	1800	S Mims
1.26.08	S Mims	35	Fearman	Harriet his wife	1802	S Mims
1.40.18	S Mims	47	Fisher	George	1790	S Mims
1.34.04	Finchley	6	Flint	Richard	1831	Finchley
1.48.18	Finchley	6	Flint	Richard	1831	Finchley
1.30.02	C Barnet	42	Foskett	Thomas	1795	E Barnet
1.30.04	C Barnet	12	Foskett	Thomas junior	1825	C Barnet
1.44.15	C Barnet	42	Foskett	Thomas	1795	C Barnet
1.14.10	C Barnet	13	Fox	Martha	1824	C Barnet
1.29.10	C Barnet	13	Fox	Martha	1824	C Barnet
1.44.08	C Barnet	13	Fox	Martha	1824	C Barnet
1.7.02	Shenley	11	Fox	Martha	1825	C Barnet
1.10.07	Shenley	4	Galloway	Susannah	1832	S Mims
1.26.01	S Mims	5	Galloway	Susannah	1832	S Mims

Calling	State	Disability?	Cause	Condition
labourer	orphan		no home	not any
errand boy	orphan		no home	
labourer	widower	infirm	illness	not any
labourer	widower	illness	not able	
haymaker	married	affection of chest	illness	belong to Cork
	bastard		deserted	
	bastard		deserted	
labourer	bastard			
	bastard		deserted	
labourer	widower	infirm	aged	not any
labourer	widower	infirm	past work	
labourer	widower	aged	infirm	none
labourer	widower	aged	infirm	none
blacksmith	single	infirm	out work	not any
blacksmith	single	illness	out work	not any
labourer	married	illness	out work	not any
labourer	married	ruptured	illness	hone
menial servant	married	able	out of place	none
casual labourer	single	illness	accident	not any
	orphan			
	orphan			
tailor	widower	illness	out of work	
	motherless	father in House	no home	
tailor	widower	weak intellect	not able	
needlework	deserted			motherless
needlework	deserted			motherless
needle work	deserted			motherless
	deserted			no mother
	bastard			
	bastard		deserted	

231

Ref no	House	Age	Surname	First name	Born	Parish
1.40.09	S Mims	5	Galloway	Susannah	1832	S Mims
1.44.12	C Barnet	71	Gillman	Ann	1766	C Barnet
1.5.03	E Barnet	71	Gillman	Ann	1765	C Barnet
1.29.17	C Barnet	71	Gilman	Ann	1766	C Barnet
1.17.04	Shenley	10	Godfrey	Charles	1827	F Barnet
1.32.03	F Barnet	10	Godfrey	Charles	1827	F Barnet
1.32.06	F Barnet	14	Godfrey	Sarah	1823	F Barnet
1.47.01	F Barnet	10	Godfrey	Charles	1827	F Barnet
1.47.01	F Barnet	14	Godfrey	Sarah	1823	F Barnet
1.8.01	Shenley	9	Godfrey	Charles	1827	F Barnet
1.18.04	Finchley	88	Goodale	Sarah	1749	Finchley
1.33.04	Finchley	88	Goodale	Sarah	1749	Finchley
1.48.04	Finchley	88	Goodale	Sarah	1749	Finchley
1.5.06	E Barnet	87	Goodale	Sarah	1749	Finchley
1.23.04	Shenley	60	Goodman	Sarah	1777	Shenley
1.42.18	Hadley	79	Granger	Sarah	1758	Hadley
1.13.02	C Barnet	21	Gray	Ann	1815	Ridge
1.24.01	Ridge	22	Gray	Ann	1815	Ridge
1.39.02	Ridge	22	Gray	Ann	1815	Ridge
1.39.04	Ridge	22	Gray	Ann	1815	Ridge
1.1.08	C Barnet	69	Green	William	1767	Hadley
1.27.01	Hadley	70	Green	William	1767	Hadley
1.42.01	Hadley	70	Green	William	1767	Hadley
1.49.01	Finchley	59	Green	Sarah	1778	Finchley
1.24.02	C Barnet	91	Gregory	Ann	1746	Ridge
1.39.03	Ridge	91	Gregory	Ann	1746	Ridge
1.54.02	Ridge	91	Gregory	Ann	1746	Ridge
1.13.05	C Barnet	90	Gregory	Ann	1746	Ridge
1.30.03	C Barnet	6	Grimes	Ann	1831	C Barnet
1.44.16	C Barnet	6	Grimes	Ann	1831	C Barnet

Calling	State	Disability?	Cause	Condition
	bastard		infirm	not any
menial servant	widow	aged	infirm	
menial servant	widow	infirm	out of place	not any
menial servant	widow	aged	out of place	none
	deserted			not any
	deserted			not any
menial servant	deserted	no home	out place	not any
	deserted			
menial servant	deserted		out place	
	deserted			
menial servant	widow	aged	infirm	not any
menial servant	widow	aged	infirm	not any
menial servant	widow	aged	infirm	
menial servant	widow	aged	infirm	
washerwoman	married	able	deserted	not any
menial servant	widow	aged	infirm	none
menial servant	single	illness	out of place	none
menial servant	single	illness	out place	not any
menial servant	single	illness	out place	not any
menial servant	single	illness	out place	not any
ploughman	widower	rheumatic		
ploughman	widower	infirm	rheumatic	not any
ploughman	widower	aged	infirm	none
washerwoman	married	able	out of employ	separated from husband
washerwoman	widow	infirm	aged	not any
washerwoman	widow	aged	infirm	not any
washerwoman	widow	aged	infirm	not any
washerwoman	widow	infirm	age	some years kept by son
	bastard		deserted	
	bastard			

233

Ref no	House	Age	Surname	First name	Born	Parish
1.46.09	E Barnet	58	Grubb	George	1779	E Barnet
1.19.01	Shenley	11	Gwillim	Charles	1826	Finchley
1.33.10	Finchley	11	Gwillim	Charles	1826	Finchley
1.8.03	Shenley	13	Gwillim	John	1823	Finchley
1.8.08	Finchley	10	Gwillim	Charles	1826	Finchley
1.48.10	Finchley	11	Gwillum	Charles	1826	Finchley
1.8.05	Shenley	10	Haires	John	1826	Finchley
1.18.07	Finchley	11	Hairs	John	1826	Finchley
1.33.07	Finchley	11	Hairs	John	1826	Finchley
1.48.07	Finchley	11	Hairs	John	1826	Finchley
1.12.03	E Barnet	71	Hale	Mary Ann	1765	Shenley
1.23.01	Shenley	72	Hale	Mary Ann	1765	Shenley
1.37.10	Shenley	72	Hale	Mary Ann	1765	Shenley
1.26.09	S Mims	74	Hall	Joseph	1763	S Mims
1.26.10	S Mims	54	Hall	Sarah his wife	1783	S Mims
1.40.14	S Mims	74	Hall	Joseph	1763	Mims casualty
1.40.15	S Mims	54	Hall	Sarah his wife	1783	S Mims
1.23.05	Shenley	15	Harris	Henry	1822	Shenley
1.23.06	Shenley	13	Harris	George	1824	Shenley
1.23.07	Shenley	8	Harris	David	1829	Shenley
1.34.03	Finchley	40	Harris	Eliza	1797	Finchley casualty
1.48.17	Finchley	40	Harris	Eliza	1797	Finchley casualty
1.49.07	Finchley	40	Harris	Elizabeth	1797	Finchley casualty
1.47.01	F Barnet	30	Haselgrove	John	1807	F Barnet
1.16.07	E Barnet	60	Hawkes	Hugh	1777	E Barnet
1.31.05	E Barnet	60	Hawkes	Hugh	1777	E Barnet
1.27.10	Hadley	32	Haynes	Esther	1805	Hadley
1.42.09	Hadley	32	Haynes	Esther	1805	Hadley
1.6.09	E Barnet	31	Haynes	Esther	1805	Hadley
1.12.01	E Barnet	76	Hedge	Sarah	1760	C Barnet

Calling	State	Disability?	Cause	Condition
labourer	married	aged	infirm	not any
labourer	deserted		no home	not any
labourer	deserted		no home	not any
errand boy	deserted			
	deserted		no home	
labourer	deserted			
errand boy	orphan		no home	
	orphan		no home	
labourer	orphan		no home	not any
labourer	orphan		out place	
charwoman	widow	infirm	rheumatism	all poor
charwoman	widow	infirm	rheumatic	none
charwoman	widow	aged	infirm	not any
casualty	married	illness		
casualty	married	illness		
labourer	married	illness	out work	not any
washerwoman	married	able	out work	not any
labourer - belongs to Sarah Goodman				
belongs to Sarah Goodman				
belongs to Sarah Goodman				
menial servant	single	illness	out work	
menial servant	single	illness	out work	
laundress	single	illness	not able to work	not any
groom	single	able	out of work	
baker	widower	illness	out of place	not any
baker	widower	illness	out of work	
menial servant	single	nearly blind	out of place	not any
menial servant	single	bad eyes		none
menial servant	single	nearly blind	out of place	
menial servant	widow	infirm		all poor

Ref no	House	Age	Surname	First name	Born	Parish
1.14.03	C Barnet	77	Hedge	Sarah	1760	C Barnet
1.29.03	C Barnet	77	Hedge	Sarah	1760	C Barnet
1.44.02	C Barnet	77	Hedge	Sarah	1760	C Barnet
1.1.03	C Barnet	75	Hedge [XX]	Sarah [XX]	1761	C Barnet
1.9.04	Shenley	6	Hennersey	William [XX]	1830	Finchley
1.1.09	C Barnet	80	Hill	Joseph	1756	Shenley
1.22.01	Shenley	83	Hill	Joseph	1754	Shenley
1.37.01	Shenley	83	Hill	Joseph	1754	Shenley
1.52.01	Shenley	83	Hill	Joseph	1754	Shenley
1.22.07	Shenley	52	Hipgrave	Ann	1785	Shenley
1.37.06	Shenley	52	Hipgrave	Ann	1785	Shenley
1.52.06	Shenley	52	Hipgrave	Ann	1785	Shenley
1.10.02	Shenley	9	Holloway	Celesha	1827	S Mims
1.25.07	S Mims	10	Holloway	Celesha	1827	S Mims
1.40.05	S Mims	10	Holloway	Celesha	1827	S Mims
1.10.04	Shenley	6	Howard	Sarah	1830	S Mims
1.10.05	Shenley	4	Howard	Margaret	1832	S Mims
1.10.06	Shenley		Howard	Elizabeth		S Mimms
1.25.09	S Mims	7	Howard	Sarah	1830	S Mims
1.25.10	S Mims	5	Howard	Margaret	1832	S Mims
1.40.07	S Mims	7	Howard	Sarah	1830	S Mims
1.40.08	S Mims	5	Howard	Margaret	1832	S Mims
1.40.16	S Mims		Howard	Elizabeth	1752[?]	S Mims
1.1.10	C Barnet	61	Hull	Edward	1775	Hadley
1.2.01	C Barnet	31	Hull	Edward	1805	Hadley
1.27.02	Hadley	62	Hull	Edward	1775	Hadley
1.27.03	Hadley	32	Hull	Edward	1805	Hadley
1.42.02	Hadley	62	Hull	Edward	1775	Hadley
1.42.03	Hadley	32	Hull	Edward	1805	Hadley

Calling	State	Disability?	Cause	Condition
menial servant	widow	aged	infirm	
menial servant	widow	aged	infirm	none
menial servant	widow	aged	infirm	none
menial servant	widow	infirm		
	bastard		deserted	
labourer	widower	lame		
labourer	widower	lame	infirm	not any
labourer	widower	aged	infirm	none
labourer	widower	aged	infirm	none
menial servant	single	idiot	not able	not any
menial servant	single	aged	infirm	none
menial servant	single	idiot	not able	none
menial servant	orphan	cripple		
	orphan			
	orphan	cripple	infirm	not any
menial servant	widow	able to work	the mother pays 9d p week with each child	
mother pays 9d	fatherless		deserted	
mother pays 9d	fatherless			
	fatherless		infirm	not any
	fatherless		infirm	not any
menial servant	widow	illness	out place	not any
groom	married	weak eyes		
gardener	single	sore legs		
groom	married	bad eyes	infirm	not any
gardener	single	bad legs	out work	
groom	married	bad eyes	infirm	none
gardener	single	bad eyes	infirm	none

Ref no	House	Age	Surname	First name	Born	Parish
1.45.06.	C Barnet	0	Jarvis	Elizabeth	1837	C Barnet
1.22.08	Shenley	68	Jiltro	Susannah	1769	Shenley
1.37.07	Shenley	68	Jiltro	Susannah	1769	Shenley
1.52.16	Shenley	68	Jiltro	Suzannah	1769	Shenley
1.13.03	C Barnet	60	Jones	George	1776	Finchley
1.19.06	Finchley	61	Jones	George	1776	Finchley
1.33.15	Finchley	61	Jones	George	1776	Finchley
1.18.01	Finchley	77	Knight	Abraham	1760	Finchley
1.2.02	C Barnet	76	Knight	Abraham	1760	Finchley
1.33.01	Finchley	77	Knight	Abraham	1760	Finchley
1.48.01	Finchley	77	Knight	Abraham	1760	Finchley
1.25.02	S Mims	15	Lambert	Charles	1822	S Mims
1.3.06	C Barnet	14	Lambert	Charles	1822	S Mims
1.40.02	S Mims	15	Lambert	Charles	1822	S Mims
1.2.03	C Barnet	73	Layton	William	1763	Shenley
1.22.02	Shenley	72	Layton	William	1765	Shenley
1.37.02	Shenley	72	Layton	William	1765	Shenley
1.52.02	Shenley	72	Layton	William	1765	Shenley
1.15.06	C Barnet	16	Lenman	Christopher	1821	C Barnet
1.29.14	C Barnet	16	Lenman	Christopher	1821	C Barnet
1.3.09	C Barnet	50	Long	Francis	1786	Ridge
1.4.04	C Barnet	57	Lord	Thomas	1779	Shenley
1.22.10	Shenley	58	Lord	Thomas	1779	Shenley
1.37.09	Shenley	58	Lord	Thomas	1779	Shenley
1.29.18	C Barnet	71	Maddams	Jane	1766	C Barnet
1.44.13	C Barnet	71	Maddams	Jane	1766	C Barnet
1.1.02	C Barnet	70	Marshall	Abel	1766	C Barnet
1.14.02	C Barnet	61	Marshall	Abel	1776	C Barnet
1.29.02	C Barnet	61	Marshall	Abel	1776	C Barnet
1.44.01	C Barnet	61	Marshall	Abel	1776	C Barnet
1.29.06	C Barnet	15	Mercham	John	1822	C Barnet

APPENDIX III

Calling	State	Disability?	Cause	Condition
washerwoman	widow	infirm	aged	not any
washerwoman	widow	aged	infirm	none
washerwoman	widow	aged	infirm	none
labourer	single	illness	unable to work	all poor
gardener	single	illness	bad arm	not any
gardener	single	bad arm	illness	not any
footman	single	infirm	out of place	not any
footman	single	infirm		
footman	single	aged	out work	not any
footman	single	aged	infirm	
labourer	bastard	able	out of place	not any
shepherd	bastard		out of work	
labourer	bastard	able	deserted	not any
labourer	widower	infirm		
labourer	widower	infirm	aged	not any
labourer	widower	aged	infirm	none
labourer	widower	aged	infirm	none
labourer		illness	out work	
labourer		illness	no home	
labourer	widower	consumption	illness	
gardener	single		out of work	all poor
gardener	single	infirm	out work	not any
gardener	single	aged	infirm	not any
washerwoman	widow	blind	aged and infirm	none
washerwoman	widow	blind		
shoemaker	married	deaf		
shoemaker	married	deaf	infirm	
shoemaker	married	deaf	infirm	son 3s a week
shoemaker	married	deaf	infirm out of work	son able
labourer	deserted		out of work	none

Ref no	House	Age	Surname	First name	Born	Parish
1.29.15	C Barnet	17	Mercham	Alfred	1820	C Barnet
1.44.05	C Barnet	15	Mercham	John	1822	C Barnet
1.1.06	C Barnet	14	Merchum	John	1822	C Barnet
1.14.06	C Barnet	15	Merchum	John	1822	C Barnet
1.15.07	C Barnet	17	Merchum	Alfred	1820	C Barnet
1.2.04	C Barnet	83	Mitchell	Joseph	1753	Shenley
1.22.03	Shenley	84	Mitchell	Joseph	1753	Shenley
1.37.03	Shenley	84	Mitchell	Joseph	1753	Shenley
1.52.03	Shenley	84	Mitchell	Joseph	1753	Shenley
1.37.16	Shenley	10	Montgomery	Caroline	1827	Shenley
1.37.17	Shenley	8	Montgomery	Ann	1829	Shenley
1.37.18	Shenley	5	Montgomery	Emma	1832	Shenley
1.52.12	Shenley	10	Montgomery	Caroline	1827	Shenley
1.52.13	Shenley	8	Montgomery	Ann	1829	Shenley
1.52.14	Shenley	5	Montgomery	Emma	1832	Shenley
1.52.15	Shenley	3	Montgomery	Martha	1834	Shenley
1.37.19	Shenley	3	Montgomery	Martha	1834	Shenley
1.16.06	E Barnet	24	Morris	Mariah	1813	E Barnet
1.31.08	E Barnet	22	Mullen	Mary	1815	Ireland EB casualty
1.31.09	E Barnet	0	Mullen	female infant	1837	Ireland EB casualty
1.46.07	E Barnet	22	Mullen	Mary	1815	E B Casualty Ireland
1.46.08	E Barnet	0	Mullen	female infant	1837	E B Casualty Ireland
1.26.06	S Mims	17	Newby	Helen	1820	S Mims
1.40.12	S Mims	17	Newby	Helen	1820	S Mims
1.10.03	Shenley	8	Nightingale	Mary	1828	S Mims
1.25.08	S Mims	9	Nightingale	Mary	1828	S Mims
1.40.06	S Mims	9	Nightingale	Mary	1828	S Mims
1.53.02	Shenley	18	Nixon	Adam	1819	Shenley Casualty
1.2.05	C Barnet	67	Nutkins	Robert	1769	Elstree
1.21.01	Elstree	68	Nutkins	Robert	1769	Elstree

APPENDIX III

Calling	State	Disability?	Cause	Condition
labourer	deserted	illness	no home	none
labourer	deserted		out place	
labourer	deserted			
labourer	deserted		out of work	
labourer	deserted	illness		
horse keeper	deserted	rheumatic		
horse keeper	deserted	rheumatic	infirm	not any
labourer	deserted	aged	infirm	none
labourer	deserted	aged	infirm	none
not been out	deserted	father and mother gone to Margate for health BOB		
not been out	deserted	father and mother gone to Margate for health BOB		
not been out	deserted	father and mother gone to Margate for health BOB		
		father & mother gone to infirmary		
		father & mother gone to infirmary		
		father & mother gone to infirmary		
		father & mother gone to infirmary		
not been out	single	the father and mother gone to Margate for health BOB		
menial servant	single	pregnant	out of place	casualty
tramp	married	illness	pregnant	delivered few hours before
tramp	married	illness		delivered few hours before
tramp				
useless	single	idiot		father
useless	single	idiot	out work	father
	bastard	cripple	deserted	
	bastard			
	bastard		infirm	not any
labourer	single	sickness	not able to work	Irish man
bricklayer	widower	infirm		
bricklayer	widower	infirm	aged	not any

THE DIARY OF BENJAMIN WOODCOCK

Ref no	House	Age	Surname	First name	Born	Parish
1.51.01	Elstree	68	Nutkins	Robert	1769	Elstree
1.10.01	Shenley	58	Parkes	Elizabeth	1778	S Mims
1.25.06	S Mims	59	Parkes	Elizabeth	1778	S Mims
1.40.04	S Mims	59	Parkes	Elizabeth	1778	S Mims
1.2.06	C Barnet	76	Pearce	William	1760	S Mims
1.17.01	F Barnet	18	Peart	Paul	1819	F Barnet
1.3.07	C Barnet	17	Peart	Paul	1819	F Barnet
1.32.01	F Barnet	18	Peart	Paul	1819	F Barnet
1.47.01	F Barnet	18	Peart	Paul	1819	F Barnet
1.20.02	Totteridge	76	Pedley	Mary	1761	Totteridge
1.3.10	C Barnet	75	Pedley	Mary	1761	Totteridge
1.35.02	Totteridge	76	Pedley	Mary	1761	Totteridge
1.50.02	Totteridge	77	Pedley	Mary	1760	Totteridge
1.17.02	F Barnet	16	Peel	William	1821	F Barnet
1.3.08	C Barnet	15	Peel	William	1821	F Barnet
1.32.05	F Barnet	12	Peel	William	1825	F Barnet
1.47.01	F Barnet	16	Peel	William	1821	F Barnet
1.49.04	Finchley	62	Pepper	James	1775	Finchley Casualty
1.43.01	Hadley	32	Perin	Hubert	1805	Hadley France
1.15.04	C Barnet	45	Poulton	Nathaniel	1792	C Barnet
1.29.13	C Barnet	45	Poulton	Nathaniel	1792	C Barnet
1.5.05	E Barnet	54	Randall	Susan	1782	F Barnet
1.44.17	C Barnet	14	Rice	James	1823	CB Casualty
1.15.05	C Barnet	30	Richards	William	1807	C Barnet
1.28.06	Hadley	55	Rippon	John	1782	Hadley
1.42.14	Hadley	55	Rippon	John	1782	Hadley
1.17.05	F Barnet	67	Robinson	Jacob	1770	F Barnet
1.2.07	C Barnet	66	Robinson	Jacob	1770	Finchley
1.32.04	F Barnet	67	Robinson	Jacob	1770	F Barnet
1.47.01	F Barnet	67	Robinson	Jacob	1770	F Barnet

Calling	State	Disability?	Cause	Condition
bricklayer	widower	aged	infirm	not any
menial servant	single	idiot	infirm	
menial servant	single	infirm	weak intellect	not any
menial servant	single	weak intellect	infirm	not any
labourer	widower	infirm		
	orphan	cripple	cripple	
	orphan	cripple	deformed	
	orphan	disabled	cripple	not any
	orphan	cripple	not able	
nurse	widow	infirm	aged	not any
nurse	widow	aged	infirm	
nurse	widow	aged	infirm	none
menial servant	widow	aged	infirm	
labourer	deserted		out of work	
errand boy [XX]	deserted		out of work	
labourer	deserted	no home	out work	not any
labourer	deserted		out work	
labourer	single	illness	not any	not any
pedler	single	illness	no money	not known
widower	labourer	illness	out work	
labourer	widower	able	out of work	none
ladies maid	widow	idiot	not able to work	not any
labourer	deserted	able	out work	no home
chemist	single	illness		
labourer	single	lame	out work	none
labourer	single	lame	out work	none
labourer	single	lost use right side		not any
labourer	single	lost use of right side		
labourer	single	lost use one side	infirm	not any
labourer	single	lost use one side		

Ref no	House	Age	Surname	First name	Born	Parish
1.18.09	Finchley	9	Salt	John	1828	Finchley
1.19.07	Finchley	60	Salt	George	1777	Finchley
1.33.09	Finchley	9	Salt	John	1828	Finchley
1.33.18	Finchley	60	Salt	George	1777	Finchley
1.48.09	Finchley	9	Salt	John	1828	Finchley
1.8.07	Shenley	8	Salt	John	1828	Finchley
1.18.03	Finchley	51	Schofield	Richard	1786	Finchley
1.2.10	C Barnet	50	Schofield	Richard	1786	Finchley
1.33.03	Finchley	51	Schofield	Richard	1786	Finchley
1.48.03	Finchley	51	Schofield	Richard	1786	Finchley
1.30.05	C Barnet	27	Seagrave	Charlotte	1810	C Barnet
1.25.04	S Mims	67	Sears	Ann	1770	S Mims
1.40.03	S Mims	67	Sears	Ann	1770	S Mims
1.6.05	E Barnet	66	Sears	Ann	1770	S Mims
1.31.06	E Barnet	88	Sell	Elizabeth	1749	E Barnet
1.46.05	E Barnet	88	Sell	Elizabeth	1749	E Barnet
1.15.08	C Barnet	12	Shepherd	Edward	1825	C Barnet
1.15.09	C Barnet	11	Shepherd	Emma	1826	C Barnet
1.5.07	E Barnet	28	Shepherd	Ruth	1808	Finchley
1.51.05	Elstree	18	Shott	Eliza	1819	Elstree
1.11.02	Shenley	1	Shuttleworth	male child	1835	Hadley
1.11.03	Shenley		Shuttleworth	Mariah his mother	[XX]	Hadley
1.28.02	Hadley	2	Shuttleworth	boy	1835	Hadley
1.42.11	Hadley	2	Shuttleworth	infant	1835	Hadley
1.15.01	C Barnet	6	Simmonds	Susannah	1831	C Barnet
1.29.11	C Barnet	6	Simmonds	Susannah	1831	C Barnet
1.7.03	C Barnet	5	Simmonds	Susannah	1831	C Barnet
1.44.09	C Barnet	6	Simmons	Sussanah	1831	C Barnet
1.2.08	C Barnet	74	Skipsey	Benjamin	1762	S Mims
1.25.01	S Mims	75	Skipsey	Benjamin	1762	S Mims

Calling	State	Disability?	Cause	Condition
errand boy	deserted		no home	
labourer	married	infirm	out work	not any
labourer	deserted		no home	not any
labourer	married	aged	illness	not any
labourer	deserted		out place	
	deserted by father		no home	
	single	idiot		not any
	single	idiot		
		idiot	not able	not any
	single	idiot		
menial servant	single	illness	out of place	
nurse	widow	infirm	weak intellect	not any
nurse	widow	weak intellect	infirm	not any
nurse	widow	infirm	weak intellect	
menial servant	single	aged	infirm	
menial servant	single	aged	infirm	
not been out	deserted		no home	CB Casualty Bayford
not been out	deserted		no home	CB Casualty Bayford
school keeper	single	cripple	out of place	
menial servant	single	pregnant	out place	
	bastard		deserted	
menial servant	single	able to work		gone to service
	bastard		deserted	not
	bastard		deserted	none
	bastard		deserted	
	bastard		deserted	
	bastard			
	bastard			
gardener	married	infirm		
gardener	married	infirm	out of place	not any

Ref no	House	Age	Surname	First name	Born	Parish
1.40.01	S Mims	75	Skipsey	Benjamin	1762	S Mims
1.18.02	Finchley	50	Smith	Thomas	1787	Finchley
1.2.09	C Barnet	49	Smith	Thomas	1787	Finchley
1.33.02	Finchley	77	Smith	Thomas	1760	Finchley
1.4.03	C Barnet	32	Smith	William	1804	S Mims
1.48.02	Finchley	50	Smith	Thomas	1787	Finchley
1.23.02	Shenley	73	Spencer	William	1764	Shenley
1.37.11	Shenley	73	Spencer	William	1764	Shenley
1.4.06	C Barnet	72	Spencer	William	1764	Shenley
1.52.08	Shenley	73	Spencer	William	1764	Shenley
1.22.05	Shenley	52	Starkins	Fanny	1785	Shenley
1.37.15	Shenley	52	Starkins	Fanny	1785	Shenley
1.4.01	C Barnet	51	Starkins	Fanny	1785	Shenley
1.52.11	Shenley	52	Starkins	Fanny	1785	Shenley
1.22.09	Shenley	2	Stern	Frederick	1835	Shenley
1.37.08	Shenley	2	Stern	Frederick	1835	Shenley
1.52.07	Shenley	2	Stern	Frederick	1835	Shenley
1.19.07	Finchley	61	Stops	John	1776	Finchley
1.33.17	Finchley	61	Stops	John	1776	Finchley
1.49.03	Finchley	61	Stops	John	1776	Finchley
1.16.05	E Barnet	45	Stubbington	Thomas	1792	E Barnet
1.31.04	E Barnet	45	Stubbington	Thomas	1792	E Barnet
1.46.04	E Barnet	45	Stubbington	Thomas	1792	E Barnet
1.5.02	E Barnet	21	Sygrave	Esther	1815	C Barnet
1.23.08	Shenley	65	Taylor	Widow	1772	Shenley
1.37.13	Shenley	65	Taylor	Widow Mary	1772	Shenley
1.31.07	E Barnet	50	Thursby	William	1787	E Barnet
1.46.06	E Barnet	50	Thursby	William	1787	E Barnet
1.41.02	S Mims	53	Tinsley	Charlotte	1784	S Mims
1.14.08	C Barnet	42	Townsend	Mary	1795	C Barnet

Calling	State	Disability?	Cause	Condition
gardener	married	aged	infirm	not any
labourer	widower	blind		not any
labourer	widower	blind		
labourer	widower	blind	out work	not any
labourer	single	bad leg	accident	Enfield casualty
labourer	widower	blind		
shoemaker	widower	infirm	aged	not any
shoe maker	widower	aged	infirm	not any
shoemaker	widower	infirm	no work	all poor
shoe maker	widower	aged	infirm	none
menial servant	single	weak intellect	out of place	not any
menial servant	single	aged	not able to work	not any
menial servant	single	weak intellect	out of place	
menial servant	single	weak intellect	not able to work	none
	bastard		deserted	not any
	bastard	aged		deserted
	bastard			
publican	widower	illness	bad leg	not any
publican	married	bad leg	illness	not any
publican	married	aged	infirm	not any
blacksmith	single	illness	out work	
blacksmith	single	illness	not able to work	
blacksmith	single	illness	out work	
menial servant	single	illness		
needlework	widow	infirm	bad legs	not any
needlewoman	widow	aged	infirm	not any
labourer	single	ruptured	sickness out of work	
labourer	single	illness	ruptured	
menial servant	married	weak intellect	illness	none
	single	idiot	not able to work	

Ref no	House	Age	Surname	First name	Born	Parish
1.29.08	C Barnet	42	Townsend	Mary	1795	C Barnet
1.44.06	C Barnet	42	Townsend	Mary	1795	C Barnet
1.5.01	E Barnet	41	Townsend	Mary	1795	C Barnet
1.51.07	Elstree	0	Trott	Male infant	1837	Elstree
1.51.07	Elstree		Trott	Eliza	1819	Elstree
1.16.01	E Barnet	76	Tuckfield	William	1761	E Barnet
1.16.02	E Barnet	32	Tuckfield	Mary	1805	E Barnet
1.3.01	C Barnet	75	Tuckfield	William	1761	E Barnet
1.3.02	C Barnet	78	Tuckfield	Priscilla	1758	E Barnet
1.31.01	E Barnet	76	Tuckfield	William	1761	E Barnet
1.46.01	E Barnet	76	Tuckfield	William	1761	E Barnet
1.6.10	E Barnet	31	Tuckfield	Mary	1805	E Barnet
1.47.01	F Barnet	57	Varney	William	1780	F Barnet
1.45.02	C Barnet	40	Waller	William	1797	CB Casualty
1.3.05	C Barnet	40	Warren	Joseph	1796	S Mims
1.49.02	Finchley	63	Warren	William	1774	Finchley Casualty
1.15.03	C Barnet	49	Waterton	Sarah	1788	C Barnet
1.29.16	C Barnet	49	Waterton	Sarah	1788	C Barnet
1.44.11	C Barnet	49	Waterton	Sarah	1788	C Barnet
1.45.01	C Barnet	49	Waterton	Sarah	1788	C Barnet
1.7.05	Shenley	50	Waterton	Sarah	1786	C Barnet
1.27.04	Hadley	58	Watkins	Frank	1779	Hadley
1.3.04	C Barnet	57	Watkins	Frank	1779	Hadley
1.42.04	Hadley	58	Watkins	Frank	1779	Hadley
1.28.03	Hadley	58	Weatherley	Thomas	1779	Hadley
1.42.12	Hadley	58	Weatherley	Thomas	1779	Hadley
1.13.04	C Barnet	18	Weedon	John	1818	S Mims
1.26.02	S Mims	19	Weedon	John	1818	S Mims
1.40.10	S Mims	19	Weedon	John	1818	S Mims
1.34.02	Finchley	50	Wells	Edward	1787	Finchley
1.48.16	Finchley	50	Wells	Edward	1787	Finchley

APPENDIX III

Calling	State	Disability?	Cause	Condition
nothing	single	idiot	not able	none
	single	idiot		
	single	Idiot	unable to work	
	bastard		mother in the workhouse	
menial servant				
labourer	widower	infirm		all poor
menial servant	single	not well	out of place	
labourer	married	infirm	past work	
washerwoman	married	aged	past work	
labourer	widower	aged	infirm	none
labourer	widower	aged	infirm	not any
menial servant	single	not well	illness	poor
labourer	single	rheumatism	not able to work	
painter	married	illness	not able to work	not any
police man	married	consumption	illness	
brickmaker	widower	accident	not able to work	not any able
menial servant	single		lost place	
menial servant	single	infirm	out of place	none
menial servant	single	infirm	out of place	
menial servant	single	infirm	out place	not any
menial servant	single		lost place	
shoemaker	single	infirm	out of work	not any
shoemaker	single		out of work	
shoemaker	single	weak head	out work	none
labourer	single	infirm	out work	not any
labourer	single	dropsy	out work	none
labourer	single		out of work	father poor
labourer	single	able	out of work	
labourer	single	illness	out work	not any
labourer	single	illness	out work	none
labourer	single	illness		

Ref no	House	Age	Surname	First name	Born	Parish
1.19.02	Finchley	5	Wilding	Charles	1832	Finchley
1.19.03	Finchley	10	Wilding	Eliza	1827	Finchley
1.33.11	Finchley	5	Wilding	Charles	1832	Finchley
1.33.12	Finchley	10	Wilding	Eliza	1827	Finchley
1.48.11	Finchley	5	Wilding	Charles	1832	Finchley
1.48.12	Finchley	10	Wilding	Eliza	1827	Finchley
1.8.09	Shenley	4	Wilding	Charles	1832	Finchley
1.9.01	Shenley	9	Wilding	Eliza	1827	Finchley
1.51.04	Elstree	72	Williams	Elizabeth	1765	Elstree
1.10.09	Shenley	13	Williams	Elizabeth	1823	S Mims
1.18.05	Finchley	77	Williams	Elizabeth	1760	Finchley
1.21.03	Elstree	75	Williams	John	1762	Elstree
1.21.04	Elstree	72	Williams	Elisabeth	1765	Elstree
1.40.17	S Mims	14	Williams	Elizabeth	1823	S Mims
1.48.05	Finchley	77	Williams	Elizabeth	1760	Finchley
1.5.10	E Barnet	71	Williams	Elizabeth	1765	Finchley
1.51.03	Elstree	75	Williams	John	1762	Elstree
1.6.01	E Barnet	74	Williams	John	1762	Elstree
1.6.02	E Barnet	71	Williams	Elizabeth	1765	Elstree
1.33.05	Finchley	77	Williams	Elizabeth	1760	Finchley
1.21.02	Elstree	58	Wilshin	Mary	1779	Elstree
1.5.09	E Barnet	57	Wilshin	Mary	1779	Elstree
1.51.02	Elstree	58	Wilshin	Mary	1779	Elstree
1.49.05	Finchley	60	Winterburn	Thomas	1777	Finchley
1.11.01	Shenley	12	Woodhouse	Charles	1824	Hadley
1.27.06	Hadley	15	Woodhouse	Frederick	1822	Hadley
1.28.01	Hadley	11	Woodhouse	Charles	1826	Hadley
1.4.05	C Barnet	14	Woodhouse	Fredk	1822	Hadley
1.42.05	Hadley	15	Woodhouse	Frederick	1822	Hadley
1.42.10	Hadley	13	Woodhouse	Charles	1824	Hadley
1.13.06	C Barnet	30	Yeial [xx]	John	1806	not examined

APPENDIX III

Calling	State	Disability?	Cause	Condition
errand boy	deserted		no home	not any
	deserted		no home	not any
	deserted			not any
labourer	deserted			not any
	deserted			
	deserted			
	deserted		no father	
	deserted		no home	
charwoman	married	aged	infirm	
menial servant		able to work	lost place	
washerwoman	widow	infirm	not able to work	not any
labourer	married	infirm	aged	not any
charwoman	married	infirm	aged	not any
menial servant	orphan	out of place	no home	not any
washerwoman	widow	aged	infirm	
washerwoman	widow	infirm	not able	not known
labourer	married	aged	infirm	
labourer	married	infirm	not able	not any
charwoman	married	infirm	not able	not any
washer woman	widow	aged	infirm	not any
washerwoman	widow	infirm	aged	not any
washer woman	widow	infirm	afflicted	
washerwoman	widow	aged	infirm	
gardener	widower	rheumatism	not able	not any
errand boy	orphan	able to work	no home	
pot boy	orphan	bad ancle	out place	not any
labourer	orphan	able	no home	not any
pot boy		illness	orphan	all poor
pot boy	orphan	illness	out work	none
labourer	orphan		out work	none
post boy	single	illness	settlement unknown	removed from Hartshorn

251

Appendix IV

People appearing in text

The index that appears at the end of this volume includes references to all the people mentioned in Woodcock's diary together with those featuring in the appendices. However the editor thought it would be helpful to the reader if certain groups of people are identified separately. This is done in the following appendix.

Appendix IV

People appearing in text

List of local traders

Allen, Mr	plumber
Beattie, Mr	plasterer
Bellamy, Mr	carpenter/contractor
Bennett, Thomas,	butcher of Barnet
Bennett, William	butcher
Bowers, George	wine merchant of Chipping Barnet.
Bowers, Mrs	wine merchant
Clayton, William	Chipping Barnet, butcher, gravel
Coe, Mrs	landlady of the *Castle*
Cooper, Mr	plumber
Cornwall, Mrs	nursery gardener
Cotterell, Mr and Mrs	*Green Man*
Cowing, Mr	stationer
Dowton, Duckworth and Taplin	auctioneers
Fennell, James	master sweep of Hadley [spelt Farnell in 1841 census]
Flitt, Edmund	carrier of Chipping Barnet, made daily trips to Smithfield market
Gregory, Mr	bread contractor
Hall & Cannon, Misses	clothes suppliers
Harvey, George	faggots
Hopewell, John	grocer and cheesemonger and an elected Guardian for Chipping Barnet
Markwell,	undertaker
Marsh, Edward	of the Minories, clothing
McGregory,	bread contractor,
Nicholas, Alfred	coal and timber merchant of Chipping Barnet.
Nutkins, Robert	plumber, attended boiler
Pitkinn, Mr	plasterer
Shuttleworth, Ann and Mary Ann	clothiers in High Street, Chipping Barnet

Smith, Benjamin,	grocer and tallower chandler and an elected Guardian for Chipping Barnet
Wager, John,	carpenter and undertaker of Chipping Barnet
Whaley, Mr & Mrs	*Cross Keys,* South Mimms

List of officials and staff

Acason, William	relieving officer of Barnet Union
Adey, D G	Poor Law Commissioner
Bass, Mr,	Guardian and veterinary surgeon
Beach, John	workhouse staff
Bennet, Thomas	of Barnet
Betham, Frederick, Mr	Guardian and farmer of Ridge
Buckland, James, Mr	treasurer
Buckle, Richard	constable
Byng, General Edmund	local MP of Wrotham Park
Carrie, James	medical officer
Coe, Mr	overseer Chipping Barnet
Debenham, Mr	of the Wellhouse, Barnet
Dowton,	
Elwin, Revd Mr	
Frost, Mr	constable of Finchley
Goodyear, Mr	
Griffin, John, Mr	surveyor and architect
Hall, Mr	Commissioner from Totteridge
Hammond, William	medical officer Barnet
Hills, Mr,	
Hudson, Mr	medical officer
Humphreys, Mr	medical officer
Hunt, Mr	of Hadley,
Jacques, Mr	parishioner of Finchley
Lord, Thomas	of Shenley
Lucas, Mr, Hadley	overseer
Morrison, Walter	Union medical officer
Newcome, the Revd Mr	Rector of Shenley
Pruden, Mr	
Pye	policeman

Wells	postman
Williams, Richard	vestry clerk
Willis	workhouse porter
Wilson	overseer

Visitors

Adams, Mrs	and friends
Amersham Union	
Audsley Mr and daughter	of Finchley
Barnard, Revd Mr	of Colney
Blundell, Revd Thomas	and friends
Byng, Hon Edmund	of Wrotham Park
Caledon, Lord	of Tyttenhanger
Dickens, General	
Dury, Colonel and friends	of Hadley
Franklin, Mr James	
Goodwin, Miss	of Barnet Common
Goodwin, Mrs	
Goodyear, Mr	and two friends
Hall, Mr	commissioner, Totteridge & friends
Hall, Miss	of Totteridge, with Mr Hall
Hammond, William	medical officer, Barnet
Hardwick, Lady	of Tyttenhanger
Hays, Mrs and Miss	of Hadley
Hayward, Miss	and friends
Hendon workhouse	Master
Malden Union	Five gentlemen
Montague, Miss and friend	
Mutter, Revd G	rector of Whitchurch
Newcome, Thomas, Revd	and Miss Newcome and friend
Osman, Mr	parishioner of Finchley
Ray, Mr and two gentlemen	
Richardson, Mr and friend	
Robarts, Miss	
Robarts, Mr	
Sears, Mr	and family
Seaton, Captain	and friends
Smith, Mr	and two gentlemen
Thackery, Revd Mr	

Ward, Mr — and friends
Watford Union workhouse — clerk and master
Wood, Revd Mr & Mrs — of Shenley

Members of the Board of Guardians and the parish they represented

Bass, William, veterinary surgeon	Friern Barnet
Betham, Frederick, farmer	Ridge
Bryant, Charles, innkeeper	Chipping Barnet
Clayton, Benjamin, Esq, farmer	Shenley
Dickens, James Esq	Hadley
Elwin, the Revd Thomas Henry	East Barnet
Fox, Henry, Esq	South Mims
Hopewell, John, grocer	Chipping Barnet
Howorth, James, attorney	Chipping Barnet
Manning, Samuel farmer	Shenley
Osmond, Samuel farmer	Totteridge
Shove Chalk, the Revd William	Elstree
Smith, Benjamin, grocer	Chipping Barnet
Thackeray, the Revd John Richard	South Mims

Ex-Officio
Byng, George, Esq MP
Dury,Alexander, Esq
Lendon, Revd Abel, — clerk, rector St James, Friern Barnet

Miso Winter, John, Esq

Appendix V

Extract from Register of Paupers for whom

places in service provided

June 1836–December 1839 [HALS: BG/BAR 83]

The information included in the following two pages was extracted from the Register of Paupers for the period covered by other material included in this volume. This Register identifies the pauper for whom places in service were found, the parish from which they came, the date they entered into service and the name of the master or mistress, his or her address and trade or profession. The terms of the pauper's employment and some remarks relating to his or her subsequent employment, are also added but limited space has meant that some of this detail has not been included and words have been abbreviated. These are general standard abbreviations for months and shortened place names ie E Barnet or EB is East Barnet, FB or F Barnet Friern Barnet and C Barnet or CB Chipping Barnet.

The editor would refer readers to the original for supplementary information. The register continues beyond the period included here.

Pauper's name	Age Parish	Entered service	Master/mistress
Gwillam, John	14 Finchley	June 1836	John Frost
Williams, Elizabeth	15 S Mims	July 1836	Mrs Beatham
Gillman, Ann	69 C Barnet	22 Sept 1836	Mr Goodwin
Williams, Elizabeth	15 S Mims	11 Oct 1836	Mrs Ward
Cooper, Mary	16 Hadley	17 Oct 1836	Mrs Cornwall
Sygrave, Esther	18 C Barnet	22 Oct 1836	Mrs Wells
Collins, Job	16 Shenley	22 Oct 1836	Mr Han.. Friend
Bartlett, Elizabeth	52 Totteridge	3 Jan 1837	Mrs Nicholls daughter
Waterton, Sarah	48 C Barnet	17 Feb 1837	Mrs Acason
Godfrey, Sarah	15 F Barnet	17 Feb 1837	Mrs Tibbott
Lenman, Chris	17 C Barnet	26 Feb 1837	Mr Benjamin Clayton
Cooper, Mary	17 Hadley	20 Mar 1837	Mrs -- ditto
Williams, Elizabeth	15 S Mims	15 June 1837	Mrs Reeve
Woodhouse, Frederick	17 Hadley	21 Sept 1837	Mr Hill
Fox, Martha	15 C Barnet	8 Nov 1837	Miss Samuel
Williams, Elizabeth	15 S Mims	15 Jan 1838	Miss Tilley
Godfrey, Sarah	15 F Barnet	6 Feb 1838	James Cox
Sanders, Hannah	16 C Barnet	9 Feb 1838	Mr Newman
Sygrave, Esther	18 C Barnet	15 Feb 1838	Mrs Cottle
Hawkins, Georgiana	16 Ridge	14 Feb 1838	Mrs Melville
Smallbones, Eliza	28 Hadley	12 Mar 1838	Mr Sykes
Peel, William	17 F Barnet	6 April 1818	Mr Cottle
Childs, Ann	19 Ridge	23 April 1838	Mrs Coe
Woodby, Sarah	20 Totteridge	23 June 1828	Mrs Exgrave
Ross, Charlotte	24 C Barnet	15 July 1838	Mr Burnham
Thursby, William	49 E Barnet	18 July 1838	Mr Crawley
Brown, Anne	28 Totteridge	7 Aug 1838	Mrs Jefferies
Tedder, Eliza	18 Ridge	7 Sept 1838	Mrs Partridge
Brandon, Charlotte	46 Finchley	22 Sept 1838	Mrs Clemence
Williams, Elizabeth	16 S Mimms	22 Dec 1838	Mr Bademead
Signall, Ann	15 S Mimms	5 Jan 1839	Mrs Pepper
Sygrave, Sophia	19 C Barnet	21 Jan 1839	Mrs Beresford
Anderson, Mary Ann	15 S Mims	21 Jan 1839	Mrs Wood
Nightingale, Mary	11 S Mims	23 Jan 1839	Mrs Aser
Anderson, Mary Anne	15 S Mimms	25 April 1839	Mrs William Hill
Williams, Elizabeth	17 S Mims	22 June 1839	Butcher Mary
Slade, Thomas	15 Finchley	26 July 1839	Mr Brett
Fox, Martha	15 C Barnet	9 Aug 1838	Mrs Read
Menus, Jane	14 S Mims	23 Aug 1839	Teasdell
Signall, Elizabeth	12 S Mims	11 Oct 1839	Aser
Saunders, Hannah	18 C Barnet	25 Oct 1839	Green Man
Bartlett,	18 C Barnet	30 Dec 1839	Clark
Hammond, Mary Anne	24 Hadley	31 Dec 1839	Mrs Sykes
Walters, Joseph	63 E Barnet	27 Dec 1839	Sheffield

Abode, trade, profession	Terms of contract	Other information
Finchley, Shoemaker	apprenticed	
Farmer, Barnet Common	in approbation	
Barnet Common		
Green Street, Shenley	board lodge and clothes	
Hadley, nurseryman	£ 5 per annum	
Hadley, watchmaker	£5 per annum	
Somerstown		
London		
Barnet	1s per week	
Shenley Butcher	1s per week	
Barnet Common	4s per week	
Finchley		
Warwick Lane, London	£5 per annum	
Barnet	9s per week	
Potters Bar Farm	board lodge and clothes	
Barnet Hill	on approbation	
Whetstone, milkman		
Green Man, Barnet	£5 per annum	
Green Man Tap	£5 per annum	
Boreham Wood	board lodge and clothes	
Totteridge	£8 per annum board lodge	
Green Man Tap	board lodge 2s a week	
Castle, Barnet		
Bushey, butchers	£4 per annum	Left place at 6 oclock Morning
Totteridge, gent	£9 per annum	
Barnet Hill, farmer	£5 per annum	
Whetstone, laundress	on approbation	
Hendon, farmer	18d per week	
Barnet, shoemaker	£8 per anuum	E. Clemence - ran away from place
Elstree	£4 per annum	Mrs Bademeade
Farm Barnet	1s per week	Eliza Cope
Chipping Barnet	£4 per annum	
Grammar School	£2 12s per annum	left on 15 April did not suit
Potters Bar, clerk	board lodge & clothes	
Wool Pack, Barnet	on approbation	
Tykes Water Laundry	£5 per annum	M. Butcher
Barnet	board, lodge & clothes	J.A. Brett
Barnet, the Wellington	£5 per annum	H Read
C Barnet, eating house	board, lodge washing 1s a wk	discharged 27 November misbehaviour
Potters Bar, clerk	board, lodge, washing & clothes	
Whetstone	board and lodge £6 per annum	discharged 9 September illness
Elstree, painter etc	board, lodge and clothes	
Totteridge	board, lodge and £? per annum	
Barnet Common, baker	board lodge 3s per week	

Sources

Primary Sources

Barnet Museum

Admission and discharge books one and two, 1836 to Christmas 1839 [WE/05]

Barnet Union, Rules for guidance of labour master

Workhouse Accounts, 25 November 1837 to 4 December 1837 [WE/05 2003.A.001]

Hertfordshire Archives and Local Studies

Barnet Union Board of Guardians, Minutes 43 volumes July 1835-March 1930 [BG/BAR 1-43]

Hemel Hempstead Workhouse, specifications [DE/Ma 22]

Journal of Benjamin Woodcock, 1 September to 10 May 1838, [70876]

Letter books out letters 5 vols July 1835-November 1869 [BG/BAR 69-73]

Masters' reports 5 volumes December 1852-1863 [BG/BAR 78-82]

Ordnance Survey Map 1881 ref: OS sheets XLV3 and XLV7

Poor Law Barnet, Sealed orders of [BG/BAR 74]

Register of Paupers for whom places in service provided, 1 vol June 1836-October 1879 [BG/BAR 83]

London Borough of Barnet Local Studies and Archives Centre, Dawes Lane

Plans (L7373/1/3, 1/2, 1/1,/2-3, 31, 41/1-2, 58, 60 /1-4, 61/1-7, 62 /69)

Poor Law Union dated 23/11/1835, another with some change of names of the buildings around the periphery stamped received date 2/8/1856.

Later drawings by Mausbridge dating 1885-1892; Ambulance House in Stone Yard 1885, New Cells & Shed 1889, Roof Plan casual cells, General Plan 1891, Associated Wards and Casual Cells Elevation, Longitudinal plan, sectional and ground plans, all 1892, 4 plans New Laundry, 7 plans & elevations

Bedfordshire & Luton Archives and Records Service
Land Tax Returns 1831, 1832 [QDL Eaton Bray]
Registers Eaton Bray, [P63/1/9]

Census 1841, [HO 107/438]

Secondary Sources

Books

Forster, John, *The Life of Charles Dickens,* quoted in Book Second: First
years of fame 1836-41 (Cecil Palmer, 1872)
Gelder, W H, *Historic Barnet*, 5th edition (Barnet & District Local
History Society 2002)
Kingsford, Peter and Jones, Arthur, editors, *Down and out in
Hertfordshire*, (Hertfordshire Publications, 1984)
Knight, Judith and Flood, Susan, editors, *Two Nineteenth Century
Hertfordshire Diaries, 1822–1849* vol XVIII (Hertfordshire Records
Society, 2002)

Pigot & Co's Directory, Middlesex 1839
Pigot & Co's Directory, Hertfordshire 1839

THE HERTFORDSHIRE RECORD SOCIETY

The Hertfordshire Record Society exists to make Hertfordshire's historical records of all kinds more readily available to the general reader. Since 1985 a regular series of texts has been published.

ALAN RUSTON, Chairman
HEATHER FALVEY, Hon. Secretary
GWYNNETH GRIMWOOD, Hon. Treasurer
SUSAN FLOOD, Hon. General Editor

Membership enquiries and orders for previous publications to the Hon. Secretary, Dr Heather Falvey, 119 Winton Drive, Croxley Green, Rickmansworth, WD3 3QS

Annual Subscription (2009–2010)   £17.50

Previous publications:

I: *Tudor Churchwardens' Accounts*. Edited by Anthony Palmer (1985) O/P

II: *Early Stuart Household Accounts*. Edited by Lionel M Munby (1986) O/P

III: *'A Professional Hertfordshire Tramp' John Edwin Cussans, Historian of Hertfordshire*. Edited by Audrey Deacon and Peter Walne (1987) O/P

IV: *The Salisbury-Balfour Correspondence, 1869–1892*. Edited by Robin Harcourt Williams (1988) O/P

V: *The Parish Register & Tithing Book of Thomas Hassall of Amwell* [Registers 1599–1657; Tithing Book 1633–35]. Edited by Stephen G Doree (1989) Price £6.00

VI: *Cheshunt College: The Early Years*. Edited by Edwin Welch (1990) O/P

VII: *St Albans Quarter Sessions Rolls, 1784–1820*. Edited by David Dean (1991) O/P

VIII: *The Accounts of Thomas Green, 1742–1790*. Edited by Gillian Sheldrick (1992)   Price £6.00

IX: *St Albans Wills, 1471–1500*. Edited by Susan Flood (1993) O/P

X: *Early Churchwardens' Accounts of Bishops Stortford, 1431–1538*. Edited by Stephen G Doree (1994)   Price £6.00

XI: *Religion in Hertfordshire, 1847–1851*. Edited by Judith Burg (1995) Price £6.00

XII: *Muster Books for North & East Hertfordshire, 1580–1605*. Edited by Ann J King (1996)   Price £6.00

XIII: *Lifestyle & Culture in Hertford: Wills and Inventories, 1660–1725*. Edited by Beverly Adams (1997)   Price £6.00

XIV: *Hertfordshire Lay Subsidy Rolls, 1307 and 1334*. Edited by Janice Brooker and Susan Flood, with an introduction by Dr Mark Bailey (1998)   Price £6.00

XV: *'Observations of Weather' The Weather Diary of Sir John Wittewronge of Rothamsted, 1684–1689*. Edited by Margaret Harcourt Williams and John Stevenson (1999)   Price £19.00 (£15.00)

XVI: *Survey of the Royal Manor of Hitchin, c1676*. Edited by Bridget Howlett (2000)   Price £18.75 (£15.00)

XVII: *Garden-Making and the Freeman family A Memoir of Hamels, 1713–1733*. Edited by Anne Rowe (2001)   Price £18.50 (£15.00)

XVIII: *Two Nineteenth Century Hertfordshire Diaries, 1822–1849*. Edited by Judith Knight and Susan Flood (2002)   Price £19.50 (£15.00)

XIX: *"This little commonwealth": Layston parish memorandum book, 1607–c1650 & 1704–c1747*. Edited by Heather Falvey and Steve Hindle (2003)   Price £21.00 (£15.00)

XX: *Julian Grenfell, soldier and poet: letters and diaries, 1910–1915*. Edited by Kate Thompson (2004)   Price £22.00 (£15.00)

XXI: *The Hellard Almshouses and other Stevenage Charities, 1482–2005*. Edited by Margaret Ashby (2005)   Price £21.00 (£15.00)

XXII: *A Victorian Teenager's Diary: the Diary of Lady Adela Capel of Cassiobury, 1841–1842*. Edited by Marian Strachan (2006) Price paperback £9.99

XXIII: *The Impact of the First Civil War on Hertfordshire, 1642–1647*. Edited by Alan Thomson (2007)   Price £22.00 (£17.50)

Maps:

The County of Hertford From Actual Survey by A Bryant In the Years 1820 and 1821 (2003)   £7.50

A Topographical Map of Hartford-Shire by Andrew Dury and John Andrews, 1766 (2004)   £9.50

For more information visit www.hrsociety.org.uk

INDEX OF PLACES AND SUBJECTS

INDEX OF PLACES AND SUBJECTS

mutton; soup, 41, 95; potatoes, 14, 17, 19-20, 22-23, 27, 38, 41, 49, 56, 72, 79, 80, 87, 113, 128, 136
small hamper, 82;
garden: 28, 38, 52, 87
grass crop, 152;
kitchen, xxv;
workhouse garden, 22
Gas Company, 196, 210, 218
Green Man, 119-20, 122, 125, 132, 136, 139, 258
grindstone, 85
Guernsey, 102

Hanwell Asylum, 145, 159, 165, 167, 171, 173, 213
Hatfield, 132
health, 71
accident, 2, 28, 36, 47, 62, 67, 68, 127, 128, 136;
bath, warm, 58, 65, 91, 107;
blind, 8, 13, 16-17, 28, 30, 35, 51, 61, 82, 93, 113, 129;
blood, 28, 76;
bowel complaint, 102
consumption, 14, 69-70, 87;
cripple, 24, 40, 42, 58, 74;
doctor's list, 25
dropsy, 46, 76, 85, 90, 127
hair cut close off, 31
idiot, xxiv, 66, 74, 104, 105

inflammation on the brain, 28;
lameness, 46;
low weak state, 4, 27;
lousy, 23, 67, 112;
measles, 14, 16, 17, 18, 19;
medicine, 29;
one hand, 3;
ragged and hungry, 26;
relaxation of bowels, 5;
sick children, 48;
sinking, 4, 10, 11, 13, 17, 27-8, 44, 49, 60;
small pox, 98;
struck & knocked down, 122;
surgeon's list, 31;
surgical machine, 14
tapped, 54, 66, 76;
thigh, broken, 2, 4, 47, 127;
women's sick ward, 92
Hemel Hempstead, iv, xxv, xxvi, 25, 62, 100
Hendon Union, 55, 57, 85, 255
Hitchin Poor Law Union, 153
holiday, 14
Hospital, Lock, 29, 67, 69, 93
Hoxton Asylum, Mddx, 72, 153
Hulbech, [Holbeach], Lincs, 104

Irish Casualty, 4, 8, 10, 72, 74, 76-7

Kimpton, 131

Lincolnshire, 57, 104
London, 7-8, 15, 24, 26, 28, 62, 64,

Maldon Union, Essex, 91, 255
Margate infirmary, Kent, 69, 88, 139
Margate, St Johns, 36-7
matron, 1, 3-4, 8, 12-13, 39, 42-45, 49-50, 52, 55, 59-60, 72, 77, 80-81, 99, 102, 113, 130
Mile End, 173

outdoor relief, xviii, xxii, xxiv, xxxviii

Peacock, Islington, 82
Pigots' directory of 1839, x, xii, xviii
Poor Law, 1834, vii
poor law districts, vii
porter, 55, 66, 74, 77-8, 80-1, 84, 86, 95, 96
porter's dog, 63
porter's lodge, 87

Red Lion, xii, xvii, xviii
religion:
baptism,/christening, 9, 90, 138;
bible & prayer book, 109;
chapel, 68, 70, 79, 102, 112, 137;
chaplain, 86, 89, 138
church, 2, 12, 34-5, 37, 52, 65, 77, 102, 138;
divine service, 82, 87, 113, 132;

INDEX OF PEOPLE

INDEX OF PEOPLE

INDEX OF PEOPLE